THE TAKING OF JEMIMA BOONE

ALSO BY MATTHEW PEARL

The Dante Chamber

The Last Bookaneer

The Technologists

The Last Dickens

The Poe Shadow

The Dante Club

THE
TAKING OF

JEMIMA
BOONE

COLONIAL SETTLERS, TRIBAL

NATIONS, AND THE KIDNAP

THAT SHAPED AMERICA

MATTHEW
PEARL

HARPER

An Imprint of HarperCollins*Publishers*

HarperCollins books may be purchased for educational, business, or sales promotional use. For information, please email the Special Markets Department at SPsales@harpercollins.com.

FIRST EDITION

Designed by Bonni Leon-Berman

Library of Congress Cataloging-in-Publication Data has been applied for.

ISBN 978-0-06-293778-0

21 22 23 24 25 LSC 10 9 8 7 6 5 4 3 2 1

Dedicated to the memory of Ian Pearl,
1972–2020

CONTENTS

CAST OF CHARACTERS

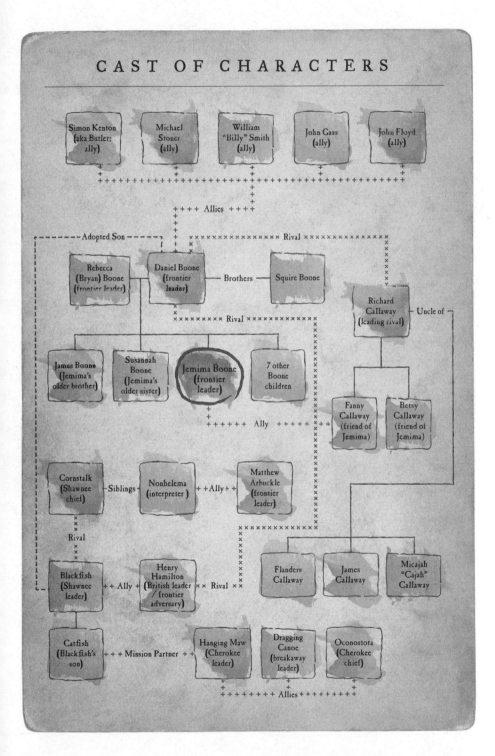

THE TAKING OF JEMIMA BOONE

PROLOGUE

REBECCA BOONE NOTICED SOMETHING MISSING as she looked out over the garrison at Moore's Fort in southwest Virginia: men. Instead, she saw the other wives of the hunters and military officers staying at the fort. The early 1770s on the frontier—the sparsely populated stretches of Virginia and the areas westward across mountainous borders—meant residing either in standalone cabins or in cabins clustered into "stations" or forts, which included protective structures to keep attackers at bay. Conflicts with American Indian tribes came at a quick and bloody clip, so most frontier men were commissioned as soldiers by colonial governments, whether or not they wanted to be.

On this summer day, those men were out of sight. Some were away from the fort playing ball; others napped in the fields. They hadn't even bothered bringing guns with them. The father of one of the men, nicknamed Old Daddy, had stayed behind, but conventional wisdom held the elderly as irrelevant to the defense of the fort—much the way women were viewed. With Rebecca was her adolescent daughter Jemima. She had raven hair and tenacity like her mother's, and a stubborn, independent streak like her father's. Daniel Boone, the accomplished woodsman, was away on a mission into Kentucky, a purported promised land to which he had been drawn for years to the point of obsession. He continued to look for a way to settle there, against odds and logic.

Responsibility for the family, as often was the case, fell to Rebecca. Faced with the distressing sight of this unguarded fort, Rebecca decided to take a stand against the men. She instructed eleven-year-old Jemima to take a rifle. If the men weren't going to use their weapons, the women would.

Rebecca and Jemima, along with Jemima's older sister, Susannah, joined the other women of the fort. Upon a signal, they fired into the air as fast as they could. Then they raced to slam both gates of the fort, one in front and one at the back, locking them.

The men came stampeding toward the fort. "They were all exceeding mad," one woman recounted of the events she witnessed as a nine-year-old. In their headlong rush, some of the men tumbled into a pond outside. One man scaled the wall—in the process unwittingly proving that this fort would not keep out enemies particularly well. He discovered the ruse. As the other men realized the trick by the ladies, they began to argue among themselves over the cause, and two or three fistfights broke out. Calls were made to have the women whipped. Jemima, holding a smoking rifle, watched the startling scene unfold around her, and the sight of this girl gripping the weapon alongside the other armed women likely squelched the idea of whipping anyone.

Rebecca had just demonstrated to young Jemima a crucial lesson. When the men in authority stumbled, women would have to rise up.

Jemima carried the lesson to Kentucky, where the family set up not just a home but a community, and she continued to build on it as she entered the folklore of the American frontier when she was kidnapped in July 1776. Theodore Roosevelt, writing in the late nineteenth century, observed that the epic story of Jemima's kidnapping "reads like a page out of one of Cooper's novels," but the Rough Rider got it backward. In fact, the real incidents inspired James Fenimore Cooper's *The Last of the Mohicans*, the 1826 adventure novel intertwining the fates of the colonists and Indians, a book that went on to become one of the most popular in the English language. But the transformation of life into literature can make the true story harder to observe independently from what it inspired. Another early chronicler of the West once complained about Cooper's advantages compared to the chronicler's attempts to gather facts about the Boones' frontier: "A novelist may fill up the blank from his own imagination; but a writer who professes to adhere to the truth, is fettered down to the record before him."

The records of the Boones' experiences are deep and complex, however. Cooper's novel and other literary and artistic interpretations retain only traces of the verve, excitement, and stakes of these original events. Nor was Jemima's kidnapping a standalone moment, but rather part of a chain reaction that included another kidnapping, all-out military combat, and a courtroom drama that effectively put those preceding events on trial. Jemima Boone was in the middle of it all from the moment that chain reaction began.

BOOK I

THE
TAKING

DUCK

ON THE DAY HER LIFE would be transformed, Jemima Boone was occupied like many girls her age—escaping chores and testing parental boundaries. This was July 14, 1776, ten days after the completion of the Declaration of Independence, but news of that turning point in the year-old Revolutionary War had not reached Jemima and her fellow settlers beyond the borders of the former colonies. While the fledgling American government was still spreading the word of its determination to form a nation independent from England, the frontier remained in limbo, caught in a struggle among Indians, settlers, the British, and nature itself.

Jemima strolled the banks of the Kentucky River with two friends downhill from the hardscrabble settlement where they had moved with their families. That year-old settlement was Fort Boone—or Boonesboro, as it was increasingly called—named for Jemima's father, Daniel, but gesturing at her whole family's contributions. Alongside Jemima walked Betsy and Fanny Callaway. Betsy, sixteen, had dark hair and complexion, and Fanny, fourteen, would be described as a "fairy blonde." At thirteen, Jemima was the youngest of the trio and, having arrived before Betsy and Fanny, had eagerly welcomed companions near her own age.

They constituted a significant portion of the girls at the settlement, the total population of which was fluid but not more than a hundred. Childhood came with considerable autonomy on this frontier, but it also absorbed pressures and responsibilities. Considered an adult at sixteen, Betsy had recently gotten engaged, and the younger girls began to attract suitors. Now that they were in their teens, they were expected to contribute to one of the settlement's scarcest resources: children.

Late the previous year, Dolly, an enslaved Black woman brought to Boonesboro by the Callaway family, had given birth to a son, the first non-Indian known to be born in Kentucky. Dolly's motherhood is one of many early milestones achieved by members of the community who had no say in their arrival to this wilderness. Jemima's older sister, Susannah, had by now given birth to a daughter, making Jemima more conspicuous in her status as next in line among Boones to start a family. In the short history of settlers pushing into Kentucky, there had yet to be a wedding. The teens and their families were still among the only non-Indians settled in Kentucky—the result of the controversial westward expansion that now faced obstacles at every level.

With summer blazing, the girls had felt confined at home, and this excursion broke up the monotony. It also held out the possibility of coming home with flowers, which could spruce up the spartan cabins in the settlement. The Callaway girls' half sister, Kezia, who was seven and known as Cuzzy, and some of the other younger girls begged to go along, but the older ones sent them home disappointed. The trio kept walking until they reached the settlement's lone canoe. One of the eligible young men at the fort, twenty-four-year-old Nathan Reid, had offered to row them out when he had heard about their plans earlier. But Reid never showed, and they may have already forgotten about his offer. The three friends didn't need anybody's help with the canoe or the river. Jemima had earned the childhood nickname Duck for taking to the water so naturally.

Climbing into the unadorned vessel, the three girls floated along the dark water, vegetation stretching above magnificent cliffs into the sky. Jemima had recently hurt herself stepping on a sharp stalk, the same kind of cane stalks lining the river's edges. Draping her leg over the side of the canoe into the water soothed her but left her guard down.

THE BOONES HAD led the way to Kentucky before the Revolutionary War as they balanced a desire to stake out a new phase of life against portents of violence, which were often ignored. On one of Daniel Boone's early expeditions through the treacherous passages, including the Cumberland Gap, he had encountered members of the Shawnee tribe, for whom the vast natural resources of Kentucky had not only material but also spiritual importance. The Shawnee creation origin story stressed the value of isolation and independence, envisioning the tribe on an island as the only people in the world. Kentucky, at least up to this point, might as well have been that mythic island. On this occasion, an Indian known to the explorers as Captain Will—a Cherokee by heritage who had shifted tribal allegiance to the Shawnee—warned Boone and his companions against incursions into this untrammeled territory, which was separated from Virginia by mountain ranges and rivers and had only recently begun to be mapped.

"Now, brothers," Captain Will said, "go home and stay there. Don't come here anymore, for this is the Indians' hunting ground, and all the animals, skins and furs are ours; and if you are so foolish as to venture here again, you may be sure the wasps and yellow jackets will sting you severely."

The American Indians who frequented Kentucky, including from the Shawnee and Cherokee tribes, faced the prospect of the first permanent incursion into an area they had inhabited for some ten thousand years. The eighteenth century had brought with it greater but still limited exposure to outsiders, through European trade and religious missions. Boone and his fellow explorers represented a sea change, an attempt to set a course toward seizing Kentucky. The exact meaning of the name Kentucky has been lost, but it's believed to mean the "Land of Tomorrow" in one Iroquoian dialect, unintentionally matching these colonists' objectives, a grave threat to the local tribes' futures.

The solemn warning from Captain Will failed to dissuade the explorers, who continued to marshal resources for additional scouting trips into Kentucky. Daniel Boone occupied a role during this formative moment of American history harder to categorize than the politician or the military commander, though at times he served as both. Boone was a *settler* in the most literal sense of the word. That was his true vocation—to settle areas new to him and often to the colonists. Hunter, woodsman, explorer, surveyor: these skills all helped make him this consummate settler. Though Boone generally sought peaceful coexistence with Indians, he relentlessly pushed into other people's territories, prompting conflict—thus his preoccupation with Kentucky.

Boone's early, temporary excursions into the "Land of Tomorrow" gave him a sense of the beauty and unknown dangers he could expect. On one hunting jaunt, he and fellow woodsmen read from Jonathan Swift's *Gulliver's Travels*, a fantasy voyage into unknown lands. The edition they read from likely contained a map of Brobdingnag, land of giants, situated by Swift somewhere in North America. The trips also led to property claims on the land by the travelers, in turn prompting a demand for surveyors to record those claims. One such team of surveyors put their lives on the line to parcel off two thousand acres below the Elk River for George Washington, then a representative to the Virginia legislature, and in two other spots recorded seven thousand acres for another legislator, Patrick Henry, who was ready to carve out a large piece of property in a place unknown to him. Washington and Henry, like other influential politicos, believed they could get rich from pushing into the territory. Joining the rolls of early surveyors was Hancock Taylor, whose nephew Zachary later became president of the United States. As he traveled in 1774, Taylor stopped to christen a spring with his daughter's nickname, Jessamine. While Taylor's team floated down the Kentucky River, Indians riddled their canoe with bullets, killing one of Taylor's men and shooting Taylor twice. As an indication of the vital importance ascribed to land claims by the settlers, Taylor was brought the survey book on his deathbed. Another surveyor "told him he ought to sign them," according to a later deposition, "and he did" before he passed away. With lives risked and lost through these explorations, actually living in Kentucky seemed about as farfetched as settling Brobdingnag.

Fanciful notions gave way to material plans as the settlers completed a series of treaties with tribes in the mid-1770s, sometimes forced onto the Indians by the military might of the settlers. For one of these negotiations, a group of land speculators had asked Boone to help draw up an agreement with the Cherokee over lands on the south side of the Kentucky River. "This I accepted," Boone later remembered, as related by his biographer. This brought Boone to an assembly of Cherokee and colonial representatives at the Watauga River, in present-day Tennessee, in the spring of 1775, shortly before the Revolutionary War began. Even when strife with Indians spread, Boone usually came off as fair-minded, poised, and hospitable, a natural ally to them. He advised another settler about how to comport himself. Approach Indians, Boone opined, "frankly and fearlessly, showing not the slightest sign of fear or trepidation. By kind acts and just treatment, keep on the friendly side of them." For Boone, philosophy doubled as strategy. Among the like-minded leaders of the Cherokee was the aged Oconostota, who had been lobbying for peace with colonists for decades.

This crowd gathered at Sycamore Shoals, named for its giant trees, on the southern bank of the Watauga. Richard Henderson was among the colonists' leaders in the venture. Henderson, thirty-nine, was an attorney and judge who had pushed back against restrictions on land expansion, especially into Kentucky, where by this point settlers had a track record of false starts and aborted explorations. Henderson saw a chance to make a fortune with a new colony. He spearheaded the weeks-long treaty negotiation. Along with the delegates, witnesses, and other attendees, the scenery filled out with wagons overflowing with goods and weapons, payment by the settlers for the Cherokee land. Covering twenty million acres in parts of what are now two states, the treaty was one of the largest land exchanges in American history. It paved the way for Boone and others to call for permanent settlement.

Another pioneer who arrived at the gathering, Richard Callaway, would have been taken for a ghost by others present. Though only in his fifties, Callaway had been on his deathbed with a serious illness the last time most of the attendees would have heard of him. He had rushed out a final will, which reflected property transactions over two decades amounting to thousands of acres. An orphan at a young age, Callaway had followed his older brothers in accumulating land and serving in a variety of governmental and bureaucratic roles, which helped the clan consolidate power and influence. Tall and muscular with streaks of gray growing into his black hair, Callaway was a man proud of his family name and accomplishments, and with the unexpected recovery of his health came renewed ambitions for a larger fortune and more power. No level of societal respect or wealth ever seemed to be enough for Richard Callaway.

The settlers took pains to appear fair, having translators present from both sides, but not everyone approved of the dealings. Some observers later claimed settlers plied tribal negotiators with alcohol, despite other testimony that insisted liquor was kept away until after the treaty was finalized. Even putting aside the contested integrity of the proceedings, some members of the Cherokee community disagreed in principle with concessions made by their leadership, especially what they considered to be the egregious surrender of vital tribal hunting grounds in Kentucky.

Dragging Canoe, part of the younger generations of Cherokee leaders, broadcast his displeasure. The man had received his name—Tsi-yu'gunsi'ni—from an incident in his boyhood, when he had insisted that he could haul a canoe for a war party but instead could only drag it. His strong will carried over into adulthood. He stamped his foot and gave a scathing speech about the land deal, though he did not stand in the way of its completion. He called the Kentucky lands involved in the deal "bloody ground" that would be "dark" and difficult to settle. Dragging Canoe's declaration got the settlers' attention, as did its ambiguous wording. Some who heard his speech thought the "bloody ground" referred to a history of violence in Kentucky among competing tribes; others interpreted it as a warning of violence to come against the settlers. Dragging Canoe added some details that supported the latter interpretation when he remarked that even if the Cherokee respected the settlers' new claims, other tribes certainly would not—the Shawnee a prime example. Truth was, Dragging Canoe himself had no plans to accept this turn of events.

Years earlier, the British had forbidden private purchase of lands from American Indians such as the one Henderson engineered, having cited "the great dissatisfaction of the said Indians" involved in such transactions. During this final stretch before war broke out between the colonies and their motherland, authorities came down hard. The royal governor of North Carolina, the colony from which Boone and many of the others involved in the Sycamore Shoals treaty had traveled, rushed out a proclamation against the "unwarrantable and lawless undertaking" by Henderson, taking pains to point out the inferior classes of people the new settlement could attract. "A settlement may be formed," read the proclamation, "that will become an Asylum to the most abandoned Fugitives from the several Colonies." The leaders of the venture now faced the prospect of becoming fugitives themselves. Lord Dunmore, the royal governor of Virginia, added a proclamation that "Richard Henderson, and other disorderly persons, his associates" (Daniel Boone would have counted chief among these) who had made "pretense of a purchase made from the Indians," should be "immediately fined & imprisoned."

Such brewing controversies loomed, but at the same time felt far removed geographically and philosophically from Watauga. To observe Daniel Boone during those days was to see a man surrounded by friends and admirers, settlers and Indians alike, a trailblazer watching his long-gestating dream to push into Kentucky turn into reality. While in Watauga at this formative moment, the Boone family lived in a cabin bustling with activity. Daniel and Rebecca, who was pregnant at the time, were joined by their six children, including daughters Jemima and Susannah, along with Susannah's new husband, William Hays.

Jemima had grown into a precocious twelve-year-old with long dark hair that reached almost to her feet. Her personality tended toward being hopeful, bold, and strong-willed—in her own way, as strong-willed as Dragging Canoe, who had refused to admit he couldn't carry his tribe's dugout. With the backdrop of historic events and meetings, Jemima actively engaged with the many new people who passed through the treaty grounds.

Since the time Jemima was a baby, the family had relocated from Virginia to North Carolina, with a detour by her father to journey into Florida and secure land there; instead of going south, the brood moved several times to remote spots with simple cabins. Jemima's was a life of constantly changing and widening horizons. When Daniel was with his family, he danced at celebrations and holidays, played tricks on his loved ones, and provided meat for feasts. But just as often he was off on hunts and expeditions, at one point being away for the better part of two years. When they would move and say good-bye to older family members, it came with the knowledge they'd probably not see them again—as when Jemima, at ten years old, last saw her grandmother, Sarah Boone, a farewell filled with tears.

Their family now prepared for yet another transformation, with a change of scenery almost entirely unique among settlers in the history of the American colonies, and with little idea what to expect.

BEFORE BEGINNING HER own journey, Jemima, as usual, had to watch her father leave without them. The treaty was not even complete when Daniel started for Kentucky with an advance team. He left so abruptly that some later debated whether or not he ever was present at Sycamore Shoals. Though bidding good-bye to him had become routine, this particular trip carried different connotations than earlier ones. Boone, who had served the interests of military and political leaders, now chased a purpose at once grander and more personal. He was staking claim to a new community built on his values and those of his family and collaborators, resting upon a vision of industrious citizenship and personal independence. There were ample reasons to doubt the wisdom and viability of pushing into Kentucky, including the proclamations that declared them outlaws subject to arrest. One member of the North Carolina government, hearing of the Kentucky project and related settlement plans hatched by Boone's benefactor, Richard Henderson, reportedly asked "if Dick Henderson had lost his head." Such profound doubts about their success would only have motivated Boone, who thrived on overcoming challenges, sometimes to his detriment. The act of proving himself tended to put Boone in increasingly difficult circumstances, in which he then had to prove himself again and again, until losing touch with his original purpose.

Boone's thirty-person advance party into Kentucky included his younger brother, Squire, Rebecca's cousin Billy Bush, a young clerk named Felix Walker, Captain William Twitty, and Richard Callaway, the stern colonel of the North Carolina militia. Once successful, Boone planned to return for his family. During the group's trek, they used blades to cut through thickets, unifying trails previously forged by Indians and settlers with "buffalo traces" made by migrating animals, and thus cleared fresh passages through the dense wilderness. The way ahead was never easy; as one traveler wrote, it was "either hilly, stony, slippery, miry, or bushy." Mountains surrounded them, towering hundreds of feet overhead. Part of what appealed so strongly to Boone and his compatriots about Kentucky were these inhospitable but majestic qualities—its representative status as a frontier.

"Delightful beyond conception," one early settler phrased his impression of the land. At one point in the early days of exploration, Boone's party saw a vast plain filled with buffalo (these were American buffalo, or bison), between two and three hundred, a mix of calves and adults, moving at different paces, some rushing, others loping—a gorgeous demonstration.

"A new sky and strange earth seemed to be presented to our view," Walker later wrote. Walker, twenty-one, had bright blue eyes and stood about as tall as Boone. Crossing into Kentucky confirmed the stories he'd heard from trailblazing explorers including Boone. Wild game and rich vegetation seemed to be everywhere. "It appeared that nature, in the profusion of her bounty, had spread a feast for all that lives, both for the animal and rational world." Being in the front guard of this expedition felt like being with Columbus and crew coming upon America—the mythologized version of that odyssey, at least—and, at times, even felt like being the first to enter the Garden of Eden (without, in Walker's sunny view, any forbidden fruit). Boone, according to a likely dramatized account passed on by one of his grandsons, turned to the group and likened their circumstances to another biblical episode, that of the compassionate landowner Boaz: "We are as rich as Boaz of old, having the cattle of a thousand hills." Walker, in a somewhat odd juxtaposition that did not bode very well for success, also thought to compare their party to that of Don Quixote. The Bible, Columbus, Cervantes—the choice of references reflected the feeling of epic importance they attached to the journey.

Conceiving of themselves as versions of Columbus perhaps should have tipped off the settlers about how the native population could see them: destroyers. On March 25, 1775, a few days after crossing into Kentucky, gunfire woke up the party during the night. Bullets struck Twitty, an enslaved man named Sam, and Walker. Sam fell into the fire, dead. Indians stormed the campsite. Twitty's bulldog locked onto the neck of an attacker. The Indians killed the dog with a tomahawk, but the dog's attempt to protect Twitty had slowed the onslaught and injured one of the attackers. The Indians retreated with some of the settlers' horses. Boone later recounted, through his biographer, that his party had been "surprised and taken at a disadvantage."

Entirely isolated and in peril, Boone and the others felled trees to construct a makeshift cabin around the injured men who could not be moved. Walker pulled through but Twitty, shot through the knees, died and was buried alongside Sam and the bulldog.

Boone wrote weeks later of the attack as "our misfortune," as though bad luck had befallen them. But he had been caught off guard when he should not have been. On the one hand, Felix Walker remembered Boone as "my father, my physician, and friend" for the way he cared for him after his gunshot injury. But Walker also bluntly identified the man's Achilles' heel. He "appeared void of fear of consequence," Walker observed, exhibiting "too little caution for the enterprise." Boone misconstrued the fact that Kentucky possessed wide, unpopulated expanses as a reason to overlook how the Indians would react to this latest and most serious plan for settling it. Even given the overt signs of deadly conflict—Dragging Canoe's warnings, as well as attacks on other settlers in Kentucky—Boone viewed the skirmishes as reasons to *hasten* settlement, not to rethink it or change strategy. Problems motivated Boone. "Now is the time to flusterate their intentions," he wrote to Henderson of the Indians on April 1, 1775, "and keep the country whilst we are in it. If we give way to them now, it will ever be the case." Henderson, in turn, wrote to supporters advocating "the absolute necessity of our not losing one moment" in shoring up Boone's position.

Into these combustible circumstances arrived Jemima and the rest of their family. The fledgling Boonesboro marked a western extension of America and a remote country in itself. The not-yet-finished layout encompassed a mix of cabins and common-use buildings. Henderson and fellow stakeholders soon joined Boone, as did curious visitors, such as thirty-year-old Dr. John Ferdinand Smyth, who boasted a medical degree from Edinburgh University and explained that he was doing research for a book on America. New faces were welcomed, even those only passing through. Visitors might provide help in defense or a particular skill, such as Smyth's medical expertise, as well as novelty and breaks in routine. For his part, Dr. Smyth characterized himself as reluctantly impressed. "Although the inhabitants are in reality a rude, barbarous and unpolished set of men," he wrote, "yet you will frequently find pleasure in their conversation; their ideas are bold and spirited." Smyth eventually noted in the travelogue he wrote that Boonesboro then had seemed a "particularly dangerous" place.

THE FAR BANK of the Kentucky River presented an almost biblical diorama of temptation during the three girls' afternoon canoe cruise of July 14, 1776: grapes, ripe and juicy, and beautiful flowers. Jemima, who sat and steered while the two Callaway sisters stood and rowed, reminded her friends that they were not allowed to cross to the other side, where Indians were known to hunt. This led to light teasing. Was Jemima so afraid of Indians? Or are you afraid, one of her friends asked, of "disobeying your father"—the great Daniel Boone? The teasing was charged. Boone's personality loomed large over settlement life. And Boone's rival for the hearts and minds of Boonesboro happened to be these girls' father, Richard Callaway, who had built one of the larger family cabins at the settlement, an emblem of importance. The friendly taunt reflected the friction between their fathers.

Maybe Jemima caved to the pressure, or swifter river currents conspired with the idea, but the canoe shifted toward the forbidden side of the water. The girls neared what would later be called Black Fish's Ford after the Shawnee warrior Blackfish, a man who would soon have an impact on the Boones' lives and fates. Jemima's fears, passed on to her from her family, were well founded.

Changes had swept the region since they had arrived. Late the previous spring, news of the Battle of Lexington had reached Boonesboro, unfolding a new reality as the Revolutionary War began. The colonists in Kentucky suddenly were no longer outlaws to the neighboring British colonial authorities—in fact, those authorities, such as Virginia's Lord Dunmore, now had to flee for their lives, and the colonists were technically not colonists at all anymore, but settlers and nation builders. Having defied the British at such an important turning point, Boonesboro in wartime stood in the vanguard of a larger rebellion, which was steered by the Continental Congress and its Continental Army. But as all parties regrouped, so did tribes that had been overwhelmed in previous clashes on the battlefield when the colonists and British authorities had been unified.

Despite their teasing of Jemima, when the other girls realized they would soon be out of view of their settlement, they became nervous, too. They all worked together to turn the vessel around. These girls knew how to guard against danger when necessary. They had traversed some of the most unforgiving territories with their families, pulling their own weight and then some. But they had little time to react when their worlds turned upside down.

A figure thrashed into the water and latched on to the boat. In a blur of cultural confusion, the girls first thought he was an enslaved man who had run away from Boonesboro. Dangers to the enslaved individuals had been brought to the fore by the death of Sam during the initial arrival of Daniel Boone's party. Later, one of the enslaved men at Boonesboro, Grampus, took the mare of his enslaver, John Luttrell, fled the fort on horseback, and then, as Richard Henderson put it, "was totally gone." Henderson suspected several settlers had assisted Grampus's flight. Luttrell rounded up three men to help him "overtake" Grampus, but no extant records suggest they ever found him or identified settlers who abetted him.

The vast wilderness that put the enslaved residents in special danger also provided cover.

In thinking the thrashing man in the water might be a runaway, the Boonesboro girls would likely have thought of Grampus. Then, seeing it was not him, they thought the man might be an Indian who had stayed with them at Boonesboro of whom little is known, beyond that his name was Simon—at least, that was his Anglicized name, as Indians were sometimes known one way by settlers and another by their tribes. Relations between settlers and Indians on the frontier ranged in a wide spectrum; they could be allies, could live among one another, could intermarry, or could be sworn enemies.

"Simon! How you scared me!" cried out one of the girls, before realizing this wasn't Simon, either.

As the vessel continued to pull toward shore, Shawnee warriors revealed themselves from behind cane stalks. The warrior in the water forced the canoe to shore. Fanny smashed his head and hands with her oar, frantically pounding. The girls had few options. To go into the rapid water would mean probable drowning, though by one account that's exactly what Jemima did, jumping into the river and living up to her nickname, Duck; if she could make it back to the shore where they came from, unlikely as it was with her injured foot, she could get help and save her friends' lives. If Jemima did risk the swim, it remains uncertain how far she got; the Indians caught up with her and forced her to the far shore with the other girls.

Of the braves, or American Indian warriors, holding position on land waiting for their quarry with weapons, one stood out to Jemima Boone. The regal native leader named Hanging Maw waited to greet them. The fact that he and Jemima already knew each other could mean salvation or death.

BLOODY GROUND

HANGING MAW STUDIED THE THREE girls brought to where he stood on the riverbank. This was a pivotal moment in a complex mission with a wide range of possible outcomes that could affect every settler and Indian on the Kentucky frontier. This leader was a Cherokee, belonging to the community presided over by Chief Oconostota. Years before, that chief had articulated his hopes to curb conflict with the colonists to Lieutenant Henry Timberlake, one of the colonial officers in Virginia: "The bloody tomahawk, so long lifted against our brethren the English, must be buried deep, deep into the ground." This goal set the cultural backdrop for the period in which Hanging Maw came into his own as a warrior and a leader.

During that same era, as the tribe sought equilibrium with colonists, Oconostota spoke at the College of William and Mary to an audience that included then-student Thomas Jefferson, who wrote that he was in awe of the chief, "although I did not understand a word he uttered." At the college, Oconostota studied a portrait of King George III. "I am determined to see him," the Cherokee leader said of the king. "I am now near the sea, and never will depart from it till I have obtained my desires." Oconostota proposed to Lieutenant

Timberlake a trip overseas to pursue common ground with British leadership with the objective of a lasting peace. Arriving in England in 1762, the Cherokee leader sang loudly from the bow of the boat while ships steered closer to listen, blocking the docks. Though some colonists and English focused on the amusing aspects—in their eyes—of an Indian chief's mannerisms, Oconostota's purpose struck a serious chord. His was nothing less than a bid to change history, to stop the gradual yet unmistakable erosion of American Indians' way of life and end bloodshed.

When the visitors marched into the royal hall at St. James's Palace in Westminster, Oconostota gave King George a hug, a Cherokee custom that shocked the monarch. Communication proved a problem during the meeting, more than expected. The interpreter who had traveled with them from Virginia, William Shorey, had died en route, rumored by some to have been murdered with poison—the rumor in itself capturing the high stakes involved. Timberlake did his best to bridge cultures and languages, frantically trying to stop Oconostota when he attempted to light a pipe to smoke with the king. For their part, the Cherokees were impressed by the king's youthfulness and affability.

Most of their exchange is lost to history. But an understanding passed between the powers—an allegiance to British authority by the Cherokee leaders and a promise to the Indians from the crown. Not long after, King George proclaimed new restrictions on American colonists expanding westward. But expansion continued long after that Cherokee delegation left England, empowered by colonists' increasing willingness to defy the British as they carved out an autonomous cultural identity leading up to their revolution. Warriors like Hanging Maw found themselves on one battlefield after another—on small and large scales—defending their lands and communities. When Virginia's governor Lord Dunmore reported the situation back to the crown, he might as well have been thinking of Daniel Boone and his cohort when he wrote that some colonists "for ever imagine the lands further off are still better than those upon which they are already settled." Frontier settlers saw things differently. Their lens was not unlike the one through which the Indians viewed their own motivations. "He explored new countries from the love of nature," said a relative about Daniel Boone, "to find a country . . . where he could hunt and live at ease."

THAT INCREASING DESIRE by colonists to secure land in the years after the Cherokee delegation to England inevitably led to violent clashes that called on talented, honorable warriors such as Hanging Maw. Those clashes could grow into blood feuds that cycled back and forth between the Indians and settlers in the region encompassing parts of Virginia, North Carolina, and Kentucky. News of incidents had to travel long distances, meaning actions and reactions could be separated by months, even years. Rumors spread faster, and could be explosive.

That pattern played itself out in particularly tragic fashion for the area's tribes in April 1774. Michael Cresap, a thirty-two-year-old rabble-rouser traveling on the Ohio River, heard that Cherokees had murdered a settler near Pittsburgh a month earlier. Provoked further by an incendiary letter from a Virginia official implying war with Indians, Cresap set out for blood, vowing, according to a contemporary newspaper, "to put every Indian to death he should meet with on the river." Rebuffing attempts to restrain him, Cresap ambushed several groups of Indians in Captina. Cresap—or, by some accounts, several of his followers—killed at least three, not bothering to identify their tribal affiliations, none of which were Cherokee. Two were Shawnee and one was Delaware.

Soon after that, forty miles north, in Big Yellow Creek, settlers got wind of Cresap's murders. Twisted reasoning came into play: attack Indians near Big Yellow Creek—went some of these settlers' logic—in case the news out of Captina stoked tribal plots for vengeance. A man in his twenties named Daniel Greathouse, who happened to be an acquaintance of Cresap's, snatched this mantle of paranoid overreaction. He rounded up a posse of thirty-two men and concealed them at the tavern of another settler, Joshua Baker, near an Indian encampment. Greathouse then crossed the river into the territory of the Mingo tribe, where a Mingo woman warned him to go away. News of the Captina murders had, in fact, reached the Indians, and the woman believed Greathouse could become a target for their anger. Her warning probably saved his life.

Greathouse left with what he came for: intelligence. He had estimated the number of Indians in the nearby camp, too many to take head-on. He needed a ploy to draw them out and weaken them. He returned to Baker's and instructed the proprietor to ply Indians who came by with alcohol. The sale of liquor had been recognized as detrimental to tribal communities, but profits had prevented the application of any significant restrictions.

Several Indians, men and women, came to Baker's and indulged more than usual, not suspecting a trap. Greathouse's posse, concealed inside the house, watched. In a macabre tableau reflecting the thin line between fellowship and violence, one of the Indians tried on a settlers' military hat and coat, calling out: "I am a white man." He was gunned down on the spot. Greathouse and a half dozen of his men stepped out of hiding and slaughtered every Indian they saw. Included among the dead was the same woman who had protected Greathouse at the Indian encampment. Other Indians, hearing the gunfire, rowed across the river in canoes toward Baker's to investigate. Greathouse's men went outside, shooting at the rowers.

When they returned from the river, they were asked what happened to the Indians in the canoes. The riflemen answered, "They [fell] overboard into the river."

According to one account of the atrocities inside Baker's, the attackers eviscerated a pregnant Indian woman, impaling the fetus on a stake. These murders shocked all sides, contributing to the start of what became known as Lord Dunmore's War, pitting the western colonies against the region's tribes.

Only one Indian in the house survived that day. A baby girl had been strapped to the back of her now-murdered mother. A member of Greathouse's group grabbed the infant by the ankles, ready to smash her head. One of the other assailants, clinging to a shred of humanity, intervened to save her.

THE FACT THAT Hanging Maw was a Cherokee guiding a group of Shawnee braves to capture the Boonesboro girls was telling but not entirely surprising, given the violence against the frontier's various tribes. These tribes had profound bonds with each other, some long-standing and some more recent. In the extraordinary history of American Indians before the arrival of the settlers, which spanned thousands of years, many of the separate tribes had come from overlapping and richly connected communities. Individual Indians also maintained their own interconnections. Oconostota, chief of Hanging Maw's Cherokee tribe, was half Shawnee. The Indian known as Captain Will, who first warned Boone to stay out of Kentucky, had shifted from Cherokee to Shawnee affiliation. The leader of the Mingoes married a Shawnee woman—slaughtered along with the others at Baker's tavern by Daniel Greathouse's marauders.

When the dust settled, the short-lived Lord Dunmore's War hurt the Shawnee as much as any tribe—and in turn motivated them.

Shawnee chief Cornstalk, taking a stance like that of his Cherokee counterpart Oconostota, generally tried to avoid armed conflict. Cornstalk was a large man who had a commanding presence,
"graceful and attractive," according to one colonial report. The
tribal structure of the Shawnee divided groups by function, and
Cornstalk guided the branch known as Maquachakes, representing
a kind of civil administration for the tribe. They resisted Christian
missionaries and other cultural intrusions, whether from Europe-
ans or from other tribes. As encroachments from the outside grew,
Shawnee settled into a policy of protectiveness, one that became a
way of life. Cornstalk did not hold high regard for his tribal peers
who thought resolution came by fighting. "I have with great trouble
and pains," he remarked during one crisis, "prevailed on the foolish
people amongst us to sit still and do no harm till we see whether it is
the intention of the white people in general to fall on us." Cornstalk
even willingly talked with Michael Cresap, whom many blamed for
lighting the fuse that ignited Dunmore's War. Though Cornstalk
steered his people toward peace, he could not overcome the call
to battle from more militant quarters in the tribe, in particular a
very vocal group of warriors. At the forefront of this movement was
the Shawnee Blackfish, ten years Cornstalk's junior, a relative hard-
liner about using force when threatened.

Whatever resistance Cornstalk put up behind the scenes, he did
not show reluctance on the battlefield. In the definitive clash of
Dunmore's War, he led the charge of Shawnee troops, by one account
riding a striking white horse. This engagement would be known
as the Battle of Point Pleasant. Cornstalk cried out "Be strong! Be
strong!" to his soldiers. But colonial military overtook Shawnee
troops, who likely included Blackfish and his militant allies, who
had pressured Cornstalk into fighting in the first place. The losses
piled up. Casualty estimates suggest that as many as 25 percent of

Indian fighters were lost. By one possibly dramatized report, Cornstalk used a hatchet to kill one of his own men who tried to run
away from the increasingly hopeless battle.

In contrast to the conventional narrative of a rout, John Floyd,
a friend of Daniel Boone's, had a more nuanced evaluation after
witnessing the battle as part of the Virginia militia. Floyd believed
that the fight was actually a draw, and that the Indians only appeared to be at a disadvantage because they were trying to carry
off their wounded, while the colonists by chance were positioned
in the woods in a way that shielded them. Floyd also believed that
many of the colonial soldiers actually "lurked behind" and refused
to fight. The victory, in other words, may have been a by-product of
the locale and a reluctance by colonial soldiers that kept them from
becoming casualties.

Regardless of the reasons, the Shawnee retreated. In the wake
of the lost battle, Cornstalk, a skilled orator, rallied his warriors—
not to keep fighting, but to vie for peace. He called out: "Shall we
kill all our women and children and then fight until we are killed
ourselves?"

Cornstalk ended up leading treaty talks with colonists at a temporary encampment called Camp Charlotte. The agreement included provisions interpreted by settlers as part of the larger trend
toward settling Kentucky. As with Hanging Maw's Cherokees after
Sycamore Shoals, these concessions caused fissures between Shawnee leadership trying to cut their losses and factions of Indians fu-
rious about losing power and property they considered rightfully
theirs to use—even if not to "own" in the way settlers viewed property. Boonesboro and other fledgling settlements now threatened
the Shawnee community's much-needed hunting grounds in Kentucky. "All our lands are covered by the white people," Cornstalk
lamented.

From a non-native perspective, the Shawnee presence in eastern Kentucky was tied up with the legends of a man with the last name Swift—his first name varied depending on the account—who supposedly collaborated with the Shawnee in the 1760s, working a secret silver mine before going blind, when the mine was lost forever. (Some versions include Swift murdering his fellow miners.) This tale was popularized by John Filson, who would also popularize Boone's adventures. Various expeditions would be launched—and continue to be to this day—to look for the treasure. Another series of legends also promoted by Filson went further back than the stories of Swift's secret mines. These stories revolved around "White Indians" who had inhabited Kentucky long before the American Indians, before the latter killed them in battle.

The confused fable and so-called evidence of white natives invited settlers to argue against precedence of American Indians on frontier land; the Swift legends represent a romanticized mid-eighteenth-century world in which explorers united with Indians to generate indescribable wealth. In reality, settlers' ambitions put the actual Indian way of life in Kentucky in grave peril. Tribes, including Shawnee, had already relocated some of their towns west as settlers transformed and disrupted natural and economic ecosystems. Indian life often flowed with the seasons, split between cycles of hunting and growing crops, with Kentucky particularly vital to extensive winter hunting. Shawnee were migratory. When settlers claimed land, however, they demanded complete control over it and violently expelled the Indians, as well as depleting game, not based on need but instead on how much could be killed. A European traveler pointed this out with surprise, remarking how some hunters "kill six or eight deer every day, which many do merely for their skins, to the great injury and destruction of the species, and to the prejudice and public loss of the community at large." For one particular journeyer into Kentucky, the reflexive response to seeing a buffalo for the first time was to shoot at it. (In less than twenty years, the plentiful American buffalo in Kentucky seen by Boone's awestruck companion Felix Walker would go extinct because of such practices.) Without their hunting territory, Cherokee and Shawnee communities could starve, and for decades the tribes had seen countless Cresaps and Greathouses, who found excuses to slaughter American Indians and grab land.

When colonists protested British taxes and control in the Boston Tea Party in December 1773, they dressed in Indian costumes and painted their faces, and the participants called themselves Mohawk or Narragansett, as though tribal identities were interchangeable. The iconography of Indians had become useful symbols for political rebellion and a natural right to fight against authority, even while actual Indians were placed in a terrible bind by these political and military developments. With the start of the Revolutionary War in 1775, tribes had responded in a wide variety of ways with a range of positions, sometimes inside each tribe. Within Indian families and clans, alliances and conflicts sprouted up over what to do. Some tribes or groups aligned with the revolutionaries, some with the British, and some felt deeply torn, indifferent, or confused. To be stuck in the middle of a fierce war in which one's own land was directly at issue felt apocalyptic, with good reason.

A few months after Camp Charlotte had come the Cherokee concessions at Sycamore Shoals in which Hanging Maw participated. It was here that the rising tribal leader met Daniel Boone and visited the Boone family cabin, being introduced to young Jemima.

Dragging Canoe, the Cherokee renegade, had been right when he had warned those settlers at Sycamore Shoals about the Shawnee. While Cornstalk pleaded through diplomatic channels to stop land grabs, in May 1776 a group of Shawnee warriors decided on blunter action as the Revolutionary War raged on. The warriors traveled with representatives of four other tribes to the Cherokee town of Chota seeking direct action to regain land. Cherokees in particular had strategic and symbolic importance in the landscape of American Indians. The intertribal delegation marched into Chota with faces painted black, portending war.

The visitors reported to the Cherokee leaders how "they found the country thickly inhabited and the people all in arms." One of the Shawnee then presented a nine-foot-long purple war belt—a call to military action—to the Cherokees. As recorded by a British trader who was present, an unnamed Shawnee warrior spoke of how the rebel colonists had "unjustly brought war upon their nation and destroyed many of their people; that in a very few years their nation from being a great people were now reduced to a handful; that their nation possessed lands almost to the seashore and that the red people who were once masters of the whole country hardly possessed ground enough to stand on . . . that he thought it better to die like men than to diminish away by inches." The speaker insisted "that now is the time to begin" the real fight.

Oconostota, who years earlier had voyaged to England hoping for peace, refused to take on the visitors' militant cause, despite the long line of disappointments and personal losses he had absorbed over the years. Other Cherokee decision-makers also still sought a peaceful route to endure the latest upheavals caused by the Revolutionary War. But this old guard came off as frustrated, even helpless. Instead, Dragging Canoe, who had warned of the dangers at Sycamore Shoals, stepped forward to accept the symbolic belt for his breakaway faction of Cherokee. Those in favor of fighting started a chant that meant one thing: war.

Now Hanging Maw faced a hard decision. He was part of the upcoming generation of Cherokee leaders. He had fought alongside

George Washington years before in a smaller but formative conflict, the French and Indian War, when both leaders were "young
and warriors," as Hanging Maw reflected later. Daniel Boone also
crossed paths with George Washington during the same conflict to
block French expansion into British territories, when twenty-year-
old Boone served as a teamster, transporting supplies. (It was from a
fellow teamster, a well-traveled trader, that Boone first heard details
about Kentucky.)

But the fact was that the settlement of Kentucky threatened all
the tribes' futures; even if tribes were willing to move west, that
would become impossible if the settlers opened the floodgates to
their own unchecked westward expansion. The situation increasingly resembled a trap.

Though no records exist of Hanging Maw ever having defied
Oconostota prior to this, he now joined Dragging Canoe's movement. This meant being on war footing and, as it turned out, becoming part of a new and dangerous mission. Leading an intertribal
party with the Shawnee, Hanging Maw trekked into Kentucky with
four fighters, with urgency growing as the fledgling Boonesboro grew
stronger by the day. The intertribal party's ostensible goal, to use a
settler's contemporaneous description of another party of Shawnee
warriors, was "to take a look at the white people on Kentucky."
Their real purpose was to fight to save Kentucky from disappearing
into the hands of the settlers.

Not far from Boonesboro, along the south fork of Licking River,
a settler named John Cooper tended land on a modest homestead.
Cooper had come to Kentucky in a group of fifteen, around the same
time as the Henderson-backed Boone mission. Splitting off from
the others, Cooper built a cabin and, it was said, became the first
settler to raise a crop of corn in Kentucky. In some ways, his cabin
set an even more threatening precedent in the Indians' eyes than

a well-armed fort, making clear that settlers would spread out at random and control land far and wide. On July 7, 1776, a raiding party of Indians killed Cooper, while others from Cooper's original party fled north. Then on July 14, the same day Jemima Boone and friends pushed off in a canoe on the Kentucky River, another transient settler was killed near Cooper's homestead. Both of the deaths were likely the handiwork of the band of warriors led by Hanging Maw, and their biggest target still awaited them.

AS HE STEPPED out from his hiding place at the Kentucky River, Hanging Maw may have been the leader of his party, but the other four men were also formidable. Braves of the Shawnee tribe often wore clothes of bright colors with paint and feathers, and in the summer wore just a breechcloth below the waist. One of the Shawnee men was called Big Jimmy. Another Shawnee there was reportedly "a noted Indian brave" known as Catfish. They all spoke some English, possibly selected for that skill. This was not merely a military maneuver, but also a political one.

Hanging Maw recognized Jemima from Sycamore Shoals, when he had visited the Boone cabin as one of the Cherokee representatives negotiating the controversial land purchase. When she was brought to him now, Hanging Maw asked Jemima if her two companions were her sisters.

"Yes," she replied.

Here was a chance for the tribes to gain leverage on a central figure of the frontier. Hanging Maw said, laughing: "We have done pretty well for old Boone this time—got all his young squaws."

THE PLAN

FROM HER VANTAGE POINT AT the fort at Boonesboro, Rebecca Boone, thirty-seven, dark-haired and strong-shouldered, could see the banks of the Kentucky River. "She is by nature a quiet soul," a contemporary commented of Rebecca, "and of few words." The site for the fortress of cabins was chosen with proximity to the water in mind, and Rebecca knew this river well. Rebecca and Jemima were, as far as they could figure, the first female settlers who stood on the shore of the Kentucky, and for a period of weeks upon their initial arrival among the very few women amid the Boonesboro settlers. From her position, Rebecca could check on her daughter Jemima and the Callaway girls. The Boones and Callaways had shared the tense ups and downs of establishing Boonesboro.

Rebecca married Daniel when she was sixteen, just a few years older than Jemima now. Rebecca came from a large family, the Bryans, who had dispersed themselves throughout the same emerging backcountry as the Boones. In fact, Rebecca first saw Daniel at one of several Bryan-Boone weddings. As the co-head of the Boone household, Rebecca now wielded her own expert gun, oversaw a home front that changed locales regularly, and during Daniel's long absences taught the children both domestic and outdoor skills. Early in their time in Kentucky, after the controversial land purchase at Sycamore Shoals, she had given birth to a son, William. But the pregnancy had been a difficult one, and the baby died soon after. Grief and physical recovery would be interrupted by the demands of their surroundings and by taking care of their other children, including the youngest, six-year-old Daniel Morgan and three-year-old Jesse.

As she glanced down once again from the fort, Rebecca made out what appeared to be the flash of a tomahawk before the girls disappeared into the wilderness on the far side of the river. Margaret Callaway, the stepmother to the two girls with Jemima, noted the ominous disturbance, too. Then "a terrible shriek" and screams broke the air from the girls' location. The mothers' hearts sank.

In one of the cabins, Daniel Boone, now forty-one, napped in his finest clothes. It was Sunday, and the residents of Boonesboro would soon convene for the second time that day. Though typically they managed without a preacher unless one happened to be passing through, they would mark the Sabbath by gathering and setting aside time to rest or frolic, rare activities for them as they tried to build a town out of a wilderness. The fort-in-progress consisted of a dozen similar log cabins laid out in a rectangle, with a high fence enclosing it. Their favorite place to congregate was under a giant elm, the "divine tree," its enormous branches providing shade for a hundred people over a "turf of fine white clover" to sit on. Richard Henderson, the settlement's haughty benefactor, privately raised an eyebrow at these scenes. He questioned whether any religious services could help the fort's "set of scoundrels who scarcely believe in God or fear a devil."

Rebecca shouted: "The savages have the girls!" Daniel Boone jumped up with a start from his nap. He ran out, snatching his rifle on the way. Quickly taking in from the others the little that was seen and known, he launched into a run to the river to try to head off the canoe. He had not stopped to put on shoes.

Nathan Reid had forgotten to accompany the girls on their excursion. It turned out that Reid and his friend John Floyd, a twenty-five-year-old surveyor who cut an imposing figure at over six feet tall with dark hair and skin, stood talking under an elm tree. Through the woods toward them bolted thirteen-year-old Caleb Callaway, brother of the Callaway sisters who were with Jemima. "They've captured the girls!"

Floyd grabbed Caleb by the shoulders. "What are you talking about? Who captured what girls?"

"The Indians. They took Mima, Betsy, and Fanny."

Floyd and Reid took off for the fort "as fast as our legs could carry us," as Reid later recalled, and upon arriving "we found preparations making for immediate pursuit." Reid spotted Richard Callaway loading his gun.

Boone reached the river, but too late. The canoe drifted in the water, empty and overturned. A heart-stopping symbol of his daughter's possible fate and—considering that the Indians could have gotten some use out of the canoe—maybe a taunt directed at Boone. Or worse: a trap.

The settlers first needed to retrieve their lone canoe to use for a rescue attempt. But every possible move carried a degree of risk. The Indians could have been monitoring the canoe and waiting to attack anybody who tried to reach it. Other Boonesboro residents who'd heard the hue and cry joined Boone. Betsy's fiancé, Samuel Henderson, thirty, was the younger brother of Richard Henderson, who spearheaded and oversaw the fort's settlement. Samuel had been out hunting when the girls left, and was back in his cabin shaving when he heard the shouting, dropping his blade and scooping up his gun, leaving half his face unshaven. Twenty-three-year-old Flanders Callaway also arrived armed. At the river, they studied the situation and conferred with each other. "Who will swim over after the canoe?"

John Gass volunteered. He was twelve years old. The young Boonesboro resident had made a name for himself on an earlier occasion when he stood up to the dictatorial Richard Callaway and was publicly reprimanded by the settlement's authorities. Now drawing on his courage again, Gass stripped off his clothes and, despite the strong currents, dove in. He would present an easy target for a sharpshooter, but at least he was small and quick. As the boy propelled himself as fast as he could across the water, Boone and the others trained their rifles to cover his path, watching for combatants. Gass reached the overturned canoe and flipped it from underneath. Climbing into the vessel, he steered back to shore, where the others cheered.

Richard Henderson had commented a month earlier that attacks by Indians—and casualties resulting from any such attacks—could actually *help* the settlement by motivating its inhabitants to be more security-minded. He posited that such small-scale attacks would not hurt them in the long term. "A few skulkers could only kill one or two," he wrote, "which would not much affect the interest of the company." But despite Henderson's cold-blooded calculus, no one took the latest turn of events lightly. Indian warriors had captured the daughters of the two leaders of the community, with ramifications both personal and political. The group on shore grew with new arrivals from Boonesboro eager to help. In addition to Boone, Henderson, Flanders Callaway, and Gass, the rescue party rounded out with twenty-somethings Reid and Floyd, and William Bailey Smith, a thirty-nine-year-old adventurer.

Some of these settlers had been well known to Boone for years; in other cases, he now put faith in relative strangers, who might prove pleasant surprises or grave disappointments. Dr. John Ferdinand Smyth, the English visitor who had been welcomed to research a travelogue, had been an object lesson. It turned out Smyth, as he was described by a longtime acquaintance, "had always a trick of shooting from a long bow." In other words, he was a pathological liar. Stories of noble parentage almost certainly were invented, along with his medical degree itself, and records show that he had been on the run after failing to pay creditors.

In the case of John Floyd, demand for his surveying skills increased with colonists' desires to claim, settle, and sell land. Though he had received a no-frills education, he surpassed many of his contemporaries on the frontier in both writing skills and etiquette. Floyd had been loyal to Boone since an early excursion marking land in Kentucky, when Boone risked his own safety to convey a warning to the surveyors at the outset of Lord Dunmore's War. Floyd continued to look up to Boone, having reported back to Virginia a sentiment that "Boone has more influence than any man now disengaged." Like Boone, Floyd was a captain in the militia. They were now joined in the growing search party by two more captains, Nathaniel Hart, forty-two, a contrarian by nature who was a frequent thorn in Richard Henderson's side, and David Gass, forty-four, the younger Gass's uncle, who had accompanied Boone on some of his first missions into Kentucky.

Also rushing to the spot was Richard Callaway, whose rank as a major meant he was technically the most senior military official in Kentucky. Richard, the distraught father of Betsy and Fanny, was not only Boone's counterpart in terms of experience and personal stakes—the very life of their daughters—but also Boone's most formidable partner and challenger. Callaway's status, both in the military and in family wealth, outranked Boone's, yet Boone, as usual, grabbed the mantle of leadership.

Herculean legends grew around Daniel Boone, with one witness deeming him physically "gigantic." The frontiersman actually stood about five eight, slightly below the era's average, with strong shoulders and build, a wide jaw with a loose front tooth from a childhood fight, and a light complexion. But an aura hung about him that enhanced his stature. When a Virginia official sent Boone to warn the surveying team that included John Floyd about possible danger, the official declared that "it is indisputable" Boone would find them, the sort of unreasonable confidence that so many had about Boone. When problems arose, people naturally looked to him for solutions, and Boone made his name by overcoming challenges.

NOT THAT BOONE'S missions always succeeded—sometimes they ended in stark tragedy. Three years prior, in the fall of 1773, a few groups of adventurers, including one featuring Boone and a frequent hunting companion named Michael Stoner, had set off in an earlier attempt to settle Kentucky. The separate traveling parties were to rendezvous after crossing into Kentucky. The men who joined Boone's group along the way included heavyset, kindhearted William Bush, known as Billy, cousin to Boone's wife, Rebecca. One of the other parties included Boone's sixteen-year-old son, James Boone, whose fair hair that day was braided in a style inspired by the Indians. James had been a hunting partner for his father from before the age of ten, when Daniel would help his son pass through deep snow by "hugging him up to him."

In their long history of hunting in the Kentucky wilderness, Indians had developed and maintained seasonal villages, sometimes inhabited by multiple tribes. Because Indian tribes negotiated various arrangements with each other over the use of these lands, and because treaties—more and less formal—were made between separate groups of Indians and colonists, some colonists either ignored, over-looked, or remained ignorant of what to others seemed strict bound-aries. While some transgressions were blatant, at other times what one side may have believed to be legitimate movements rang out to the other side as acts of war. Individuals who crossed paths as neighbors one day became enemies with a slight location change or a heightened political climate, sometimes without warning. A terrify-ing way of life took hold for Indian and colonist alike in the frontier.

James Boone's group on this occasion included two young men around his age, Henry Russell and Isaac Crabtree, as well as four other settlers, including Samuel Drake and two enslaved men, Charles and Adam. Advisors had suggested that enslaved individuals not be allowed in the Kentucky settlements, and some political thinkers recognized the hypocrisy of complaining about being "enslaved" by British rule while directly enslaving others. But it's unlikely that a movement toward preventing slavery in Kentucky would have gained traction among the colonists. Records suggest the Boone family did not own any slaves during the times they were explor-ing and attempting to settle Kentucky, but many of those joining the Boones' exploring parties actively engaged in the slave economy and brought enslaved men, women, and children. Virginia laws re-stricted the sanctioned use of weapons by "negros, mulattos, or indians," though exceptions existed for frontier life. These enslaved individuals were often given weapons and major responsibilities on these grueling treks, putting their lives at risk and putting the lives of the others in their hands.

Evidence suggests that James Boone's party, charged with gath-ering supplies, traveled unarmed or, at most, lightly armed. After making camp for a night, James Boone woke to find his group sur-rounded by an armed party of Shawnee and Cherokee. The Indians shot several of the men dead, including Samuel Drake. One of the

Shawnee warriors, known as Big Jim, had visited the Boone home before, so he and James recognized each other. James addressed Big Jim, begging that he spare him.

According to the testimony of the survivors and details passed down through family lore, Big Jim tortured James and Henry Russell, pulling out fingernails and toenails. James's pleas for mercy changed into begging to be killed. Their attackers stabbed them to death. Before he died, James, his will broken, expressed his erroneous belief that his whole family had probably already been killed. One of the enslaved men concealed himself under debris, watching and listening to all of this unfold. He escaped to relate the horror he witnessed and James's last words, while Isaac Crabtree ran off in another direction.

Informed of what happened, a heartbroken Daniel Boone found himself helpless, a state of being antithetical to his hands-on approach to life. He journeyed to do the one thing he could: recover James's remains. Daniel and Rebecca Boone long ago had accepted that their safety and that of their children fluctuated dramatically with the political and military tides. No doubt this factored into the dark feelings and worries Rebecca shared with a visiting minister who recorded "that her heart was often restless and anxious, though then the feelings would again leave her." The constant presence of danger was encapsulated by a persistent legend that during their courtship Boone nearly shot Rebecca while hunting. Their lives never oriented around estates and establishments, appointments and pensions, but rather built themselves around journeys and discoveries, big risks and prospective rewards. In fact, after James died, Boone was still determined to move forward with the expedition that had taken his son's life—but the rest of the group overruled him.

Rebecca gave her husband blankets to bring with him to bury their son. After Boone dug graves for the dead and covered the bodies with logs, sticks carved with each deceased's initials were placed to the side as markers. The *Virginia Gazette*, one of the earliest newspapers in the region, reported the "inhuman affair," and a colonial official captured the widespread shock when he recorded that "the Murder of Russell, Boons, and Drakes sons is in every ones mouth," conspicuously leaving out the names of the less well known and the enslaved casualties. The Indian community also absorbed the news. In the aftermath of the deaths, Cherokee chiefs sought justice for what their tribesmen had done. Cherokee leaders appear to have executed at least one member of their tribe for the murders, and put another "in confinement."

One of the few members of James Boone's party to escape, Isaac Crabtree was consumed by what had happened. He reportedly vowed revenge on every Indian he could find. In March 1774, settlers and Indians held a horse race in Indian territories in western North Carolina. Crabtree staged an ambush and murdered an Indian. The victim turned out to be the brother of Oconostota, the powerful chief of the Cherokees and Hanging Maw's superior, an act that in itself could start a war. Crabtree reportedly attempted to ambush an Indian hunting party, too, but failed. Gestures toward justice crossed cultural boundaries. Just as Cherokees pursued James Boone's killers, colonial authorities announced a bounty for the capture of Crabtree.

WHEN THE INDIAN warrior towed Boonesboro's canoe to shore, Betsy and Fanny had struck their oars against him until Fanny's oar split in half. Betsy screamed loudly until one of the Indians waiting on shore grabbed her by the hair and held a knife to her head. The Callaway family always thought Betsy took after her father, sharing Richard's dark looks and the ability to command a situation.

Fanny, on the other hand, they perceived as frail and lighthearted. She cried so hard at the start of the ordeal, her throat swelled.

Jemima proved herself her parents' daughter, suppressing fear and anger, concentrating on assessing the scene and their situation. Once the girls were on shore, their captors set the canoe loose on the water, an alarming decision that made one thing clear at the outset: they weren't after just the canoe, which, on an ordinary day, would have been a prize.

Jemima took it all in, and most of all took in the Indians' apparent leader, Hanging Maw, sorting out what his presence meant, just as he did about her. Jemima remembered Hanging Maw from Watauga, where he had called on their cabin as one of the Cherokee with whom her father negotiated for land.

When Hanging Maw asked Jemima if her two companions were her sisters, she had to think quickly. If he believed the Callaway girls were Boones, he might be less likely to harm them, either out of goodwill or a hesitancy to spark the wrath of her father. "Yes," she said, lying.

His response—"We have done pretty well for old Boone this time, got all his young squaws"—left room for interpretation. Did Hanging Maw mean the raiding party had done well for the purposes of leveraging Boone, or for enacting revenge for Boone's part in the loss of their lands? Or for getting vengeance for other settlers' wrongdoings over the last several years—senseless murders by the myriad Cresaps and Crabtrees of the region—by using a high-status family as stand-ins?

After walking with their captors for a short time, Jemima refused to budge. "I would rather die," she announced. She showed her wounded foot. Every step made the injury worse. Both Jemima and Fanny—like Daniel Boone himself during the initial swirl of the events—had bare feet. One of the Indians threatened Jemima. She didn't scream, but still refused to move. At one point, one of the Callaway sisters threw coal from a nearby fire onto the feet of a captor, burning him through his moccasins; the other Indians laughed and complimented the girl's spirit.

The captors relented, providing moccasins for both barefoot girls. The braves also took hold of the bottom of their dresses and petticoats, and began slicing into them—shortening them to the knees to allow the girls to walk faster. They buried the discarded clothing under a log to avoid leaving anything behind that could give away their route to trackers. The new outfits demoralized young ladies inculcated with colonial modesty. But in addition to their tactical awareness, the Indians showed emotional sensitivity. Rather than leaving their legs bare, they let the girls repurpose spare cloth as leggings. In their strange outfits, the girls made it about six miles on the day of their kidnapping "through canebrakes, marshy grounds, old logs, briars," as family tradition told it. A few weeks earlier, Richard Henderson had noted that the area was "so fertile, the growth of grass and herbage so tender and luxuriant that it is almost impossible for man or dog to travel, without leaving such sign that you might, for many days, gallop a horse on the trail." Though Henderson no doubt exaggerated, the Indians were attuned to the risks of leaving any trail and deftly concealed their path before camping for the night. Each girl was tied with cords and rawhide to a tree with her back against the trunk. There was just enough distance between them that they couldn't reach one another.

IN THE RICOCHET of violence and retaliation crisscrossing the American frontier, Indians had taken other young men and women prisoner, and those stories circulated among settlers as cautionary tales. The experience of Mary Jemison typified the complexities involved. In 1758, fifteen-year-old Mary and her family were rounded up in rural Pennsylvania by a combined force of Shawnee and French soldiers, during the time the French unsuccessfully challenged British dominance over the region.

As captors and captives trekked into the unknown, one of the Shawnee singled out Mary to provide her with moccasins. Seeing this, her mother guessed that Mary would be spared but the adults would be killed. Mary later remembered, as dramatized by a minister who interviewed her, an emotional moment when her mother took her aside to say good-bye, emphasizing the transience of their cultural identities, at least as far as language and family went. "My heart bleeds at the thought of what awaits you," she told Mary, "but, if you leave us, remember, my child, your own name, and the names of your father and mother. Be careful and not forget your English tongue. If you shall have an opportunity to get away from the Indians don't try to escape; for if you do they will find and destroy you."

Mary's family members were brought to another part of the woods, where they were killed and scalped. The terrified girl then witnessed the "wet and bloody" scalps of her family being prepared for preservation at the fire. She ended up adopted into a tribal family. Once in the Indian town, the flip side of the blood feud came into view: people gathered grieving the loss of a young Indian man slain by colonists. The clan considered Mary reparation for the devastating loss. Family lines blurred and shifted. "She is our sister," Mary remembered being spoken of by one of the squaws who took her in, "and gladly we welcome her here."

BOONE ORDERED THE rescue party to split into two squads to conduct reconnaissance. Richard Callaway, who had arrived on horseback, agreed to lead those searchers riding horses down the Boonesboro side of the river. They galloped off. Boone, meanwhile, used the canoe retrieved by John Gass to take the remaining five men across the river to study the scene of the kidnapping. "On ascending the river bluff" on the other side, Nathan Reid later remembered, Boone wanted to cover as much ground as they could. "Boone directed us to divide in order to discover, as soon as possible, the course they had gone." Reid, Smith, and expert surveyor Floyd searched upriver; Boone, Samuel Henderson, and young Gass traveled downriver. Callaway's mounted squad crossed the river at a shallow point about a mile down, and then reversed course, regrouping with Boone's party.

Floyd's trio identified the captors' initial trail, something that could be deduced from a single bent blade of grass. This sparked the first big disagreement between the larger party's two leaders. Callaway, characterized in family lore as being "frantic with excitement" by this point, insisted they ought to follow the Indians' trail and catch up as quickly as possible. Though charging ahead would be a satisfying course of action, it wasn't the smartest, thought the methodical Boone. "Boone objected to following the trail," Nathan Boone, Jemima's younger brother, later explained, "lest the Indians having a back watch would discover them." If that happened, or even if the captors heard the sounds of oncoming horses, it would mean disaster. "The moment they discover us they will . . . tomahawk the girls," Daniel Boone warned the party, "and make their escape or give us battle; but their first act will be to tomahawk and scalp the girls."

Boone hatched a strategic plan, one that bet on the risky proposition that they'd have enough time to save the girls: Callaway would lead his riders along the river to where they suspected the captors would try to cross at Lower Blue Licks (named for the salt licks) to block any passage in that direction. Boone and the others would simultaneously follow the captors' tracks on foot as stealthily as possible. It was inherently difficult for Callaway's mounted party to move about undetected, and Boone's plan accounted for that. That didn't mean Callaway took the idea of being sidelined in stride. As dramatized in a family history, Callaway's "whole frame quivered with an ill-concealed apprehension." He and his portion of the group abided by Boone's plan, but the disagreement registered strongly enough that rumors later circulated of Callaway riding right back to Boonesboro and sulking instead of heeding Boone to try to save their daughters. When Boone later listed who was involved in the operation, he pointedly left out Callaway.

Daylight faded, the coming night slowing them down in new ways. "The dews were very heavy," a Boonesboro resident later noted about the area known for oppressive humidity this time of year, "the nights in the heat of the summer cool." Floyd recalled, "We could not that night follow more than five miles before dark." Boone's squadron moving on foot then heard a startling sound: a barking dog. They wondered—though the track hadn't indicated it, had they already come to the raiders' encampment? They marked where they had left off following the trail. Then Boone led them toward the barking, cautiously and silently, preparing to improvise an attack. They found nine settlers, some of whom previously lived at Boonesboro. They were building a cabin.

The British were launching fronts wherever they could in the war, and an area as sparsely settled as Kentucky placed the breakaway American republic in serious danger. This lone cabin was another sign of the revolutionaries' increased incentive to spread out across Kentucky as they adjusted to a war footing. For some, lone cabins also presented a fresh start from societal limitations and prejudices in the still-emerging frontier culture. Six miles south of

Boonesboro, for example, Richard Hines had set up a cabin the previous year. Hines, who may have fought in Lord Dunmore's War alongside some Boonesboro residents (Nathaniel Hart called him "as good a soldier as any we had"), was probably the first free Black settler in this early phase of settlement in Kentucky. He was growing corn and experimenting with crops no one else was raising this deep within the frontier.

Boone's party explained what happened and the cabin campers invited them to stay the night to regroup before resuming their search. The first order of business was to gather more supplies, provisions, and clothes. Boone had been barefoot since leaving Boonesboro, subjecting his feet to rough terrain in which their condition was going from bad to desperate.

Young John Gass rose to the occasion once again. The indefatigable twelve-year-old ran—in the pitch-black wilderness, no less—all the way to Boonesboro, without a trail to follow. He retrieved what he could and returned to the temporary camp before sunrise. Boone's relief can be imagined as he slipped his throbbing feet into his moccasins. Gass also brought back changes of clothing. Until that point they still wore their Sunday finest—including baggy pantaloons, stiff enough that they "somewhat impeded our movements," as Reid understated it.

By break of day Monday, when they readied to set out again, three of the campers volunteered to join Boone's dangerous expedition, and they were welcomed into the fold. Boone knew two of them well. Billy Bush, now thirty, was Rebecca Boone's cousin who had been with Boone in the party that first reached the site of Boonesboro a year earlier. Another familiar face was John McMillen, who had previously recuperated at Boonesboro from hunting injuries (brought to safety by the same precocious hero, John Gass) before setting off to help build the cabin outpost; McMillen made a memorable impression with hair so long he could wrap it around his legs. John Martin, a tall, blue-eyed veteran of the French and Indian War, joined them. These campers' quick enlistment in the cause reflected the spirit of cooperation that kept pioneers alive, and also the respect that Boone inspired in others.

In addition to having been one of the first arrivals at Boonesboro, Bush had been alongside Boone when James Boone was killed, a family tragedy that now threatened to repeat itself.

The experience and circumstances of James's death had remained raw with Boone, haunting him. On one of his trips through Kentucky before settling Boonesboro, he had visited his son's grave, a detour the reticent and stoic adventurer said left him feeling "worse than ever in his life," according to his son Nathan. Isaac Crabtree may have devoted himself to revenge after surviving the attack that killed James, but Daniel did not, even though it was his son who had died. He did not channel grief into anger. The tragedy led him to deeper introspection than was his custom, though, to be sure, he thought about his own life and circumstances more than that of the Indians who watched settlers ignore their pleas and warnings and claim land they relied upon for hunting and farming.

Daniel's striking descriptions of that visit to James's grave are likely an amalgam of the actual physical experience with a projection of his inner sorrow. By Boone's own account, he discovered that wolves had tried to dig down to the bodies, so he dug into the ground with a handspike, placing his saddle blanket above the bodies and repairing the graves, but then the clear sky suddenly turned into a fierce storm. He claimed to find fresh blood on the body. As one of his granddaughters dramatically related the story, Boone observed that "the wounds commenced bleeding afresh." He called this seeming echo of Christ's stigmata "singular." It turned out that a group of Indians had been approaching Boone that same night.

He later said the storm had saved his life, having slowed down the Indians enough for him to finish his work at the gravesite before stealing away. Otherwise, he believed, he would have been fatally outnumbered and would have died at his son's grave.

IN THE IMPROVISED team that formed around Boone to find the missing Boonesboro girls were men with a wide range of backgrounds, ambitions, and motivations.

William Bailey "Billy" Smith, two years younger than Boone, was described by an early historian of the Kentucky frontier as "unstable"—meaning, in this instance, apt to change his purpose and conviction. When residing in North Carolina, Smith attended the March 1775 treaty negotiations with the Cherokee at Sycamore Shoals alongside Boone and Callaway. He then accompanied Richard Henderson's party to rendezvous with Boone and the others at the newly founded settlement, for a while acting as a surveyor.

At six feet, Smith stood very tall for his era, with light hair and blue eyes and a larger-than-life conviviality. A bachelor untethered to the concerns that came with family, Smith seemed up for any undertaking, but that also bestowed on him an air of jolly recklessness. He was said to be a drinker. He was sometimes quicker to act than he ought to be. And Smith thought very highly of himself and his own value as a hunter, explorer, and military leader.

In the case of John Floyd, the mission to find Jemima represented a way to repay Boone for risking his life to warn Floyd and the other surveyors of danger two years earlier. "You know what Boone has done for me," Floyd wrote to a confidante, "for which reason I love the man." The Floyd family cherished their "Indian blood"— Floyd's maternal grandmother was part Indian, possibly from the Powhatan tribe—an interesting attitude to coexist with contemporary characterizations of Indians as "savages" and with the frequent tactical operations against them, including the current one to find Boonesboro's lost girls. Like Smith, Floyd was tall for his day, and was described with reference to his "unusually dark" complexion, dark hair and eyes and strong cheekbones. Members of Floyd's family were identified as being of mixed race, leaving some ripples of controversy in the public records. His work ethic overcame most knee-jerk reservations. Nothing had ever been handed to him; he secured his first surveying job at age twenty only by agreeing to be a schoolteacher first to prove he possessed the right "temper, diligence, habits, and trust-worthiness." An associate recommended Floyd as a "very sober industrious young man."

Floyd married young, but his wife died in childbirth soon after. He named his daughter Mourning as a memorial to that grief— then left her to be raised by his mother-in-law. The loss of his wife appears to have motivated his decision to turn his back on a comfortable life in Virginia for a less settled existence of exploration. As a land surveyor more familiar with Kentucky than almost anyone else, Floyd correctly worried about the catastrophic consequences of "ruining" tribal hunting grounds. In addition to his topographical expertise, Floyd had experience in law enforcement, having served as a deputy sheriff in Virginia, with duties that included tracking down criminal suspects. Jemima was only a few years younger than Floyd's wife had been when she died, perhaps imbuing his part in the quest to rescue her with added significance.

Some members of the rescue party, including Flanders Callaway, had family ties with the girls. Flanders's father, James, was one of Richard Callaway's brothers, so Fanny and Betsy were cousins to Flanders. By one account, Flanders had run away from home in Virginia against his parents' wishes to join his uncle's family in their Kentucky adventure. Jemima could find in Flanders the same kind of will to adventure that motivated her father. He was a "tall, spare, thin-visaged, swarthy man" with striking dark eyes. Around the fort, he'd admired Jemima. Daniel had fifteen years on Flanders, but Boone's youthful appearance and Flanders's serious, weathered mien made the two men look about the same age.

JEMIMA HAD A SECRET. She believed she had a penknife in her pocket. She spent part of the night trying to reposition her bound hands to reach it, but eventually gave up, unable to loosen her restraints.

The captors were sleeping in a circle around the girls. No chances were being taken, nor was anything done by happenstance. A plan was in place. The howls and cries of dangerous animals filled the night air. When the girls were not crying, they comforted each other, led by Betsy, the oldest.

The girls' thoughts raced. Betsy pined for her fiancé, Samuel Henderson, whose older brother had been instrumental in the establishment of Boonesboro and their presence out in the wilderness. It was later said Samuel broke down in tears when he realized Betsy was gone from the fort and her life in danger. In Betsy's mind, Samuel *had* to be coming for them. Then there was Betsy and Fanny's father, Richard Callaway, the hotheaded military officer heavily decorated from his service in the French and Indian War, who had recovered from serious illness to become part of the Kentucky frontier. But Jemima and her friends knew the one person most likely to reach them, the man renowned and respected in both Indian and settler circles for his tracking and hunting abilities, and for his stubborn perseverance. That was Daniel Boone. He was their lifeline, and they needed a way to conspire with him from afar.

The Indians told the girls they were being taken to the Shawnee towns. To the hostages, this revelation implied a number of possible fates. They could be killed in a revenge ritual or a call to war. They could be chosen as "adoptees" for the tribe, considered replacements for those killed in combat or murdered in cold blood.

Legal consequences for the unjust deaths of Indians were elusive. For example, colonial authorities finally caught up with Isaac Crabtree, whom they had been looking for since he'd murdered Oconostota's brother at a horse race. According to family lore, at trial Crabtree defended himself by claiming that he recognized the Indian he ambushed and killed as one of the perpetrators of the brutal raid against Crabtree's group, along with Big Jim, the Shawnee who killed James Boone. To this unprovable assertion Crabtree added another. He claimed that his own brother John had been present during the raid that left James Boone dead. He said John had escaped but then disappeared forever, presumably taken or killed by the Indians. That story also did not appear to have ever been verified. Despite Crabtree's dubious defense, one Virginia official correctly doubted the prospect of a conviction, writing, "I am persuaded it would be easier to find 200 men to screen him from the law, than ten men to bring him to Justice." Whether Crabtree sufficiently clouded the facts in a fog of confusion or the settlers did not have the heart to condemn one of their own in such tense times, Crabtree was acquitted, and Hanging Maw's tribe was left with another unacknowledged loss. Symbolically "adopting" settlers, especially women and children, helped tribes rebuild their communities and families.

Another scenario presented itself. The Revolutionary War increased pressure on tribal factions to commit to alliances or become enemies of one side or the other. The girls now could become political pawns, a possibility that Hanging Maw understood when asking if they were all Boones and that Jemima likewise grasped when deciding how to answer.

The girls' minds raced through all that had happened. There was reason to think the Indians had been watching them before they were captured, and Fanny came to believe that flowers had been placed near the water deliberately in order to attract them to land. The kidnapping may have been planned well before that. Jemima thought back to the treaty at Sycamore Shoals, with both Hanging Maw and Dragging Canoe in attendance. Moreover, although the girls could not have known, it turned out that one of the seemingly innocuous visitors to Boonesboro, "Dr." John Smyth, not only had lied about university degrees and large land holdings, but also had been a spy for the British. According to one account, Smyth had been recruited to pave the way to "sweep Virginia and her Kentucky territory clean of 'rebels.'" Smyth had gone from Boonesboro to the Shawnee, providing intelligence that may have contained diagrams of the settlement and routines of residents, including Jemima and the Callaway girls. Smyth later boasted that Henderson, whom he identified as Boonesboro's leader, was "void of military talents," though Smyth also admitted that he couldn't actually tell who was in charge of what in Boonesboro. "There seems to be no such thing," Smyth complained, as "insubordination." By the time the girls were taken, Smyth was long gone, supporting the loyalist cause back in Maryland (he later wound up imprisoned in Fredericksburg).

The captors informed the girls that a group of fourteen Cherokee warriors—almost certainly more of Dragging Canoe's renegades— had been dispersed along the Kentucky River ready to do "mischief." This was a clear warning, reminiscent of the captive Mary Jemison's mother exhorting her not to "try to escape." Escape would bring the girls into the hands of their captors' allies, and, potentially worse, the "mischief" could be channeled toward Boonesboro if the girls undermined their captors' plan to use them as bargaining tools.

Whether or not Jemima ever found her pocketknife, the knowledge reshaped their outlook. Escape could accelerate death.

The next day as they walked with their captors, the girls, scratched and bleeding from the rugged terrain, enacted the beginning of an unspoken plan to counteract the Indians' ingenious methods to leave no traces. The girls broke twigs. Betsy, wearing her wooden shoes, dug her heels into the dirt and mud to make marks. They also tried tearing off small scraps of clothing and dropping them to create a trail. Betsy carried a perfect accessory for these purposes: a handkerchief embroidered E. CALLAWAY. Tearing off pieces, she gradually dispersed the letters of her name into the woods. Jemima had nothing with her name on it, but she had another idea. She tied knots into a string from her bonnet to indicate the number of their captors, then let it fall.

Some of this escaped the captors' attention at first, but they began to notice transgressions. When a girl flattened a weed or leaf, the Indians would methodically straighten it, or bend it in a direction that could mislead a tracker. The captors chose barren land whenever possible to avoid leaving behind trampled undergrowth. When they realized Betsy's gambit with the handkerchief, according to Callaway family tradition, one of the Shawnee grabbed it and "trampled [it] furiously beneath his feet. A tomahawk was then suspended over her head . . . she was threatened if it was repeated." They also chopped the wooden heels off of Betsy's shoes, then demanded that the girls walk in each other's tracks to leave fewer signs of their passage. When the Indians noticed broken branches, the girls explained that they were so tired, they had to grab onto the branches to help them walk.

The Cherokee culture to which Hanging Maw belonged prized women's contributions and long rested on matrilineal traditions, tracing lineage through maternal ancestors. Exposure to European

societies gradually eroded these practices in favor of a more patri-
archal hierarchy. Overall, while Indians and settlers alike counted
on women's fortitude on the frontier, they both tended to relegate
women to what were considered domestic spheres, rugged though
they were. In the Shawnee traditions in which Catfish and the other
captors came of age, women were in charge of agricultural duties,
preparing game, and sometimes constructing housing. At times
there was a kind of "auxiliary" chief role held by a woman, particularly to preside over issues affecting women. In a sophisticated
strategy by Jemima and her friends, the female hostages unleashed
their strengths by playing on the perception of female weaknesses
that existed in both colonial and Indian cultures. Jemima threw
herself down, an excuse to scream as she fell, hoping to provide a
signal to the rescue party they prayed was coming for them. One
of the warriors ran over waving his tomahawk. Jemima blamed her
wounded foot for the incident. Every second she managed to delay
their progress was a small victory. Every second could bring Daniel
Boone closer.

Jemima urged the other girls to catch fresh water in their hands
to drink when crossing streams, to maintain their health and keep
up their strength. In some accounts of what happened during the
kidnapping, the captors began to drag the girls forcibly across difficult crossings.

The captors needed the women to move faster, knowing they had
to gain space from any pursuit by Boone in order to reach the Shawnee towns. Meanwhile, as Hanging Maw interacted with Jemima,
she saw something besides urgency in his eyes, something unexpected. A hint of affection.

ENDS OF THE EARTH

BOONE'S PARTY, NOW COMPOSED OF nine men, trekked to the suspected Indian trail they had discovered and marked the previous day. They came upon a new clue, a recently extinguished campfire. The captors had camped here with the girls overnight, the pursuers missing them by hours. "By daylight we were on their track," John Floyd later wrote. Boone's doggedness through this process would become the stuff of legend. Theodore Roosevelt, in his heavily researched though bias-prone elegy of the frontier, *The Winning of the West*, described how Boone "followed the tangled trail like a bloodhound." By this point, Boone was also trying to decipher from the path taken which tribe held the girls. For a student of the wide range of political circumstances among different communities of Indians, this could provide clues about not only where the captors were headed but also their motivations.

Serious problems presented themselves: the trail that led from the apparent camp not only split into multiple directions—which appeared to be another tactic to throw off the pursuers—it also went through thick cane that made tracking all but impossible. "They had totally prevented our following them," wrote Floyd, recording their frustration. What signs they could analyze indicated that the kidnappers were moving swiftly.

Boone had decades of experience with Indians and the wilderness. On one of his other expeditions, Boone's skills impressed his companions not only because he found tracks, but also because he correctly determined that the warriors were stepping in one another's footprints to conceal their numbers. Even so, and in spite of the faith he had in himself and inspired in others, relying on tracking was a long shot. Just months before searching for Jemima, in a similar setting, Boone had tried to track two young settlers who had disappeared during an apparent attack. He never found more than a few footprints. One body was later found, scalped; the other was never recovered.

"It would never do to follow them in this way," Boone concluded as they searched for the three girls, as recalled by Nathan Reid, pointing to the fact "that they were making tracks faster than we were." They could try to follow multiple possible courses, but that would slow their search down too much. Boone gambled. Instead of trying to account for as many scenarios as possible, he would place himself in the mind-set of his adversaries. He would guess where the captors were going based on his knowledge of the terrain. But if he miscalculated, they could lose the girls forever.

Away from the overgrown cane, they made progress through a more passable route, with Boone leading, "followed by the men in perfect silence," as Reid recalled. The journeyers stopped for the night, Reid capturing their level of exhaustion when remembering "we threw ourselves on the ground to sleep." They revitalized themselves with jerked venison that Gass had brought back from Boonesboro, which had already been low on food before this latest crisis. Resuming at dawn on Tuesday and "pushing on with all might," they stopped at a stream around ten a.m. Boone studied the environs. He predicted they were nearing a spot where they would intersect with the Indians' tracks. Though he seemed to be operating by some second sight rather than evidence, he turned out to be right.

Two hundred yards farther, the water in the stream was muddy, suggesting it had been crossed. Realizing they were getting closer, the mood tensed. They knew the girls' safety hung in the balance, and, as Reid put it, "one imprudent step on our part might lose them their lives." They were now some forty miles into coarse thicket and razor-sharp cane. As soon as they crossed the stream, Boone was able to confirm that the path was a "war path," a route that lent itself to more stealth than hunting paths, which connected Cherokee and Shawnee territories. That location spoke volumes. Both tribes included factions bent on halting the settlers' most aggressive expansion yet.

The bad news for the pursuers was that the captors would be safer on their own grounds, but that also meant that the captors would *feel* safer. As Floyd wrote later about that moment, "We then supposed they would be less cautious."

Continuing through the sweltering heat, Boone and his party came upon fresh blood staining the leaves and grass. His heart raced with dire images of his daughter, fatally wounded. They traced the blood to the carcass of a buffalo, partially skinned, with meat taken from the hump. (An entire hump weighs up to two hundred pounds, too heavy to transport.)

That carcass represented a chilling sight in its own right. It meant the captors saw their journey as coming to an end, forcing the rescuers to commit to a plan of action.

"Our study had been more to get the prisoners," wrote Floyd, reflecting anxiety about any possible violence about to come, "without giving the Indians time to murder them after they discovered us, than to kill them."

With the captors' pace slackening, Boone's party knew Jemima and her two friends might already be dead. Boone was not a man who tended to articulate feelings or fears. He planned rather than emoted. He turned to Floyd and the others and announced: "To-night we will recapture the girls, dead or alive."

A renowned hunter, Boone could derive important information from an animal's remains. His interests and expertise in animals extended beyond hunting skills. He was part of a committee at Boonesboro formulating strategies to preserve the population of game animals, which was being devastated rapidly, as well as volunteering to help improve the breeding of horses.

To Boone, the buffalo indicated that the captors would stop to cook when they reached the next body of water, before the meat spoiled in the warm weather. American buffalo (or bison) was pivotal to this formative moment for Kentucky's future. For one, it was a favorite of the Shawnee, and may have been too tempting to pass up even while hurrying with the girls. Reid had observed this before: "The Indians would frequently break out of the war path into the buffalo paths, pursue them some distance, and then fall back into the war-path again, in order to elude pursuit should any be made." If a chance encounter with game had slackened the Indians' pace, it would give Boone just the opportunity for which he had waited.

Callaway family legend later indicated that around this same time Richard Callaway, leading the secondary front of men on horseback, found a separate track left behind by the captors near Licking River and, concealing himself, began his own stealth operation. Callaway may have fantasized this in his frustration at being left out. In reality, he was nowhere to be seen. Only Boone's party was in position to reach the girls, and time was running out.

The troubling parallels with the 1773 death of James Boone multiplied, some of which Daniel Boone would have known and others he could not. The Indian party involved in each incident was an intertribal combination of Shawnee and Cherokee; in James Boone's case, the young man was captured and killed by a Shawnee called Big Jim, and the girls' captors included a Shawnee warrior named Big Jimmy. (These, of course, were their Anglicized nicknames.) Both incidents were sparked by the settlers' push into Kentucky and their inability or refusal to accept clear warning signs about repercussions.

If Boone's intuition proved right and Hanging Maw's party would stop for the night to cook, it meant the captors were becoming less fearful of detection. Either they were confident they had shaken their pursuers, or they had decided to kill the girls—or had already killed them. The motives and plans of the captors could only be guessed at from the clues, much like the path they had taken. The sun waned. Boone's team could not lose a moment.

Even those members of the party who had not known Boone before this mission quickly came to trust him, and according to family lore a consensus settled on "leaving it to Boone how to act." As usually happened, life-altering responsibilities landed on Boone's broad shoulders. Many people relied on his help. Back at the fort, for example, food shortages had become common. Just as the Indians had predicted, Boonesboro's hunters had begun to drive away game from the area, a problem that Boone was tasked to improve. Residents looked to Boone in matters of defense, though even he could not motivate enough of them to complete all the log cabins and stockades (barrier fences) needed to help keep them safer, whether because of wishful thinking that Indians would not attack directly or a "spirit of indolence," as Richard Henderson labeled it. Making his way through the wilderness, Boone could hardly bring himself to think of the terror his daughter and Richard Callaway's poor girls experienced. On top of that, these men with him, friends new and old, depended on his leadership. One misstep and they all could be wiped out in an ambush.

Boone stopped again when he found a snake, skinned. It writhed. Like the hump of the buffalo, the condition of this reptile's remains gave off vital clues: the Indian warriors had been through here very recently. They were coming so close to their quarry, but as they reached a stream at around noon, the trail once again split into two before all visible signs of the Indians' course vanished. "No sign of it could be found on either bank," according to Reid.

Boone directed the group to divide up again, putting themselves in more jeopardy, proceeding with the knowledge that they could encounter their opposition at any moment. They prepared rifles. They had to blend into the environment, a skill possessed by Indian hunters that Boone respected and emulated. The leader also had to account for Flanders Callaway. On the one hand, Boone considered Flanders "the best shot he ever knew under pressure in an Indian fight; he was cool and collected." But he worried Flanders could act rashly to try to save his cousins, Betsy and Fanny—and to save Jemima, for whom Boone suspected the young man had feelings. He put Flanders in the rear of the party.

They discovered items on the ground and in the underbrush that made their hearts leap. Scraps of fabric. The girls were alive, and they were fighting to be discovered. "This we saw," remembered Reid, "and well knew the purpose for which it was done." Without the branches broken by the girls at risk to their lives, the pursuers could not have kept up with the trail. William Bailey Smith, the "rollicking" seat-of-the-pants adventurer, later remembered what he called the intricate chain of evidence they had to follow, like a ribbon through a labyrinth: "The bended blade of grass, the crushed lichen, the smallest stone displaced, were unerring guides in the pursuit." Among the clues now eagerly collected along the way Boone had found something striking. It was the string from Jemima's bonnet. He studied the knots she had tied into it. Five knots—it meant something. There were five captors, Boone explained to the others, correctly interpreting Jemima's meaning. He announced to his men the number he planned on taking down himself: "Allow me two."

FOR THE HOSTAGES, the prospect of being brought to an Indian town not only stoked fears of permanent removal from one's family, but of becoming an enemy to one's family. The recent Battle of Point Pleasant in late 1774 was a striking example. When Chief Cornstalk led the Shawnee in that last stand of Lord Dunmore's War, a man fought alongside him called White Wolf, or John Ward. White Wolf had once been a settler. He had been kidnapped as a child, raised in the tribe as a Shawnee, and now died on a battlefield fighting with the Indian army against his biological family. His brother recognized his body. His father, on the colonial side, was a casualty of the same battle, killed by a bullet that may have been fired by his son.

The Girtys were four Pennsylvania-born brothers taken by Indians as young men during wartime; settlers recovered one of the Girty boys, while the other three were brought up in three different tribes. Simon Girty ended up among the Senecas, the same tribe into which Mary Jemison had been kidnapped and adopted. When Michael Cresap unleashed the chain of events that brought the frontier to the brink of all-out war, Girty was asked by colonial leaders to talk to Indian chiefs in an attempt to placate them; after that conflict erupted, Girty was said to have served as interpreter at the treaty with Cornstalk and other tribal leaders that ended Lord Dunmore's War. He continued to be a key interpreter and scout for Indians and the British in their conflicts with the insurgent colonists.

Simon Girty's fellow Seneca adoptee, Mary Jemison, had an increasingly disorienting experience as the Revolutionary War took hold. By that point, she felt at home in the Seneca community. She married and had children. But in a typical pattern seen during the war, the Senecas were first encouraged by the rebels and the British to be neutral until, abruptly, they were pressured to take sides. In Mary's Indian town, the side taken was against the colonists' rebellion. The British actually tricked the Senecas into sending warriors to the battle of Fort Stanwix, where they were used as an expendable front line. Mary (also known at this point by her native name Dehgewanus) described "doleful yells, shrieks, and howlings" when the town's warriors returned and reported more than thirty men dead.

Officers for the British army—men who had not only killed soldiers from the colonial community where Mary came from, but whose manipulation also caused the deaths of the Indians whom she now considered her family—camped out at Mary's home among the Indians and expected to be waited upon. "Many and many a night," she recalled, as recorded by her ghostwriter, "I have pounded samp [a type of corn] for them from sunset till sunrise, and furnished them with the necessary provisions, and clean clothing, for their journey."

As the war progressed and intensified, a regiment of Revolutionary soldiers made its way toward the Seneca town, and word reached Mary that the rebels were "burning and destroying the huts and cornfields; killing the cattle, hogs, and horses; and cutting down the fruit-trees belonging to the Indians throughout the country."

Terrified that the members of the community into which she was born would kill them all, Mary and the others in the Seneca town fled for their lives.

NEWS ABOUT THE Boone and Callaway girls reached Virginia's Fort Randolph, which at this point in the Revolutionary War was commanded by a hardy and proud officer, Captain Matthew Arbuckle. The fort rose up from the point where the Ohio and Kanawha Rivers met. The American fort was named in honor of the deceased Peyton Randolph, who in a technical sense could be viewed as America's first president, having led the Continental Congress. From its choice of names to memorialize to the high standards of its blockhouses and cabins, Fort Randolph styled itself as the vanguard of a new epoch for a new nation, and a continued warning to nearby Indian communities who had been swayed to side with British forces. Arbuckle was a true believer in the cause of the Revolution. He vowed in a letter that he would "Loose [sic] the Last Drop of My Blood in Defence of My Country when fighting for that Blessed Enjoyment Called Liberty."

Arbuckle had been a key commander in the Battle of Point Pleasant, which had sealed the colonial victory over the Shawnee in Lord Dunmore's War. Another soldier who fought there attributed "much of the success" of the battle to Arbuckle's "bravery and fine military talents." Two years later, the aspiring nation was now at war with England, and Arbuckle had constructed Fort Randolph on the site of the Battle of Point Pleasant, where he had earned military glory. Of Scottish descent, the strapping Arbuckle, who was described as being as "large in spirit" as he was in stature, prized family as much as battling Indians. His pregnant wife, Frances, lived in a house about a mile from the fort with two young sons from his first marriage, which had ended with his first wife's death from illness almost five years before.

Fort Randolph was recognized as a key military bulwark against the British strategy to channel Indian hostilities against the former colonies. On May 6, 1776, the Virginia Convention—one of many assemblies meant to formalize and organize the Revolutionary War—had passed an ordinance funding Arbuckle's operation, backed by the rationale that "there is too much reason to apprehend the enemies of America are endeavoring to kindle an Indian war on our frontier, which ought timely to be provided against."

Right around his thirty-fifth birthday, Arbuckle received intelligence about Shawnee and Cherokee warriors killing "cabiner" (isolated settler) John Cooper and kidnapping three girls near Boonesboro. "Two of the women were daughters of Col Callaway at Cantuckie," Arbuckle reported in a letter to his superior officer, "and the other a daughter of Col Boone's at Cantuckie." The fort's captain considered this a matter of national importance and security. Arbuckle rounded up three of his men. Though he had plenty of soldiers to choose from—other officials accused Arbuckle of recruiting too many men to Fort Randolph—many were too frightened of Indians to leave the fort. Selecting his trio, Arbuckle dispatched them to the Shawnee with orders regarding the girls: *Demand the prisoners.*

"THE GIRLS WERE caressed frequently," David Henry, a militiaman at Boonesboro, was later told, "and complimented as 'pretty squaws.'" Rumors suggested that Hanging Maw fell in love with Jemima during their odyssey through the Kentucky backwoods and that he contemplated bringing her home to make her his squaw.

A similar outcome could be found in the story of Blue Jacket, a Shawnee leader, who married a Virginia woman taken prisoner by the tribe. By one account, Hanging Maw's Shawnee partners in his operation decided more than once to kill Jemima for leaving clues behind. Hanging Maw stopped them each time and made them understand they would face his wrath if they hurt her. Just as Daniel Boone and Richard Callaway began to split apart in the course of their journey, so did Hanging Maw and the Shawnee who were with him—and Jemima was one cause of the schism. Hanging Maw's formidable presence during the kidnapping would be dramatized in a poem by Rebecca Boone's cousin, Daniel Bryan: "He was a Chief in Manhood's vigorous prime; / Of stature lofty, strait, and dignified— / Strong, Muscular and springy were his limbs; / And haughty elevation mark'd his step."

Hanging Maw admired Jemima's dark hair, which nearly touched the ground. In tribal tradition, long, flowing hair signaled spiritual strength. He began to call her "my squaw." But if he entertained any romantic notions, he never made physical advances, and did his best to ensure that Jemima and the Callaway sisters felt comfortable and respected. Offered dried beef, Jemima had no appetite, but she was struck by how the Indians had treated her honorably. Moments of humor even slipped through the tension. The Shawnee warrior whom Fanny had beaten with her oar took ribbing from the other Indians for having been battered by the young woman.

The Cherokee warrior's difficult position moderating among competing, multitribal interests became more pronounced as questions lingered about what to do with the girls. Hanging Maw had allied himself with Dragging Canoe's breakaway renegades, but by nature he was a political rather than military operative. The girls could be held hostage to negotiate terms for the invaders to retreat from Boonesboro and the other settlements. But the rage among the Shawnee for years of atrocities weighed against that course, putting the hostages in imminent danger. Neither Hanging Maw nor the girls could know what transpired to the east as word spread to Captain Arbuckle at Fort Randolph. Depending on how the timing panned out, the captors could be reaching Shawnee territory around the same time as Arbuckle's three soldiers arrived to demand the prisoners be "immediately" turned over. Boone and his men were a kind of stealth force, but Arbuckle's troops tended to be nervous and trigger-happy, often undisciplined infantrymen who considered themselves first and foremost "Indian fighters." If Arbuckle's men met the captors before Boone's did, the crossfire could kill the girls.

To help them climb the steep hills, the girls were told to hold on to the Indians' backpacks. The girls' delaying tactics evolved. Fanny had a painful thorn in her foot and had trouble walking. Anything to slow their progress helped, but Jemima feared what the captors would do to a genuinely incapacitated Fanny, so she urged her friend on. The Indians found an emaciated old white pony that they offered to Fanny to ride. Fanny refused, but Jemima managed to communicate to her that this was another chance to stall, increasing their odds of being overtaken by rescuers.

At one point, all three girls climbed onto the pony. They found ways to rile up the animal to ensure they would be thrown off. Because the pony had been tied up during the Indians' mission to capture the girls and was already (as later recalled) "ill and spiteful," it was not hard to aggravate the animal, which came with risk. The pony bit Betsy hard, bloodying her arm. The ploy added another injury but also added time to the journey, including a stretch when one of the braves mounted the pony to show the girls how well he could ride the same animal.

When they reached a place by a stream to camp for the third night, the girls were placed in a clearing on a bluff. Thick woods ringed around them, the trees stretching into the darkening sky. Hanging Maw asked Jemima to check his head for lice. This was a routine necessity among settlers and Indians alike spending time in the woods, but Hanging Maw's choice to ask Jemima reflected the rapport they had developed. She agreed. He sat on the ground and she ran a comb and her fingers through his hair. "It was our policy to do whatever we possibly could to conciliate them," Jemima said later. "Every such thing tended to delay their progress, and . . . we felt sure that father and friends would exert every avenue for our rescue."

She also had reason to reinforce Hanging Maw's feelings toward her and her family. Though no record exists of what they spoke about as she combed through his hair, the interaction let them speak with as much privacy as they ever had on the journey. The act itself was a subtext. She was far too excited to "have felt [a louse] had it been as large as her thumb." Both Jemima and Hanging Maw had reason to see the situation hurtling toward a violent climax, and neither, all clues suggest, wanted the other one hurt.

Whatever sentiments—and possibly warnings—may have been passed to each other, Jemima steeled herself.

"I will go get some water to drink," she said to the Cherokee warrior at the end of their exchange.

Hanging Maw insisted that he would get the water instead. He picked up the kettle and climbed down from the bluff toward the creek. Before he left, he dropped to his knees, putting his ear to the ground and listening for a long time, a timeworn method of detecting approaching riders on horseback.

After Hanging Maw had walked off to fetch the water, Jemima thought she heard a rustle. In the wilderness it was hard to tell usual sounds from unusual, but she had a knack, just like her father. The world around her seemed to come to a stop. She braced herself and took careful stock of their surroundings.

TWO INDIANS DOWN below by the stream stacked rifles and worked to build a fire to roast meat from the buffalo. It becomes hard to sort out accident from intention in those heightened moments after Hanging Maw left Jemima's side and disappeared from sight. Had she meant to remove Hanging Maw from danger, knowing he would go fetch the water himself once she brought the subject up? Or had he made sure to remove himself, having heard something that sounded out of place, both to protect himself and to give Jemima the chance for rescue? Hanging Maw had seen the possibility of beneficial political outcomes fade. Both Jemima and Hanging Maw navigated the hard-line expectations enveloping them. The Callaway sisters viewed their captors as evil, and evidence suggests at least some of the Shawnee warriors in that party saw the girls that way; to each other, they were red savages and white devils.

With Hanging Maw on his errand and another Indian gathering firewood, three captors remained. Two worked on the fire and the cooking, including Big Jimmy, who, safe to say from his nickname, presented an imposing figure. One brave from that group was on his knees as he stoked the flames. The other stood guard, gripping his rifle. Tomahawks were at hand. From the braves' gestures and actions, the girls interpreted the captors' plan easily enough: if the captors were taken by surprise, this would be the spot they would scalp the girls and escape into tribal territory.

"There the girls were," went the family tradition, "with their dresses cut above the knees, their legs scratched and bleeding; their eyes swollen." Betsy Callaway sat on a log, the skin peeling from her hands and settling into blisters from breaking so many branches and briars on their journey, her arm in pain from the pony's bite, a risk for infection. If the older Callaway girl suffered physically, Fanny was crumbling emotionally, all the assurances of rescue made by the other girls having gone unfulfilled. The sinking feeling among the girls was that by stopping and cooking, their captors showed they were safe from all settlers. They had reached an unthinkable point. For the first time, they had lost hope. Fanny folded into Betsy's arms. Jemima also sat on the log, putting her head onto Betsy's lap, the older girl trying to comfort Jemima and Fanny at the same time. Exhaustion weighed down all three, debilitating them as much as the fear.

When Jemima, her face at this low position, peered into the dusk, she met a pair of eyes. Creeping on the ground, Daniel Boone looked to her like a snake. He had his rifle in hand. He reached his hand out and then signaled to her with his finger to remain quiet. He was waiting, though she did not know for what, or if anyone was with him. Her body went numb.

"That's Daddy," she whispered to the other girls.

The nearby Indian sentry now looked through his pack for materials to mend his moccasins, possibly the ones singed when Fanny Callaway threw coal into them during their forced trek. Frustrated by not finding what he needed, the sentry made a fateful decision to check at the campfire for materials. He leaned his rifle against a tree.

LEADING UP TO this moment, Daniel Boone's squad had spotted tracks in a buffalo trace, where the marks intentionally left by the girls proved easiest to find. In another two miles, Boone had pushed ahead of his men. They all kept their eyes locked on him. As they got closer to where Boone suspected they'd find their quarry, he reminded them that their priority would be "only caring for the girls," not fighting the kidnappers. They were approximately forty-five miles into their journey. As Boone moved through the woods, he saw a sign of the Indians—smoke. They had camped.

The search party had journeyed to what seemed to be the ends of the earth, and in fact the precise site where the pursuers and captors finally met has not been positively identified to this day. Contemporary clues suggest that the girls were on a ridge at the mouth of Miner's Branch, a remote tributary of Flat Creek, emptying into Licking River.

Boone signaled them to prepare their rifles, but had insisted "no man to touch a trigger until he had received the sign" from him. He gave another signal, at which all got in a line down on the ground, then crawled upon their stomachs. A soft touch on the back from one man to the next would mean the captors were in sight. When Boone saw Jemima through a clearing in the trees and cane, every fiber in him wanted to come out firing, but he knew he had to be patient. The situation met the criteria Boone earlier had laid out to his fellow pursuers: "We must wait until the Indians consider themselves safe from pursuit." But patience came with risk. Every passing minute saw the light fade behind the trees. With darkness, they would lose sight of the girls and be unable to free them.

Concealed by the trees, Boone signaled to two of his men to train their weapons on the pair of Indians by the fire, one of whom was on his knees blowing into the embers. The plan was to fire simultaneously. Then Billy Smith pulled back his rifle lock, making a click. Accounts differ from one another, in part, no doubt, a result of the fog of battle. In some of these accounts, Smith fired aimlessly and missed; in others the click itself gave away their presence. Smith's action may have been a "stupid" mistake, as Reid called it, or Smith may have hoped leading the charge of a rescue would impress one of the girls, for whom he later implied romantic feelings. Either way, eyes of combatants met from across battle lines. "We discovered each other," Floyd later wrote, "nearly at the same time." Boone now knew there would be no chance to avoid casualties.

The Shawnee chopping wood for the fire—possibly Catfish—realized at once what was unfolding. He launched his hatchet at Fanny, grazing her head. He then grabbed a rifle. A shot from Boone pierced him and he fell dead, facedown. Jemima held her head down to avoid gunfire.

The girls started across the ridge toward the rescuers, blocking their shots. Boone yelled, "Fall down!" Flanders Callaway rushed to Jemima's side. One of the rescuers, John Martin, charged toward Betsy Callaway while raising his rifle as a club. She was nearly unrecognizable, with a red handkerchief over her head and torn and sodden clothes, and other settlers had been mistakenly attacked or killed when wearing clothes that clouded their cultural affiliation. Martin thought Betsy was one of the Indian captors. "For God's sake, don't kill her," Boone cried out, slowing him down enough for him to realize his mistake.

Big Jimmy, who had been lighting a pipe at the fire, had jumped to alarm at the first sounds of disturbance. Before he could reach for a weapon, he turned his large frame toward the girls. Fanny saw "blood burst out of his chest" before even hearing the shot from Floyd's rifle that hit him. By some accounts, he fell into the fire. The mission had been drawn up to avoid violence if possible, and yet impulses of vengeance undoubtedly competed with this intent. Boone's request to "allow me two" was one example, and Floyd later acknowledged the temptation to take a clear shot at a fleeing captor.

The other two Shawnee warriors escaped into the woods, while Hanging Maw was not seen during the confrontation. He ultimately made it back to Cherokee territory. The girls were ecstatic, but for what seemed like a long while could not speak. The rescue party found moccasins, knives, and tomahawks left behind. Floyd studied a war club, a carved weapon designed to deliver a fatal blow. By one account, Floyd also recovered some silver objects left behind by the Indians, which he would later melt down into silverware that would remain in his family for generations. He identified the objects as Shawnee. Once the girls had regained their bearings, they shared the intelligence they'd gathered, including the identity of Hanging Maw and specific Shawnee words they had heard spoken and had committed to memory.

The rescuers gave the girls blankets and a little food. From his haversack, Boone shared some dried venison and cakes. Even amid their immense relief, the girls had reason to feel self-conscious now that they were in the presence of family and suitors. Though outsiders to the frontier would remark on the rugged style of clothes worn by settlers—with Kentuckians sometimes called "white savages"—the girls still were raised with an eighteenth-century European sense of decorum. Their hair and clothes were in disarray, and their legs showed more skin than they ever would have chosen to reveal. Jemima later said they "stuck to their blankets as close as any squaws ever did," a fascinating identification with Indian women at a time when they had straddled two cultures so closely, but she stressed that she felt "no sense of shame."

The faction of rescuers on horseback had rendezvoused with those on foot, and the girls were placed on the horses. Exhausted and hungry, they sometimes fell behind, and the party prioritized their comfort. For at least part of the journey, Betsy rode on the horse of Samuel Henderson, her previously distraught fiancé. They "lay all night," as Boone later recalled, near Flat Creek, "at the mouth of a Small Branch" of the river, the geographical details always imprinted in his mind because of their connection to "retaking my daughter." Boone sent some of the men to hunt for meat, but Jemima refused to let her father out of her sight. "She would not let him leave her one minute," and did not want him to leave her side ever again, as family tradition had it, though fate had different plans in store.

As they neared the river and their settlement, Boone hollered out to signal their approach. All the residents in Boonesboro seemed to rush forward at once to celebrate the girls, and there was "not a dry eye" among them. Rebecca Boone laughed and cried as she embraced Jemima. Expectations that the ordeal was behind them, however, would be tempered as details continued to emerge. The drive to protect and avenge family would not end with Jemima and Daniel Boone: an Indian killed in the rescue, reports suggested, was the son of War Chief Blackfish, one of the Shawnee's most feared leaders and strategists.

BOOK II

RETALIATION

Chapter

5

FALLOUT

WORD OF THE KIDNAPPING AND rescue rippled through
the region. The year before, Richard Henderson had dismissed
whatever impact could come if a few "skulk[ing]" Indians were to
kill one or two settlers. Now people far and wide learned that the
daughters of Boonesboro's top commanders had been abducted in
broad daylight in plain view of their families. The event struck a
chord. "The situation of our country is much altered," John Floyd
reported in a letter to his benefactor a week after the rescue, before recounting how they found the girls and detailing additional
evidence of Indian presence and activity in the area. "The Indians
seem determined to break up our settlement," Floyd warned, recognizing a crisis in stability and security. "Unless it was possible
to give us some assistance . . . the greatest part of the people must
fall a prey to them." Boone, according to his first biographer, characterized the contemporaneous violence highlighted by the girls'
kidnapping as "extremely distressing to the new settlers."

In Boonesboro and the isolated outposts and cabins in Kentucky,
as many as thirty settlers took flight soon after the girls' rescue,
scrambling for safety before they got caught in the crosshairs. "A
war was expected," Boonesboro settler Levi Todd (grandfather of

the future Mary Todd Lincoln) wrote about the fallout, "and many went from the Countrys." Outward flow of population since settlers first arrived was nothing new. By one estimate, three hundred people had left over the last year and a half (total population numbers from the time are harder to pin down). Part of that transience stemmed from the mind-set of settlers who elected to push into the frontier in the first place. Henderson stewed about the fickleness and selfishness he saw in many early Kentucky settlers, who he believed sought little more than another adventure to brag about. "The fact is," he wrote, "that many of them are single, worthless fellows, and want to get on the other side of the mountains, for the sake of saying they have been out and returned safe, together with the probability of getting a mouthful of bread in exchange for their news." During the Revolutionary War, some men also left Kentucky to fight the British closer to the front lines.

But the exodus in the wake of the girls' kidnapping ushered in a distinct period of dire straits. The leaders of the settlement all but pleaded with those fleeing to reconsider, to no avail. The outflow rendered them nearly defenseless. If wider hostilities were to break out, Floyd wrote, "our situation is truly alarming," and he wondered whether "any thing under Heaven can be done for us." Boonesboro was left with fewer than thirty men. The number of males was considered the chief metric for defense, explaining in part the incomplete records kept of how many women and children lived there at this time. To remain in place meant risking one's life and, for those with children, risking young lives, too. No wonder that Floyd, in his letter reporting the kidnapping, closed with a sign-off that was unusual for him, one hinting at doom: "affectionately, to my last moments."

Much of what kept the core figures of Boonesboro in place was psychological. Those leaders knew that if they fled Boonesboro now, "there is scarcely one single man who will not follow the example," as Floyd wrote. Henderson had established martial law to keep order and discipline in the settlement, but even that couldn't force anyone to weather the storm that was rushing in.

CORNSTALK, THE SHAWNEE chief, took his mission very seriously. He toured the region to meet with fellow Indian leaders as well as American and British diplomatic agents, who were competing to court Shawnee support for their respective sides in the Revolutionary War. He passed through a number of Indian towns and rendezvoused with other chiefs, along the way also making plans for future counsels.

This diplomatic tour began before the kidnapping. While in Mingo territory along the Scioto River, Cornstalk and his traveling party stopped at Upper Chillicothe, also called Pluggystown after the Mingo chief, Pluggy, who, like Cornstalk, had been a key figure in the conflicts with the colonies during Lord Dunmore's War. One night during Cornstalk's stay, an Indian came running into town with what one witness described as "the alarm halloo." Cornstalk rushed to hear what the newcomer had to say. The news ended up directly relating to him and to the Shawnee tribe.

The messenger explained that a party of Shawnee and Cherokees had taken prisoners from the Kentucky River, and that settlers killed some Shawnee during a rescue. Though the details appear to have been garbled by the time the message reached Cornstalk, evidence indicates the report must have been about the kidnapping of Jemima and the Callaways. One of the Shawnee kidnappers who survived Boone's assault apparently had returned to Indian territory explaining that "the white people pursued them, came up with them . . . and killed two of the Shawanees."

Cornstalk, as it turned out, had had no involvement in planning the kidnapping. Such tactics were inconsistent with his overall endeavor to settle problems without violence. If any of the Shawnee leadership had been aware of a plan to take hostages from Kentucky, it had been a competing faction, not Cornstalk's. As a matter of policy, the chief would not shy away from denouncing unsanctioned acts of violence by Shawnee and tended to accept whatever fate might come to them. Less than a year earlier, Cornstalk personally tipped off settlers about rogue Shawnee warriors who he believed could pose a danger to them. A contemporary reported that Cornstalk warned that those renegades "might do some mischief, and that if any of them should get killed by the whites he should take no notice at all of it."

Now as he heard the news of the girls' kidnapping in the summer of 1776 from the messenger, Cornstalk responded in a similarly even-keeled manner. The Mingoes who listened to the news alongside him appear to have expressed anger that Daniel Boone's party had killed the Shawnee kidnappers. Cornstalk disagreed. He explained that the Shawnee-Cherokee party who engineered and carried out the plot should be held responsible for any deaths, including their own, under such circumstances, that it was "they who had killed [Cornstalk's] young men and not the white people"— because they had committed the initial transgression. In fact, even Hanging Maw, who had led the kidnapping operation from the Cherokee side, distanced himself from the mission. Though he had been allied with Dragging Canoe's renegade campaign against settlers, after the girls' kidnapping, no evidence suggests that Hanging Maw continued his involvement in Dragging Canoe's shadow wars. As Dragging Canoe launched other missions against the ex-colonists, Hanging Maw reintegrated himself into mainstream Cherokee leadership and was on track to become one of Dragging Canoe's principal nemeses.

Meanwhile, when the three soldiers from Fort Randolph sent by Matthew Arbuckle reached Shawnee territory to demand that Jemima and the Callaway girls be freed, Cornstalk was still away touring Indian towns and couldn't receive them. Urgency dissipated for Arbuckle's soldiers when they learned that the young women were no longer Shawnee prisoners. However, although the girls had reached safety, the matter remained too serious to let rest. Even without the benefit of Cornstalk's guidance, Shawnee leadership knew the situation required diplomacy. One of Cornstalk's brothers, probably Nimwha (Munseeka) or Silverheels, decided to journey to Fort Randolph with the soldiers to explain personally to Captain Arbuckle what had transpired. Both brothers had ample previous experience: Nimwha had helped negotiate significant treaties for the tribe, and a few years before, Silverheels had risked his life to help Cornstalk save several traders during Lord Dunmore's War.

The three soldiers and the Shawnee chief reached Fort Randolph on August 15, 1776. Arbuckle greeted them, eager for a report. The fort's captain had not received any messages from Boonesboro since the kidnapping, and this was the first he heard about the rescue. The Shawnee chief explained to Arbuckle how Daniel Boone's party managed to trace the kidnappers and described the clash that followed. The chief confirmed that two of the Shawnee involved had been killed. Reports indicated that one of the Shawnee killed—possibly by Boone—was the son of Blackfish. That category was not restricted to biological children, as Blackfish also had adopted children and could have considered someone else part of his family who was not related by blood.

For the moment at least, the news that one of the deceased warriors came from an influential family did not spark another blood feud. Cornstalk's power and influence still overshadowed Blackfish and the more hawkish factions of the Shawnee. Cornstalk's brother, as Arbuckle later reported, "promised to hold to a lasting peace." Still, Arbuckle remained suspicious. He had heard about Cornstalk's diplomatic tour and knew it included meetings with British officials. Arbuckle considered the fact that Cornstalk entertained both sides in the Revolutionary War a sign of wavering, which Arbuckle described as a rhythm "constantly backwards and forwards . . . So that the peace with them I look upon it not to be lasting and am ever on my guard for fear of a surprise."

What Cornstalk actually did around this time contrasted sharply with Captain Arbuckle's suspicions of his fickleness. The Shawnee chief *prevented* another kidnapping. When he stayed in Pluggystown during his tour, Cornstalk parlayed with two of the American "Indian agents," officials assigned to negotiate alliances with tribes. The agents were William Wilson, who had a Shawnee mother, and Joseph Nicholson, who had been an interpreter for George Washington when the politician had traveled through Indian country several years earlier. Meanwhile, a group of Mingoes, led by Pluggy, formulated a plan to kidnap Wilson and Nicholson and transport them to Fort Detroit, where British operative Henry Hamilton would reward them for handing over such high-profile prisoners. Cornstalk successfully advised Wilson and Nicholson how to escape and where to go to stay out of the Mingoes' reach.

Not knowing of this dramatic intervention, Arbuckle fixated only on the news that Cornstalk was going to Fort Detroit, the British enclave at the vanguard of strategizing against America's western territory. Paranoia ran deep on both sides as the Revolutionary War continued to escalate. As long as Cornstalk spoke to their enemies—at least from Arbuckle's perspective—he may become an enemy, too.

JEMIMA RETAINED HER poise and spirited personality as she entered a new phase of her life. One anecdote that took place after the kidnapping caught up with some of the Boone family as they crossed a flooding stream on horseback. Jemima, who had an eight-year-old girl riding behind her on her saddle, told her father to get ready because she was going to lead the way. Plunging into the water, her horse got spooked by something drifting in the stream and threw Jemima and the girl headfirst into the water. The men in the party dove in but found no sign of Jemima or the child. Then the two girls resurfaced. The younger one had to be helped to catch her breath. Jemima—reinforcing her childhood nickname of Duck—seemed perfectly fine. She "seemed to enjoy the misfortune," a witness said.

"A ducking is very disagreeable this chilly day," she said, putting the group at ease, "but much less so than capture by the Indians."

With the joyous return of the girls and the rescue parties in mid-July 1776, the remaining population of Boonesboro felt the larger winds of change. Though the Declaration of Independence had been adopted in Philadelphia in July, less than two weeks before the kidnapping, the news took time to reach the settlement. Two Virginia newspapers (each called the *Gazette*) published the document, and a settler brought one of these to Boonesboro in early August. The stunning document was read aloud to a gathering, probably around the divine elm, and met with "cheers and war-whoops" by the residents. The community held a bonfire that night in commemoration of the moment. The Declaration confirmed that the Revolutionary War was not simply a push to realign the colonies' rights, but rather a full break from the British Empire. On the one hand, the sentiment spoke directly to the spirit of the Kentucky settlers; the prefatory phrases of the founding document—". . . to assume among the powers of the earth . . . the laws of Nature and of Nature's God"—argue for territorial autonomy based on natural rights (for whites, of course), much like the way many of Boonesboro's settlers phrased their own claims. On the other hand, the Declaration escalated the potential for scorched-earth campaigns by the British, and the isolated outposts of Kentucky were conspicuously vulnerable targets. "The pursuit of happiness," a linchpin of the document's philosophy, though an abstraction, spoke to the hopes that had spurred relocation to the frontier, hopes that often went unfulfilled.

With the girls' kidnapping behind them, residents at Boonesboro sought normalcy. One settler described the Boonesboro community thus: "In a word, they were as a large family." In the earliest days of the settlement, Richard Henderson had commented that there was "no scouring of floors, sweeping of yards, or scalding of bedsteads here," though Henderson himself made the unusual decision to have shingles put on his own cabin roof. By late summer 1776, domestic scenes became more feasible.

Just weeks after the girls' return, on August 7, Betsy Callaway and Samuel Henderson got married in one of the cabins. This was the very first wedding among Kentucky settlers. Some accounts point to Squire Boone, Jemima's uncle who later became a preacher, as officiating for the couple, while others name the girls' lead rescuer—Daniel Boone—as presiding. Henderson's hunting shirt had seen better days—likely he had worn it during the arduous rescue; for his nuptials, he reportedly borrowed a shirt from another member of that rescue party, Nathan Reid. Betsy, whose mangled dress had looked so odd to her rescuers that they nearly pummeled her, now wore a "plain Irish linen dress." Nineteenth-century historian George W. Ranck wrote, "There was dancing to fiddle-music by the light of tallow 'dips,' and legend says the guests were treated to home-grown watermelons, of which the whole station were proud." Evidence suggests that the watermelons came from Richard Hines, the free Black cabiner and groundbreaking farmer located south of Boonesboro, who grew Kentucky's first known watermelon and muskmelon crops. Nine months later, the newlyweds welcomed their first child, Frances, who was also the first child born to settlers married in Kentucky.

Whether Daniel or Squire Boone officiated, Richard Callaway worried about the legitimacy of his daughter's marriage. With questions remaining about the overall legal status of Richard Henderson's colony—which Henderson had officially called Transylvania— Callaway wondered whether a wedding sanctioned by the breakaway colony's authorities would be recognized elsewhere. Callaway received a promise from the participants that the authenticity of the marriage would be confirmed outside of Kentucky. Callaway's skepticism likely signaled as much about his resistance to the leadership of the Boones in the wake of the girls' rescue as it did about the settlement's legal status. Despite assurances from Betsy and Fanny, Callaway also stewed over worries that the Indians had "violated" his daughters, another reason to hoard anger against Boone. It was Boone's strategies for the rescue—however successful ultimately—that had extended the duration of the kidnapping and, in Callaway's mind, had given the captors more time to commit harm.

The other girls liberated in July also married after returning to Boonesboro. One account from family lore had Jemima and Flanders Callaway's courtship actually occur when Flanders "sought and won the heart and hand" of Jemima on the way home from the rescue. Though not so immediate, whatever suspicions Daniel Boone harbored during the rescue about Flanders's feelings toward Jemima were correct. Jemima reciprocated. No doubt the experience of the rescue itself served to strengthen emotional alliances and seed romantic connections. Jemima and Flanders married when she was fourteen and he was twenty-four. Fanny Callaway married John Holder, thirty-three, a recent arrival who would be described as a handsome man of commanding appearance with "a good deal more than an ordinary share of agility and strength." He stood six feet tall with stone-gray eyes. By one account, these two couples married in a double wedding, though other clues point to the Holders marrying later. Because Holder was widely—though inaccurately—incorporated by many into the story of the girls' rescue, the tale of the joint wedding came to represent a kind of ceremonial consecration of the bonds formed during the kidnapping and rescue. This time, Richard Callaway officiated. The seesaw of authority and power between Boone and Callaway tilted once again, at least symbolically.

Progress was made on fortifying the settlement now that the abduction demonstrated the dangers when settlers let down their guard. With fewer people, opportunity arose for those remaining to spread out. John Floyd witnessed arguments multiply over land claims in the area. As a surveyor responsible for marking and recording plots and property lines, Floyd saw firsthand how disagreements turn into threats. He reported settlers warning him that "they will drive me and the officers to hell" if he and his fellow Boonesboro leaders did not approve claims. Floyd already had longed to leave Kentucky; he had no family present to hold him back, but he still felt torn. He vowed to stay to help the other residents. "When I think of the deplorable condition a few helpless families are likely to be in," he had written, "I conclude to sell my life as dearly as I can, in their defense rather than make an ignominious escape." But high-minded ideals eroded in this charged environment. Only a few months later, Floyd, Boone's right hand in the rescue of Jemima and the Callaway girls, headed back to Virginia.

As so many fled Kentucky, Boonesboro residents welcomed reinforcements and new arrivals, sometimes greeting them with a celebratory volley of gunfire. Captain James Estill came with his family, bringing an enslaved man named Monk, who would impress the settlement with his ingenuity. Reminiscent of the agricultural experimentation of Richard Hines, Monk planted the first apple orchard at Boonesboro. Michael Stoner, who had accompanied Boone a few years before to warn the unsuspecting surveyors, rejoined his friend at the settlement after spending time raising crops in a more isolated area. Though carrying a reputation for being clumsy, Stoner knew the territory as well as Boone did, maybe better. Orphaned at a young age, he was a hearty thirty-year-old of German descent with enough influence from Pennsylvania Dutch (Deutsch) country that he was often known as the Dutchman. He was "a low chunky man," as one of Boone's sons later described him, who was said to laugh in Dutch.

Another Boonesboro newcomer introduced himself as Simon Butler and epitomized the settlement's potential as a place for a fresh start. "Tall, lithe, straight, auburn-haired, blue-eyed," as a descendant would describe him, the twenty-one-year-old Butler had a secret that started with his name. He was actually Simon Kenton. A wandering spirit with a sharp temper, Kenton in his teenage years had courted a young woman in his native Virginia who chose another suitor, a friend of Kenton's named William Leachman. Kenton attended the wedding, intentionally provoking Leachman and his brother, who gave Kenton a beating. On April 10, 1771, Kenton challenged Leachman to fight. Locked in fierce hand-to-hand combat in an isolated section of forest, Kenton was on the ground and appeared defeated until he wrapped his opponent's braided hair around a tree, using the constraint to turn the tide. Kenton battered his rival so badly that Leachman collapsed, blood gushing out of his mouth and nose. Kenton's efforts turned from trying to disable Leachman to trying unsuccessfully to revive him. Weighing his bleak options, Kenton fled into the night, shoeless, splattered with blood, and without a possession to his name.

Moving from one outpost to another, Kenton took pains to conceal his past, starting by adopting the alias Butler, while learning skills as hunter and woodsman from pioneers and Indians. While engaged in military operations during Lord Dunmore's War, he met Simon Girty, the settler serving as Indian interpreter for the British after years living among the tribes. Though Butler felt safest in solitude, he also saw the winds of change blowing from the Revolutionary War, noting that "the Indians became very harsh on us." After hearing of several incidents, including when Indians "took two daughters of Col. Callaway and one of Col. Boone at Boonesborough," Butler later recalled, he "quit raising corn" in isolation and began aligning himself with the settlements. After encountering Stoner and first hearing about "Taniel Schpoon's Fort" ("Daniel Boone's fort," filtered through Stoner's accent), Butler made his path through the shadows to Boonesboro. The settlement had already had experience with a man bearing a false identity— Dr. Smyth, who had ended up betraying them. Had the settlement's detractors known Butler's story, they would have had a field day: a fugitive fleeing murder charges proving this was a haven to those rejected by society.

Boonesboro faced major disappointment as Richard Henderson tried to strengthen the legal status of his proposal for Transylvania Colony, which included Boonesboro. The mastermind of the

westward push into Kentucky had already been frustrated by reports of various political figures debating the validity of their land
purchase, or as Henderson phrased it with irritation, the "minute
circumstances of our contract with the Cherokee Indians." Though
in private Henderson lamented what he saw as the poor class of
settlers in Kentucky, he also chafed at others who viewed them as
a "lawless train of abandoned villains," while to the settlers themselves, Henderson stressed their "noble and honorable purpose."
Four months after the kidnapping, Henderson traveled to Virginia
to argue for official recognition. With the war in full swing, Henderson no longer had to worry about British disapproval of his enterprise, but when the Declaration of Independence turned colonies
into states, the new Virginia legislature claimed Kentucky for itself,
and Henderson's Transylvania was literally "stricken from the map."

Henderson, at a loss, moved from Boonesboro and didn't return for three years. Boonesboro was now without legal status and
drained of key leaders, a no-man's-land "surrounded on all sides
with difficulties," vulnerable to all enemies.

HENRY HAMILTON, FORTY-TWO, set his sights on bringing
down Boonesboro. Hailing from Ireland, Hamilton had been stationed in the American colonies loyally serving British interests for
almost twenty years. He had seen Indians up close as both ally and
foe to the British during the French and Indian War, and he had
grown personally interested in tribal life and culture. Cultivating
drawing as a hobby, he'd sketch portraits of Indians as well as land-
scapes of the vast natural spaces he encountered. Eventually appointed lieutenant governor of Fort Detroit, the British stronghold
on the Detroit River near the border with Canada, Hamilton was in
strategic position to influence the western territories. That influence

could take various forms. At times he forged alliances and bonds with Indians; at other times he manipulated them.

Hamilton was a bureaucrat at heart—a man who followed orders. At the brink of the insurrection of the colonies that became the Revolutionary War, his superiors directed him to use his perch at Fort Detroit to prompt Indians into "making a diversion and exciting alarm on the frontiers." Hamilton accepted. The message that Fort Detroit supported unrest undoubtedly spread through official and unofficial channels and would have indirectly empowered missions like the one Hanging Maw, Big Jimmy, and Catfish carried out when kidnapping Jemima and the Callaway girls in July 1776. Almost as soon as Hamilton had his bearings at Fort Detroit, some Indian parties applied to him for support for more aggressive action "to make war upon the frontiers," but Hamilton, as he later recalled, "declined . . . not having received positive orders on the subject." With his experience and expertise in Indian cultures, Hamilton was poised to escalate the efforts coming out of Fort Detroit beyond mere provocation to all-out warfare, but the timing had to be right.

Enlarged repeatedly since the British took over the property from the French in 1760, Fort Detroit now could house three to four hundred soldiers in its barracks. An imposing arsenal featured four six-pound cannons and two batteries consisting of twelve guns facing the river. Structures on the grounds included a hospital and a guardhouse. Here was a far cry from the collection of log cabins that was Boonesboro.

Later Hamilton would recall his "frequent conferences" with Indians and "the personal knowledge I had gained of their chiefs and principal speakers." He exhibited pride in what he considered his immersion in American Indian culture, which included participating in rituals and dances, as well as fulfilling desires for alcohol, which came into Fort Detroit in large quantities for that purpose. Hamilton sometimes paid Indians with rum in return for information and errands. According to one contemporary, Hamilton actively lobbied his superiors to expand his abilities to deploy Indians against settlers. While he waited for that authorization, he had to sway Indian delegates and visitors to vest their loyalties with the British rather than the breakaway colonies.

Cornstalk would be an especially valuable ally, and a perfect opportunity for Hamilton to court him arose when the Shawnee leader traveled to Fort Detroit about a month after the Boonesboro kidnapping. The Shawnee had a reputation for military skill that could be unleashed with great consequence. The very act of having the meeting had a strategic effect in sowing the seeds of distrust between settlers and tribes. Matthew Arbuckle, an American counterpart to Hamilton in his post at Fort Randolph, had been frustrated and leery to learn that Cornstalk was en route to see the settlers' nemesis, Hamilton.

During Cornstalk's visit to the British base, Hamilton gave a speech to the visiting Indian leaders gathered there. Hamilton used the paternalistic vocabulary common in addresses to Indians. "Children, I am your father, and you are my children," he said. "I have always your good at heart. I am sent here to represent the great king over the waters, and to take care of you." He identified the insurgent colonists as common enemies and announced that the British would not tolerate unsanctioned Indian cooperation with them as the Revolutionary War raged on. "When the great king is pleased to make peace with his rebellious children in this big island I will then give my assistance in making peace between them and the Indians, and not before." In other words, the tribes could pursue friendly relations with the rebels only if and when the British told them they could.

Hamilton had intercepted a symbolic peace belt brought by William Wilson, the half-Shawnee negotiator who had shortly before dodged a kidnapping plot with the help of Cornstalk—a plot that would have involved bringing Wilson to Hamilton. After Hamilton's speech, the fort's governor tore up Wilson's peace belt and "contemptuously strewed it about the council-house," as Wilson reported.

Hamilton had another belt brought over to Cornstalk and asked the Shawnee chief if he knew what the belt meant. Cornstalk replied that he did not. A strange moment followed. Here was a British official usurping tribal symbolism and glossing it, explaining to Cornstalk that the "tomahawk belt" represented a chain of tribes joining "the English in the general cause." Hamilton requested—or more likely *ordered*—Cornstalk to carry the belt to the Shawnee to demand their allegiance to the British.

Hamilton displayed his attitude toward Indians who refused to cooperate. White Eyes, a leader of the Delaware tribe, was present at the fort at the same time as Cornstalk. Hamilton believed that White Eyes wanted to dissuade other tribes' delegates from siding with the British.

Hamilton attempted to intimidate White Eyes, as recorded in a letter by William Wilson: "He ordered [White Eyes] to leave Detroit before the sun-set as he regarded his head; that he would lose the last drop of his blood before [Hamilton] would suffer any nation to come there and destroy the union which was brought about by so many nations." This served as a warning not only to White Eyes but to any other tribal leaders who considered defying him. White Eyes did not reply, quietly departing from Fort Detroit, after which he called Hamilton a fool, noting that Indian armies could make Hamilton "tremble for his head" if they turned against him.

Wilson, whom Hamilton banished from Fort Detroit at the same time as kicking out White Eyes, was convinced that Hamilton was raising a proxy Indian army. Cornstalk's reply to Hamilton's tomahawk belt gesture is not in the historical record, but it would fit with Cornstalk's overall philosophy if he chose to remain just as silent as White Eyes, frustrating Hamilton as much as he had frustrated Captain Arbuckle by journeying to the British fort at Detroit in the first place. But Hamilton had reason to understand that the Shawnee had diverse factions, some of which veered from Cornstalk's anti-militaristic stance. Those more militant factions, such as the ones who followed Blackfish, waited in the wings.

American policy inadvertently aided Hamilton's cause. After raids against settlers by Dragging Canoe—the breakaway Cherokee leader with whom Hanging Maw initially had aligned himself—leaders ordered a retaliatory campaign against Cherokees in the fall of 1776 using troops out of Virginia and North Carolina. Indian towns that resisted surrender, recalled one of the Virginia soldiers, "were entirely destroyed, together with all their corn, stock and other property that could be found." In this kind of destruction of land lay a divergence between British and American policy toward Indians during the Revolutionary War—with the caveat that neither policy was consistent in conception or in practice. There were the usual gestures of justice and vengeance—Dragging Canoe drew on that ire—that made up the age-old blood feuds. But the former colonists also increasingly had interest in removing populations of Indians altogether in order to take the land and provide strategic position against the British. A year earlier, one delegate from South Carolina called for soldiers deployed into Cherokee country to "cut up every Indian cornfield, and burn every Indian town," arguing that the Indian nation would be "extirpated, and the lands become property of the public." The British, by contrast, had incentive to keep Indians in place to block the expansion of rebels, presenting themselves as more natural allies, however imperfect, to Indians under siege.

ON APRIL 24, 1777, Simon Butler, the young man who had fled Virginia under that alias fearing a murder charge, stepped out of the gates of Boonesboro with a small party of men, prepared for a morning hunt. Butler had begun earning Boone's confidence "as a spy and woodsman." But before Butler could get very far, he realized something was awry.

Boonesboro's dire circumstances are reflected in a letter sent to Virginia around this time from Harrodsburg, one of the few other Kentucky forts: "We are surrounded with enemies on every side; every day increases their numbers. To retreat from the place where our all is centered, would be a little preferable to death. Our fort is already filled with widows and orphans; their necessities call upon us daily for supplies . . . a rueful war presents itself before us." Even as the residents worked to fortify their structures in the wake of the girls' kidnapping, a series of stealth operations by Indian warriors, including a roving contingent led by Blackfish, had killed settlers around Boonesboro and Harrodsburg. Few choices remained, none of which inspired confidence.

On this morning in April, Butler and the other Boonesboro men heard a commotion outside—rifle fire and the sounds of a chase. Butler and his party rushed ahead to find a resident of the settlement, Daniel Goodman, pinned down by Shawnee warriors, being scalped with a tomahawk in broad daylight. Butler quickly took aim with his rifle and shot down the brave wielding the tomahawk. But it was too late for Goodman. He was dead. As the other warriors fled from the fort, Butler and his party gave chase.

Boone and as many as a dozen other armed men—including

trusted friend Michael Stoner—stormed out of the fort to join the pursuit. There was a treeless lane that they followed to the edge of the cleared grounds, where all seemed quiet. The quiet was deceptive. Studying the area, Butler spotted a hidden figure preparing to fire. Butler once again fired before his opponent, killing the would-be shooter, but they were not safe. They had walked into an ambush. A contingent of Indian warriors appeared out of hiding— behind tree stumps and fence posts—now blocking the lane to the fort. A contemporary recorded that the Indian fighters numbered between forty and fifty. On the ground at the time, it may have seemed far more; through his biographer, Boone recalled "a party of above one hundred in number" on the Indian side.

"Boys, we are gone," Boone said, evaluating impossible odds. "Let us sell our lives as dearly as we can!" Boone led the party in a slow, head-on march into the ambush in the direction of the fort, firing as fast as they could reload their rifles. Stoner rushed ahead of the pack with his rifle, which may have been one with special meaning. When Boone had taken on the summer 1774 mission to warn the surveyors in Kentucky of danger, he had handpicked Stoner to come with him, but Stoner did not have a gun at the time. "Well, Mike, you shall have mine," Boone said, "and I'll get another." A high-quality frontier weapon could cost two months' wages. Stoner named the weapon Sweetlips.

Now while raising his rifle to take aim in the middle of the ambush, Stoner was shot. The ball entered his elbow, passing between two bones and sending his weapon to the ground. As he groped for it, he was shot again, this time in his right hip. He was immobilized, an easy target.

Back inside the fort, Jemima tried to observe what was happening outside. If she spotted a chance to help, she was ready to jump into action.

Two braves were approaching Stoner to finish him off. Moving closer to Stoner's position, settlers gunned them down. By one account, Richard Callaway helped lift Stoner off the ground, telling him to "make the best speed he could to the fort, that he and his little band would try and keep the Indians back." Billy Bush, Rebecca Boone's cousin who had aided in the rescue of Jemima and the Callaway girls, ran to Stoner and put his arm around him to help him walk toward the fort, and he may have been assisted by William Hays, husband of Susannah Boone, Jemima's sister. "For God's sake," Stoner said, "let me go." One man was enough to shoot at, the Dutchman said. "They will shoot us, we are too big a mark, we are too big a mark." Whatever reassurances Bush or Hays might have given, it was highly unlikely they could reach the fort's gates alive at the pace of the stout, severely injured Stoner. As the Indian warriors zeroed in on them, Bush was forced to move away from Stoner. Then Monk, the enslaved man who had come to Boonesboro with James Estill, stationed himself at the gates and began to fire, driving back the braves. Monk gave Stoner enough cover to make it to the gates. As Stoner slipped inside, "a volley of balls" riddled the gateposts.

Inside the fort, Jemima rushed over to Stoner, who was losing blood fast. He fainted. She bathed him with water until he regained consciousness. "What are you doing?" Stoner asked. Jemima explained what had happened. "By my life," he said, "my gun . . . my gun." Given his rifle back, Stoner insisted on doing his part in their defense, which he could do by shooting through embrasures, the strategically placed openings in the walls of a fort. Jemima began to "run" bullets for him—that is, she molded ammunition out of molten lead. Due to the teamwork between the Dutchman and Jemima, Stoner, as family legend recorded, hit several opponents with his weapon. In surveying the ongoing gunfight, Jemima could also see something terrifying—her father in peril.

As they tried to reach the fort, Boone and the others had to stop every few steps to avoid being hit and to reload, aim, and fire. In addition to hitting Stoner, gunfire struck Boonesboro pioneers Levi Todd and Isaac Hite. Boone was "shot through the left ankle," his son Nathan later recorded, which "broke the bone." He collapsed to the ground. An Indian warrior approached with tomahawk raised. Butler fired, hitting the brave just as a second warrior approached Boone with a knife to take his scalp. Butler turned his rifle backward to use it as a club, knocking the second combatant down. Butler then lifted Boone and "miraculously," as a descendant of Butler's put it, carried him closer to the gates. Jemima, having seen her father wounded, rushed out of the fort into the gunfire. Boone leaned on her and she rescued him by conducting him through the gates. Once he was safe in the fort, a bullet was extracted from Boone's ankle, probably with Jemima's help. "The ball," as Nathan Boone described it, "mashed as thin as a knife blade was drawn out from the opposite side of where it entered."

In the melee, twenty-two Indians—as the tribe itself reportedly later assessed—had been killed. Before Boone and Jemima retreated into the fort, the chaos gave way to some clarity about who was behind the campaign. The small army of warriors was Shawnee. And their leader was Blackfish, whose son Boone reportedly killed during the rescue of Jemima; now Blackfish had watched as his son's killer and that man's daughter Jemima, who seemed always at the center of every maelstrom, disappeared behind the gates.

This was likely the first time Blackfish, Jemima, and Daniel saw one another. Even though Cornstalk had refused to pursue those who killed Blackfish's son, a plan of retaliation had begun to unfold. Skirmishes and raids multiplied, but Rebecca Boone would later identify this clash on April 24, 1777, as a watershed, a turning point, the first direct attack against the fort.

RISE OF BLACKFISH

HENRY HAMILTON FINALLY RECEIVED THE message from his superiors that he had been eagerly anticipating since the start of the Revolutionary War. It was mid-June 1777, almost a year after the Americans declared independence from England and less than two months after the landmark ambush by Blackfish at Boonesboro. The lieutenant governor now had authorization to send Indians directly to attack the rebel colonists. The news could not have been more welcome to the British strategists who wanted to further tighten alliances with the tribes. Some Indian leaders and factions already had gone firmly over to the American side of the conflict. Hamilton had done himself no favors when he'd driven out White Eyes, the Delaware chief, from Fort Detroit the year before. Shortly after that incident, White Eyes visited the Continental Congress in Philadelphia. There the chief was lauded for his faithfulness to the Revolutionary cause. The Congress sent White Eyes back with a message to carry to the tribes: "We desire you will make it known among all the Indian nations to the westward that we are determined to cultivate peace and friendship among them." The Americans, just as the British did, promised never-ending allegiance to Indians as long as they did exactly what they were asked.

Hamilton decided to unveil his news to a group of Indian delegates at Fort Detroit in a staggered fashion. First he gathered together the representatives—which included Shawnee, Delaware, and Miami tribes—and drank to the king of England's health. Hamilton then described victories by the redcoats over the Continental Army and American militias. This required some dramatic license. Since the British captured Fort Lee late the previous year, George Washington had directed Revolutionary War victories in the areas of Trenton and Princeton, New Jersey, and then in the Battle of Ridgefield. These setbacks made Hamilton's mission all the more urgent. Hamilton stressed to his audience the rebels' "obstinate disobedience" and "their threats regarding the Indians." Adding a touch of suspense to his presentation, Hamilton promised to tell those gathered about "his real sentiments"—in other words, his most important news—the next day.

When they gathered outside the British fort the following day, the Indians formed two lines stretching from the river to the woods. Hamilton, described by an observer as "painted and dressed like an Indian," finally revealed his big announcement. He declared he was now "authorized to put the hatchet into the hands of the Indians." He made clear that the arrangement had a hierarchy. The fort's leader said he "expected an implicit obedience to the order of His Majesty." It is probable—though a contemporaneous account appears to be misdated—that at this same occasion Hamilton was presented with the head of an ox, being used to represent the rebelling colonists, with a tomahawk lodged in it. Hamilton, in a symbolic gesture of his leadership, was invited to take the tomahawk from the head. Brandishing this, Hamilton led the singing of a war song, dancing with the Indians and other British officials present, before moving to the fields, where a feast awaited everyone.

The assemblies and ceremonies lasted nearly a week, after which

Hamilton continued to eagerly mark this new phase. He created incentives for Indians to wage successful campaigns against the rebels and applied enough pressure that some of the Indians taking part in his proxy war would later admit "they did not go to war of their own wish, but because ordered to do so by the governor of Detroit." Hamilton's methods earned him a scornful nickname from settlers—the Hair Buyer, for his apparent payments for American scalps. Truth be told, scalps were prized and ritualized by both sides of the war, and British and American fighters took scalps just as Indians did. But the caricature stuck to Hamilton, who later insisted that he actually urged Indian fighters not to kill unnecessarily. "I constantly addressed the Indians," he wrote, "pointing out to them the advantage which must in the future result to them, from sparing the lives of their prisoners."

Hamilton also encouraged the braves to spread his message in a unique, macabre way. It revealed itself that summer on the Kentucky frontier, when an American militiaman named Ambrose Grayson was gunned down. In addition to being scalped, Grayson's body had a "proclamation" from Hamilton left on it by the braves. The letter on the corpse unconvincingly promised rebels that "all those who would come off with their arms & use them in defence of his British Majesty should be human[e]ly dealt with."

Captain Matthew Arbuckle, as leader of Fort Randolph on the Ohio River, keenly observed the changes in the air. He was on edge over Fort Detroit's convocation and Hamilton's incendiary messages conveyed through the British-allied tribes. Arbuckle had been sending his spies to watch for Indian activities, though as trackers and woodsmen they generally came across as much less impressive than Boone's men; so it was no surprise when Arbuckle's covert scouts were spotted by their enemy and when his marksmen widely missed their targets and dropped a gunpowder horn as they scrambled away. With news reaching him that the Indian parties to Detroit "unanimously agreed (by accepting of the war belt and tomahawk) to distress this place," Arbuckle envisioned a scenario in which Hamilton's proxy army would attempt to destroy Fort Randolph and "then proceed to the frontier inhabitants." Arbuckle had vowed to his superiors to "endeavor to protect the inhabitants on the frontiers to the utmost of my power" in fighting what he called "the damned savages." Though he certainly lacked the capacity for cultural immersion shown by Daniel Boone or even Henry Hamilton, Arbuckle's reputation as an "Indian fighter" also is an oversimplification. In fact, Arbuckle cultivated a special advisor inside Fort Randolph with whom he could consult on Indian affairs at this critical juncture: the sister of Shawnee chief Cornstalk.

Standing at a purported height of six foot six, Nonhelema's strong build earned her the nickname Grenadier Squaw from settlers, referring to soldiers chosen for upper-body strength to lob grenades at enemies. She was also known by another name, Katharine, given to her by a missionary, shortened to Kate or Ketty. One witness described her as a "good looking woman of commanding presence." For a time, Nonhelema led her own village on Scippo Creek about half a mile from the Shawnee town headed by her brother Cornstalk. For reasons lost to history but possibly related to her baptism by the missionary, Nonhelema began to associate with colonists, an allegiance intensified by the Revolutionary War. Nonhelema may well have seen with clarity, earlier than her brother, that the time for maintaining diplomacy with both sides of the Revolutionary War quickly expired. A choice had to be made.

Eventually—probably by the summer of 1777—Nonhelema moved with her daughter, Fanny, into Fort Randolph, where Nonhelema could act as interpreter for Captain Arbuckle and the other officers in their dealings with Indians. Because Cornstalk was such a key figure in relations between Shawnee and the settlers, the presence of his sister gave Arbuckle a chance to stem the tide of Henry Hamilton's recruitment campaign. She became a confidante and, in all likelihood, the woman Arbuckle spent the most time with during this period. His wife, Frances, remained in Greenbrier, roughly a mile away.

By incorporating Nonhelema's insights, Arbuckle could better understand the strengths and vulnerabilities of Hamilton's position and strategize accordingly. One insight—overlooked by many, including at times by Arbuckle himself—was that no tribe was monolithic. Arbuckle wrote to his superiors that there were Shawnee who he remained "convinced are as yet our friends," despite what happened at Fort Detroit. He made clear how heavily he relied on Nonhelema's intelligence. He even passed along information Nonhelema had obtained—which she had said would put her life at risk if ever linked to her—that an American officer (her paramour Alexander McKee) was in the process of betraying the Revolution and bringing secrets over to the British. Arbuckle's superiors, however, doubted the word of an Indian woman and delayed action, possibly opening themselves up to espionage.

Arbuckle, suspicious by nature, increasingly found it difficult to know whom to trust. A few weeks after hearing about Hamilton's intertribal meeting at Fort Detroit, two Shawnee arrived at Fort Randolph wishing to confer with Arbuckle. Despite their "strong protestations of friendship," Arbuckle ordered the visitors detained.

CORNSTALK HEARD ABOUT the Shawnee taken hostage by Captain Arbuckle, yet another fire he had to try to snuff out. By this point, the tireless Shawnee chief was constantly scrambling to protect his tribe from being crushed between the British and the

Americans, and he continued to push for diplomacy whenever possible. He decided to send his son Elinipsico ahead to Fort Randolph to meet with Arbuckle. In the meantime, Cornstalk himself began to make his way to the fort. In the crisis stoked by the kidnapping of the Boone and Callaway girls, Cornstalk's brother had gone to the fort to try to appease Arbuckle, while Cornstalk took pains to persuade other parties that the fault rested with the renegade Shawnee warriors; now other family members shaped the situation from the inside, starting with Cornstalk's sister, Nonhelema. When Elinipsico reached Fort Randolph, he made no progress freeing the hostages, but he informed Arbuckle that his father and other Shawnee leaders would be there soon. Having delivered his message, Elinipsico departed.

Rather than looking forward to having an audience with the Shawnee chief, Arbuckle made an arrogant decision. As he put it to one of his superiors while waiting for Cornstalk, he decided not to release his Shawnee hostages. Instead, he planned to take *more*. "I have the two still detained," he wrote, "and intend detaining & confining as many as fall into my hands . . . until I have further instructions from you." The hostages represented leverage to push away perceived enemies from encroaching on the territory he oversaw—not much different from how Hanging Maw had originally perceived the Boonesboro girls. Arbuckle convinced himself without any apparent evidence that the two Shawnee visitors he'd already taken into custody had been spies, and his mistrust devolved into paranoia. "I am well satisfied," Arbuckle wrote, "the Shawnese are all our enemies."

Cornstalk arrived at Fort Randolph with another Shawnee leader, named Red Hawk, and they explained to Arbuckle their highly conflicted position on the war. An officer who was present at the fort at the time recalled Cornstalk's presentation: "He made no secret of the disposition of the Indians; declaring that, on his own part, he was opposed to joining in the war on the side of the British, but that all the nation, except himself and his own tribe, were determined to engage in it; and that, of course, he and his tribe would have to run with the stream." Arbuckle remained committed to his haphazard paranoia. He took Cornstalk and Red Hawk prisoner, ostensibly "to prevent the nation from joining the British." Nonhelema's role in Arbuckle's decision to hold her own brother prisoner remains unclear, though clues support her consistent presence at the fort and ongoing counsel to Arbuckle on Indian-related issues, of which this diplomatic crisis was now the prime example.

The imprisonment of Cornstalk baffled more than one higher-up in the Continental Army ranks, who recognized Cornstalk as "the most active of his nation to promote peace." Elinipsico soon made yet another trip from the Shawnee towns to Fort Randolph, this time to check on his father's safety. From the river near the fort, Elinipsico cried out for his father; Cornstalk, hearing his son from inside the fort, called out in reply. Elinipsico entered and embraced his father. Now Arbuckle had Elinipsico locked up, too.

Cornstalk cooperated with demands by the fort officials. He gave a speech, explaining his philosophy on death. "When I was a young man and went to war, I thought that might be the last time, and I would return no more. Now I am here amongst you; you may kill me if you please. I can die but once; and it is all one to me, now or another time." When asked to draw the placement of Shawnee towns, he complied. He sketched a map with chalk on the floor.

Having anticipated an Indian siege against Fort Randolph, Arbuckle had urged superiors to send reinforcements, though he did not have enough supplies to sustain more troops in residence. A portion of those troops had arrived while Cornstalk and the other hostages were being held. Without sufficient provisions, some of the soldiers defied orders and scattered to hunt deer. Away from the protection of the fort, a small group was shot at by Indians who were in the woods. Gunfire struck one soldier, Ensign Robert Gilmore of Virginia, and killed him. One of the newly arrived officers now warned Arbuckle that the soldiers "would be for killing the hostages" in retaliation. Arbuckle bristled. They wouldn't lash out at an innocent party—ran the captain's logic—who had nothing to do with Gilmore's death. But Arbuckle's draconian decision to imprison all Indians now made those hostages easy targets for vengeance.

"Let us kill the Indians in the fort," came a rallying cry from the troops, exactly as the newcomer predicted. Arbuckle and some others tried to block their entrance, Arbuckle saying "that they should not be killed, as they were his prisoners." The troops "cocked their guns" and threatened to kill Arbuckle if he did not stand aside.

The commotion sent a woman inside to warn the prisoners. Captain John Stuart, who was stationed elsewhere but had arrived with the reinforcements, referred to this woman as an "interpreter's wife" who had left captivity among the Indians to stay at the fort and had become emotionally attached to the hostages. But without record of anyone matching this description, it is probable the woman was Nonhelema, who was romantically linked with an interpreter, Alexander McKee, and had recently left her life in her Indian town. If indeed this was Nonhelema, she now rushed into the hostages' cabin to tell her brother and nephew what was happening and to say good-bye. Rationales had formed and hardened among the troops, she reported. It was said that Elinipsico had brought with him the Indians who shot down Gilmore. Hearing this from the woman, Elinipsico denied the allegation and trembled with fear.

Cornstalk "encouraged [Elinipsico] not to be afraid, for that the Great Man above had sent him there to be killed and die with him."

Rushing inside their chamber, the troops shot Elinipsico off a stool where he sat. Red Hawk was killed as he tried to climb a chimney to get to safety. Cornstalk calmly rose to meet the attackers, who riddled him with "seven or eight bullets." All three prisoners died.

DANIEL BOONE CONTINUED to recover from the wound he suffered in the April ambush when Jemima rescued him outside of Boonesboro's fort. When he became fatigued, he complained of the pain where his ankle had shattered. Jemima and Flanders spent their newlywed months trying to arrange basic comforts in a settlement that felt increasingly isolated. An early historian of Boonesboro described the typical cabin, with belongings hanging from antlers and wooden pegs on the wall. "A shelf over the fireplace was reserved for medicine, the whisky jug, tinder box, ink bottle, and quill pens, the Bible, almanac, and a few other books, which, in some cabins, included *The Pilgrim's Progress* and Shakespeare." Like many women on the frontier, Jemima was never taught to read or write, so she would have enjoyed the stories as read aloud or paraphrased and repeated. Mirrors allowed residents to check on their appearances, and sewing equipment kept clothes in good repair. The younger generation of settlers took pride in shaping the community and establishing traditions. When Fanny Callaway and John Holder had a daughter, officials reportedly offered a thousand extra acres of land to the couple if they named her Kentucky— which they declined to do.

Most of all, young couples began their domestic life by learning how to survive. Boonesboro's storehouses were running low on provisions. What little was there was going bad. Salt, used to preserve meat and other rations, as well as for medicinal purposes, was scarce. It was extremely risky to leave the immediate area of the fort to hunt or gather.

In the wake of Cornstalk's death, American officials struggled to make sense of how one of the few Shawnee advocates for peace, the buffer against Blackfish's militants, was murdered in their custody. Perhaps reaching for a sense of its inevitability, Captain Stuart, who had been present at the fort, quoted Cornstalk's comments that "I can die but once; and it is all one to me, now or another time" as a premonition of the events to come, though they actually show a savvy warrior's understanding of a treacherous situation. A later tradition had Cornstalk placing a curse on the region right before his murder, the effects of which supposedly lasted generations. Without any supernatural help, the murder turned Arbuckle's dire utterance about all Shawnee being enemies into a self-fulfilling prophecy.

Colonel William Preston of Virginia fretted when he heard about the murders. "I am apprehensive this conduct will be followed by very bad consequences to the frontiers, by engaging us in a war with that revengeful and warlike nation and their allies." Conciliatory gestures were made, however small compared to what Preston called the "catastrophe" of the killings. Arbuckle reportedly provided a "respectful burial" near the fort. Money was raised for the victims' families—albeit from the sale of the victims' own possessions. George Morgan, the Indian agent for the Continental Congress, wrote to the "chiefs and warriors of the Shawanese Nation" to apologize for the "wicked murder," though also endorsing a conspiracy theory that rival tribes, the Mingoes and Wyandots, had engineered the killing of Ensign Gilmore in order to stir the troops to kill the Shawnee hostages. Officials sent some of their communications to the Shawnee nation through Nonhelema.

Shawnee war chief Blackfish, who previously had chafed at Cornstalk's restrictions, now found his powers unfettered. His rise coincided with Henry Hamilton's authorization to escalate Indian military efforts against ex-colonists. Although Hamilton received garbled facts about Cornstalk's murder, the information he possessed suggested to him chaos and dissension among the American troops. "Cornstalk and his people were seized on by force," Hamilton wrote, "taken out of the Fort and put to Death, that the Commandant [Arbuckle] dissatisfied with this act of violence had gone off to Philadelphia." Arbuckle had not gone to Philadelphia, but the captain had indeed found himself powerless and at a loss for how to react. To Hamilton, the bedlam at Fort Randolph meant opportunity.

Blackfish's warriors had already staged operations in the Kentucky settlements, Shawnee counterparts to Dragging Canoe's Cherokee raiders. Boone saw signs of strategic coordination in Blackfish's maneuvers. "The Indians had disposed their warriors in different parties at this time," Boone recounted through his biographer, "and attacked the different garrisons to prevent their assisting each other." So many incidents riddled the area that 1777 came to be known as the year of the bloody sevens. Only twenty-two men, along with family members, remained at Boonesboro. "We passed through a scene of sufferings that exceed description," Boone recalled.

Only when militias entered the area did Boonesboro temporarily have support to carry out hunting expeditions to replenish the food supply for the residents. The arrival of a Virginia unit late in 1777 gave the fort a solid boost. As one of the militiamen put it, the newcomers "acted in the capacity of defenders of the fort against the enemy and also as Indian spies." The fort's leadership now felt sufficiently confident in their numbers to send a contingent to make salt at an area of the Licking River known as the Lower Blue Licks.

Militia members had brought iron kettles for the purpose. Saltmaking was a time consuming, intensive process. A bushel of salt could require up to eight hundred gallons of spring water. Boone headed the expedition, composed of thirty men drawn from the militia and the residents of Boonesboro and the few remaining Kentucky outposts. Though Richard Callaway stayed behind at the fort, the Boonesboro contingent included three of his nephews, Flanders (Jemima's husband) and his brothers Micajah and James Callaway. For at least a month, the fort would be left without its most proven leader, and Jemima would be separated from her father and husband.

SALTMAKERS WOULD COLLECT sediment-rich water from the spring in the kettles, which would then be brought to a fire to be boiled to produce salt. The wood fire would be assiduously maintained and fed frequently. Packers would then prepare the salt for transport, and couriers would run it to Boonesboro and the other forts. Guards patrolled the area for any signs of a problem, and scouts and hunters—Boone and son-in-law Flanders among them—would leave camp to look for signs of Indians and hunt for meat to bring back to the other saltmakers.

At the encampment, Boone woke up on Saturday, February 7, 1778, having had a distressing dream. He dreamed that his father was angry. Squire Boone, whose name was passed on to Daniel's younger brother, had been a Quaker who had a knotty relationship with the religious authorities; when delivering discipline, Squire would beat his children until they asked for forgiveness, which Daniel, being Daniel, never would. Boone attached ominous significance to dreams that featured his angry father.

Eeriness continued beyond the dream. This was a cloudy, snowy day, a little more than a month into the tedious saltmaking expedition. After hunting on his own, Boone packed up hundreds of pounds of fresh buffalo meat on his horse, requiring him to lead the horse back toward camp rather than ride it. Man and horse navigated a narrow passage, slowing down from the heavy snowfall and a fallen tree blocking the way. After getting beyond the obstruction, Boone's horse seemed scared. Boone, now on alert, peered through a haze of snow. Thirty steps away, he spotted four Indians hiding behind the fallen tree. He had seconds before they'd realize he had seen them—seconds to plot what to do. He considered pulling down the meat from his horse so he could mount it, but the tugs—green fasteners made from buffalo hide—had frozen and wouldn't budge. He reached for his knife, but the blood on the blade had frozen it to the scabbard.

Boone launched into a run. Two of the Indians gave chase on either side, while one cut Boone's load free and climbed onto the horse, riding after their quarry. There was no way to elude pursuers over the fresh snow—Boone's prints, as son Nathan recalled, "could easily be followed." He ran approximately a mile and a half. The Indians began to fire at him, bullets crashing into the snow and sending white powder flying into the air around him. One ball came so close to him that it cut the strap of his powder horn, which held gunpowder. Boone understood that shots that came so near without hitting him were intended to stop him, not kill him. With the Indians on his heels, Boone realized "it was impossible to escape." He leaned his rifle against a tree and surrendered. As Boone summed it up in terse fashion through his biographer: "They pursued, and took me."

The warriors seized Boone's weapons and brought him three miles to an encampment eight miles below the Lower Blue Licks. Boone was ushered over to Pompey, a Black man, formerly enslaved, who was fluent in English and Shawnee. Pompey acted as interpreter. The sight that greeted Boone was overwhelming. By his estimate, a hundred Indians were gathered there, during a time in winter when settlers expected tribes to send out only small hunting parties. High-ranking Shawnee approached their captive. They reminded him of his history in Kentucky. Captain Will, who had confronted Boone on his first Kentucky expedition to warn him not to come back, was present.

"How d' do, Captain Will?" Boone said.

Captain Will, taking a moment to remember his first encounter with Boone, repeated his warning that "the wasps and yellow jackets" would sting him if he tried to settle Kentucky. Arguably, his point was proved by Boone's circumstances.

Looking around, Boone saw James and George Girty, brothers of Simon Girty and, like Simon, former Indian captives–turned–trusted members of the tribal communities. Also present was Nimwha (also known as Munseeka), Cornstalk's brother, who succeeded Cornstalk as head chief, and may have been the same Shawnee who went to Fort Randolph to denounce the kidnapping of Jemima and the Callaway girls. Two French operatives working for the British, Charles Beaubien and Louis Lorimier, accompanied the Indian party. This pair had tried to engage the Miami tribe in a mission against Kentucky settlers before succeeding in recruiting this group of Shawnee, already energized by personal and strategic motives.

Pompey then escorted Boone over to Blackfish, the war chief, and in many ways Boone's counterpart as frontier strategist. Blackfish, according to Boone family tradition, "was truly one of nature's noblemen." He was known to wear a *cappo*, a long, dark, hooded European cloak. It was Blackfish who'd led the ambush at Boonesboro the previous April, when Boone was wounded. It was Blackfish whose son died in the rescue of Jemima and the Callaways—by

Boone's own gun—and whose raiders had been terrifying Boonesboro since. With Cornstalk gone, no dissension within the tribe
held him back from personal reparations or from trying to reclaim
Kentucky for use of the tribes. Blackfish asked if the men at the Pe-
memo Lick—what the settlers called Lower Blue Licks—had come
with Boone.

"How do you know that there are any men there?" Boone asked.

They made clear to Boone that their scouts had seen them.

Boone admitted that the saltmakers had come with him. Blackfish replied bluntly: he was going to kill them.

Chapter

7

FAMILIES

BOONE HAD NO GOOD CHOICES. If he resisted Blackfish, the Indians could toss him aside and overwhelm the saltmaking camp at the Lower Blue Licks without warning. He needed to find a way to appease Blackfish while avoiding that bloodshed. Boone's son Nathan recalled his father's thinking. "The enemy [had] four times the number of the salt boilers, the latter, ignorant of their discovery, would find it impossible to escape; & the next day, when the Indians proposed going there, being Sunday, [Boone's men] would be loitering about off their guard." Even if some of the saltmakers managed to slip away from a surprise attack, the fresh snow, now rising to knee height, would lead Indians right to them, just as it had stymied Boone's attempted escape. Boone made an extreme move. He proposed that he would surrender his men if the Indians agreed not to mistreat them or make them run the gauntlet—a potentially fatal military punishment.

With his conditions accepted, Boone was brought the next day by his captors to a hill opposite the salt spring, where the saltmakers rested. As Boone expected, they were literally caught lying down—sunning themselves in the snow. Boone appeared alongside an Indian and hailed them. Seeing the Indian, the saltmakers grabbed for their weapons "ready for battle," as one of Boone's men later recounted. In a moment that had to send a shock through them all, Boone cried out: "Don't fire! If you do, all will be massacred." He explained that Indians surrounded them and that he had negotiated surrender in return for good treatment. Boone warned that "it was impossible for them to get away" and "begged of them not to attempt to defend themselves." The settlers yielded, though whether all agreed with how Boone "gave up" (as one captive bluntly put it) would be a matter for debate later. But for now there was no time. Indians emerged from every direction.

The captives were taken from their camp and gathered together, their weapons thrown into a pile. They were ordered to sit. The Indians assembled a council and weighed what they would do. That Boone's deal already seemed to have been voided would have come as a grim surprise to him. From the Indians' perspectives, justice had been constantly under assault by settlers. Cornstalk had been the restraining influence after Boone killed Blackfish's son and in arguing that the death was justified to rescue the girls—but then Americans murdered Cornstalk in cold blood. No wonder Henry Hamilton had considerable success pushing tribal grievances against Americans into full-blown war.

The council of Indians decided to vote whether to hold to the bargain proposed by Boone or to execute the prisoners.

THAT EVENING, FLANDERS CALLAWAY, husband of Jemima and nephew of Boone's rival Richard Callaway, returned to the Lower Blue Licks after having been away hunting with another member of the saltmaking party. They were in for a shock. The camp was empty. At first the hunters considered the possibility that Boone and the others had started back toward Boonesboro early.

Then they found a bow with arrows, and salt tipped over into the snow. Realizing there could be no benign explanation, the two men abandoned the encampment. Reaching Boonesboro the next day, Flanders reported the mysterious development, which hit the settlement hard. A few men set out from the fort to search and picked up a trail through the snow, but they lost it at a river crossing. The missing men could be anywhere, assuming they were alive.

The night she had been rescued with the Callaway girls, Jemima Boone vowed not to let her father out of her sight again. A year and a half later, he had vanished into thin air, nothing more than footprints in the snow, and her husband had come within a hairbreadth of the same fate—in fact, two of Flanders's brothers had disappeared, too.

They all knew Daniel Boone had been in impossible situations before and had always found a way out, but now time passed with no trace or hint of survival. Days turned into weeks, then months. The men and women living on the frontier could only speculate on the fate of the twenty-eight lost men.

When a party of travelers trudged into Kentucky, they met some settlers leaving, who, as one of the travelers recalled, "informed us that Colonel Boone and 28 men were captured at the Blue Lick while making salt and carried off or murdered by the Indians." (The actual count of the other men taken, besides Boone, was twenty-seven.) The hopeless uncertainty of the settlers was encapsulated rhetorically in the two choices of "carried off or murdered." Virginia governor Patrick Henry wrote to a military official, "I don't believe all of Boone's party are lost." Henry's need to express optimism reflected the fact that others were much less hopeful, and even that more optimistic speculation was hardly rosy.

A little more than two months after Boone and his men disappeared, a small group of newcomers that included a young man named Daniel Trabue reached Boonesboro in time for Easter Sunday. The reaction of the residents to the ragtag newcomers' arrival spoke to their isolation and increasing desperation. "The people," Trabue wrote, "all ran out over Joyed to see strangers come to their town or Fort." Despite the fact that the fort was running out of provisions, the people at Boonesboro were "remarkable kind and hospetable to us with what they had," and gave them something to eat.

Trabue and his party only stayed for a short time, and the fort remained weakened, with one militiaman describing the residents as "dirty, lousy, ragged, & half starved." The structure on one side of the fort was open and vulnerable to attack. Established leaders were in short supply among the dwindling number of the men. Simon Butler (Simon Kenton's ongoing alias as he hid from murder charges) had stepped into an active role after Boone's gunshot injury in the April onslaught outside the fort that killed Daniel Goodman. Boone had called Butler over after that incident to deliver praise in his usual understated way: "Simon, you have behaved like a man today." But Butler also came to the attention of George Rogers Clark, the American officer spearheading frontier affairs, who recruited Butler away from Boonesboro to scout Indian and British operations. Adding more secrets to the ones he already kept, Butler would serve Clark as a spy—in the clandestine sense, as well as in the sense of being a scout. The hard-charging William Bailey Smith had joined the rescue mission when the girls were kidnapped—with trigger-happy results when he wielded his weapon too early—but Smith now was also away on official business for Clark, trying to drum up two hundred recruits to become soldiers. Nathaniel Henderson, a brother of Boonesboro mastermind Richard Henderson, followed his brother's footsteps in departing from Boonesboro after its legal setbacks, though remaining behind was the young enslaved man, London, whom he'd brought with him. One Boonesboro resident called London "a real soldier."

The nearby settlement at Harrodsburg, receiving the news of the saltmakers' capture, formed a company of men to travel to Boonesboro to offer help, which included Ambrose Coffee, an Irish immigrant and soldier who decided to remain at the fort. David Bundrin (also spelled Bondurant), known as a Dutchman (though like other "Dutchmen" possibly German), and his family settled amid the wilderness around the same time that Boone and the saltmakers were taken. Isolation left the Bundrins vulnerable, and within a few months they also moved into the Boonesboro compound.

In addition to these individuals and their families, the militia already staying at the fort provided trained military leaders, but they were largely out of their element in the Kentucky wilderness. Militia assignments to go into Kentucky already had been controversial, with some settlers outraged that their fathers, sons, and brothers were sent to protect the desolate reaches of the frontier instead of remaining in their own communities in Virginia or North Carolina, where they would have their own battles brought on by the Revolutionary War.

Facing the scarcity and dire circumstances of Boonesboro, soldiers began to clash. Thomas Dillard and John Donaldson, two of the militiamen, vied for command. Meat was so hard to come by that soldiers began to kill animals owned by Boonesboro families. Without the salt that Boone's expedition had aimed to provide, hunters had to use meat more quickly. One of Donaldson's allies, Lieutenant Hutchings, shot and killed a steer that belonged to Richard Callaway. Callaway, according to another militiaman, "swore that if any man killed another head of his stock, that he would shoot him." The fractures intensified, and the rift was soon considered all-out mutiny. On one side were Donaldson and Hutchings;

on the other were Dillard and, as the clues indicate, Richard Callaway. The sparse record on the militia's infighting in Boonesboro also points to another particularly formidable leader allied to the mutineers: Rebecca Boone.

Daniel Boone's absence affected all the residents, but none more so than Rebecca. As months continued to pass without any trace of the saltmakers, she came to accept the terrible likelihood that her husband was dead. It was a devastating turn. As a descendant later commented, Rebecca and Daniel had been companions in "toils, pleasures, sorrows." But Rebecca was also a woman who believed one had to be prepared, mentally and logistically, to move on at a moment's notice. Facing stark reality had been a dismal prerequisite of the life they led. With no reason to believe that Boone was alive, a "cast down" Rebecca decided to leave Boonesboro to go to North Carolina, where she and the children could stay with her side of the family. Rebecca's state of mind was described as "oppressed with the distresses of the country, and bereaved." A testament to her influence over the family, Boones' grown children and their spouses followed Rebecca's lead and prepared to go. It seemed likely to be the end, not just of Daniel Boone's immediate family in Kentucky, but of Boonesboro, at least the Boonesboro that anybody had known. The so-called mutineers, meanwhile, were described by a witness as having "went in with Colonel Donaldson and Mrs. Boone," indicating Rebecca's shared leadership with Donaldson (future father-in-law of Andrew Jackson, the military officer and eventual president of the United States) over the breakaway militiamen, who also determined to go to North Carolina.

Only one holdout prevented unanimity in the Boone family's decision to leave: Jemima. She refused to believe her father was dead. She could point to the fact that Boone had been gone for longer stretches in the past. On Rebecca's side of the argument, the fact that he had disappeared after Cornstalk's murder, in the era of Blackfish, meant that revenge had now been exacted for the Shawnee killed when liberating Jemima. On Jemima's side of the debate, her own rescue proved that Boones could find a way to come through even hopeless situations. Moreover, she had witnessed firsthand the complex dynamics between the Indians and the settlers, even in moments of intense hostility. She dug into her belief that her father was alive when she refused to obey her mother's edict to leave. Boone had maintained faith that Jemima was alive after she was taken, and now with the roles reversed she would do the same for him.

A battle of wills became a stalemate. On approximately May 1, 1778, four months after Boone had left Boonesboro with the salt-makers, Rebecca and her caravan of family and mutineers from the militia packed up and departed. It was a bleak exodus, leaving behind not only Jemima but also Boone's dream for the future. Jemima remained with her husband and an increasingly skeletal roster of Boonesboro residents. Those who stayed had to admit that Rebecca was probably right about the fate of her husband. Even Daniel's favorite cat sauntered away from his cabin and disappeared from the fort. To Jemima, watching her family recede into the horizon would have been as heart-wrenching as the bloodstained grass had been for Boone when he'd searched the wilderness against the odds for her.

JEMIMA'S CHOICE TO remain at Boonesboro was made bolder by the fact that she stood her ground even though her husband's uncle, the embittered Richard Callaway, was now the undisputed leader of the settlement. A silhouette portrait passed down through the Callaway family that some believed to be the frontier colonel shows a man in a stance of superiority, lips tightly pursed as he (perhaps) oversees his domain. Boone aspired to abide by the motto "Better mend a fault than find a fault," but Callaway had a harsher approach to friends and family. He had stewed over the respect Boone commanded even before he'd rescued Callaway's own daughters. The disappearance of two of Callaway's nephews, Micajah (also known as Cajah or Cage) and James, among the saltmakers provoked fresh outrage.

Reportedly, Callaway was a strict taskmaster to his nephews; by one account, he had physically beaten Cajah over some infraction just before the young man left on the saltmaking mission. When Dr. John Smyth, who turned out to be a spy, visited Boonesboro in its first months, he had noted that "in any of their forts it was all anarchy and confusion, and you could not discover what person commanded, for in fact no person did actually command entirely." Of course, founder Richard Henderson was more of a land speculator and politician than a leader, and Boone's tendency to lead by values and example rather than severity and discipline drew supporters away from Callaway—but now he was in charge. Moreover, Callaway could blame Boone, dead or not, for leading the disastrous mission and for whatever fate his two nephews and the twenty-five other saltmakers had met.

It was no coincidence that Callaway had been on the opposite side of the militia mutiny from Rebecca Boone. The rift between Callaways and Boones had been re-created yet again. Callaway's ascendance may well have helped drive Rebecca away. With the settlement so splintered, it stood to reason that most of those who remained behind were Callaway partisans, and his leadership style differed considerably from Boone's. Boone didn't seek out confrontation or battle when it could be avoided, while Callaway tended to resort to force by reflex, toward Indians and toward peers. If Boone was like Cornstalk, Callaway was more like Blackfish.

Though she may have felt more secure by gaining distance from Callaway, Rebecca Boone's choice to leave Kentucky did not give her an easy path ahead. First she had to reach North Carolina with limited provisions brought from Boonesboro. Dead brush and thick cane and reed had to be cut away. Narrow passes squeezed travelers between a "perplexing tangle of valleys and mountains." John Filson, Boone's contemporary and biographer, recorded how Rebecca transported "family and goods, on horses, through the wilderness, amidst a multitude of dangers." Filson surely embellished descriptions of the journey in and out of Kentucky but captured how the frontier would have appeared to be an entirely new world: "The aspect of these cliffs is so wild and horrid, that it is impossible to behold them without terror. The spectator is apt to imagine that nature had formerly suffered some violent convulsion; and that these are the dismembered remains of the dreadful shock; the ruins, not of Persepolis or Palmyra, but of the world!"

Jemima also faced what seemed to be the ruins of the past in a Boonesboro drained of allies. From this point on, it would become even more difficult to convince anyone that Daniel was alive, while her own fate could turn on how Richard Callaway governed Boonesboro.

EVEN AS DANIEL Boone awaited the Indians' council vote on his fate and that of his men back on Sunday, February 8, he had remained calm, taking in all that he could about the proceedings. Pompey, who had escaped enslavement by settlers, turned out to be not only an interpreter for the Shawnee, but also a chief of sorts, given a vote on the saltmakers' fates. Pompey had a studied style of interpreting, speaking so quietly to Boone that nobody else could hear what he said. Boone was then allowed to make a "closing speech," with the lives of his men potentially riding on his powers of persuasion. Boone addressed the assembly as "brothers," appealing to a sense of justice and demonstrating his careful study of their tribal values.

"You have got all the young men," he reportedly said. "To kill them, as has been suggested, would displease the Great Spirit, and you could not then expect future success in hunting nor war; and if you spare them they will make you fine warriors, and excellent hunters to kill game for your squaws and children. These young men have done you no harm. They unresistingly surrendered upon my assurance that such a step was the only safe one. I consented to their capitulation on the express condition that they should be made prisoners of war and treated well. Spare them, and the Great Spirit will smile upon you."

The stunned saltmakers listened to Boone's speech. Too far away from Pompey to have heard the earlier translations of the council's discussions, the saltmakers had not known their lives were at stake until they heard this plea.

Deliberations continued among the Indians and votes were announced. Boone's argument that the settlers could be integrated into tribal life as warriors and hunters had proof of the concept present among the listeners: the Girtys. The Girty brothers, who were "painted and dressed as the Indians were," voted for mercy, a stance contradicting the notorious, near-demonic reputation the Girtys had developed among settlers. Blackfish, by one account, approached the council with a private request. The vote completed, the results were proclaimed. Fifty-nine votes for death. Sixty-one to spare their lives.

They were saved, but what lay in store remained unclear. Relief was followed by toil, as the captors forced the saltmakers to carry heavy loads of supplies in a march toward the Indian towns, "an uncomfortable journey in very severe weather," as Boone told his biographer. Boone divided up the little meat he had with him among the neediest of his men. This seemed unwise to some, who couldn't imagine Boone surviving the long distances without more sustenance, but he always claimed that eating larger quantities was a habit rather than a requirement, and that he could simply "buckle his belt tighter and get along very comfortably." At one point, an Indian ordered James Callaway (Richard Callaway's nephew and brother-in-law to Jemima through Flanders) to carry a salt kettle. James, tall and ruddy, refused the command, and continued to resist until the Indian raised his tomahawk over him. "Callaway bent forward his head," remembered another saltmaker, "to receive the blow, at the same time taking off his hat and patting the top of his head with his hand, saying, 'Here, strike!'" The Indian turned away with a "dry smile" and carried the kettle himself.

Reminiscent of Jemima's line in the sand during her captivity—refusing to walk on her injured foot until given moccasins—the prisoners tested the power dynamics. Boone was also ordered by an Indian to carry a kettle and, like James Callaway, refused. The Indian pushed the kettle hard into Boone, who pushed back. The confrontation turned into a standoff and may well have come to blows.

Blackfish appeared at the scene of the dispute. Boone's physical altercation with a Shawnee could provide Blackfish with justification to enact his revenge once and for all on his son's killer. But justice for Blackfish was a concept far more complex than among those many settlers who sought an eye for an eye—restorative rather than retributive. This was the moment, as recounted by Boone's nephew, when the Shawnee chief "took Boone away and kept him under his special care and protection." As it came to be known later, Blackfish had quietly "interfered" during the Indian council's discussions of whether to execute Boone; Blackfish reportedly had "earnestly requested that Boone should be given to him to fill the place of his son who had been killed." Just as Mary Jemison's inclusion in a Seneca community was seen as compensation for a lost loved one within the tribe, ideas of reparation for a death transcended bloodshed or economic value by incorporating the person responsible into the family. For them, the word *family* crossed boundaries of tribe, culture, and bloodline.

At one point on the march, the Indians began to clear a path about a hundred yards long. Pompey explained to Boone that a gauntlet was being prepared for him. This ordeal involved arranging two columns of attackers armed with cudgels, sticks, and tomahawks, who stand in striking range of a runner who must pass through the middle. The runner is given a cudgel. The ritual could be fatal for the runner.

Boone objected, insisting that when he agreed to surrender the saltmakers, Blackfish had promised to leave aside requirements to pass a gauntlet. "No," replied Blackfish, "you made no bargain for yourself, but for your men alone." Boone had to admit to the loophole. "It was so," he said. Boone grasped at masculinity as a framework for the task: "I'm a man, and no squaw, and not afraid to run." Blackfish did not present the challenge for what in all likelihood it was: a way for Blackfish to keep Boone alive. In exchange for granting Blackfish's request to spare Boone's life, the council had insisted that the prisoner run the gauntlet.

Staring down these parallel columns of opponents was particularly intimidating. When gauntlets were organized inside towns, some of the participants striking the runner were children, but here they were all warriors. On top of that, a large portion of the participants had argued to have Boone or his men executed. Now thwarted in that goal, they were out for blood. Boone, as usual, did not show any fear. He barreled through. He zigzagged and not only eluded most of the assailants' blows entirely, but also knocked down more than one of them. Still, "heavy blows" landed against him and staggered him. One very large warrior apparently became angry to see him nearing the end of the ordeal. Breaking protocol, the warrior stepped into the middle of the path to get a clear shot. Boone lowered his head and rammed the man, sending his opponent flying to the ground. Boone was past the column of attackers; blood dripped from his body. He couldn't help but believe that some of the Indians had "seemed to favor him" and spared him more-serious injuries. Blackfish congratulated him and proclaimed him a true "brave," or Indian warrior.

The march took almost two weeks, and then the prisoners were split up to be taken to different destinations. The grueling trails brought them through deep snow and frigid temperatures. The party that included Boone crossed the Ohio River in a vessel built by Indians and held together by animal hides. During nights the prisoners were tied, as Jemima and the Callaway sisters had been. A description was later recorded of one prisoner's experience: "His arms were tied behind him, a rope or buffalo tug tied fast around his middle and then made fast to an Indian on each side of him, and the one around his arms was made to go around his neck, and tied fast to a tree, and in that position he had to sleep upon the snow." Food remained insufficient. Boone consumed slippery-elm bark followed by chewing "oak ooze" meant to calm the stomach after digesting the bark. The Shawnee were renowned for their medical knowledge and may well have been impressed to see their prisoner using remedies like their own.

They arrived on February 18 at their destination, Little Chillicothe, a key Shawnee town on a tributary of the Ohio River. They were greeted by a war dance welcoming home the warriors and celebrating the number of prisoners taken. By some accounts, more prisoners were made to run the gauntlet at this point, further weakening Boone's arrangement with Blackfish, perhaps to test which settlers would be most useful as warriors.

Boone was also in for more tests. He was tied up, brought to water, and then jerked backward whenever he tried to drink. Reportedly, he also was taken aside by a brave who had questions for him. The warrior asked Boone to recount the story of his rescue of Jemima. Did he kill a Shawnee named Catfish? The questioner, it turned out, was Catfish's son, Blackfish's grandson. Boone was now "completely in his power" and believed he was about to be killed in revenge. He replied very carefully: ". . . all the firing, it was impossible to tell who did the killing." This reply contradicted the account of one settler, who claimed Boone told him he recognized Blackfish's son when rescuing the girls. Continuing to answer without a real answer, Boone observed, "Many things happen in war that were best forgotten in peace."

Revenge was not the priority. A far more layered process was under way, one that cast a shadow on Boone's own feelings of vengeance when he'd searched for Jemima. To make Blackfish's family whole again, Boone was poised to replace the "slain son." But first, he'd have to make it past the British military and Henry Hamilton, to whom word had spread about the new prisoners.

FOR THE BOONE FAMILY, Daniel's long absence evoked many earlier stretches away from home, both planned and unplanned, including one that, according to community lore, occurred almost sixteen years before. That time, months had stretched into nearly a

year before Daniel reappeared after a "long hunt." Memories and an-
ecdotes about the timing of that absence plagued the family there-
after. By the time Daniel reappeared—so variations of this story
went—Rebecca had conceived a child, gone through a pregnancy,
and given birth to their fourth child, Jemima. In the Bible, Job
named one of his strikingly beautiful daughters Jemima, meaning
"little dove," to signify prosperity after many ordeals.

Rumors posited that the long-absent Daniel could not have been
little "Mima's" father, and that her biological father, to compound
matters, was really one of Daniel's brothers, Squire or Ned. By one
account, when told the truth by a remorseful Rebecca, Daniel
shrugged and commented that his child "will be a Boone anyhow."
Some remembered Daniel laughing over the years about the rumor,
in the process tacitly admitting to it. In some versions, Rebecca felt
light embarrassment over the topic—sitting knitting with her "nee-
dles fly[ing]" when it came up in conversation with visitors—while
in other accounts, Rebecca ribs Daniel that if he'd been home, he
could have avoided the problem.

As Boone's notoriety grew, he also could recognize that some
stories involving him—whether positive (like his gigantic physical
stature) or negative—spread regardless of their truth, leading him
to try to laugh most of them off. Theodore Roosevelt summed up
the legend this way: "Boon[e] was essentially a type, and possesses
his greatest interest for us because he represents so well the charac-
teristics as well as the life-work of his fellow backwoodsmen; still,
it is unfair not to bear in mind also the leading part he played and
the great service he rendered to the nation." This echoed James Fenimore Cooper's comment that Boone was "a venerable and hardy
pioneer of civilization." Between Boone the type and Boone the frontier leader, there was a family man watching narratives spin away
from him.

The rumors about Jemima's birth reveal acceptance of less conventional definitions of a family unit where spouses routinely died young and people disappeared without a trace and reappeared without warning. Families blended in stepfathers, stepmothers, and stepchildren; children were taken in temporarily or permanently by aunts and uncles; and people crossed back and forth over cultural lines into families made up of various ethnicities. The Boone family's timeline—as best it can be reconstructed—does not suggest any inherent conflict between Boone's expeditions and Jemima's paternity, undermining the basic premise of these accounts. But the era's versions of family planning produced legitimate confusions even among family members—birth years, and even more so specific birthdays, were often forgotten or mixed up over time. Any doubt Daniel or Jemima harbored about her paternity only makes their bond and mutual loyalty stand out, encapsulated in Jemima's vigil in Boonesboro for the man written off by the rest of the world, even within the family, as dead.

Regardless of whether the rumors had roots in fact or in fiction, jealousy toward the Boones weaponized these stories against Jemima in a time with little official documentation. Isolation for everyone—but especially women—within the forts led to a communal sense of possessions as well as a shared possession of information. "What one had, they nearly all had," commented a settler who lived in Boonesboro, "and what one knew, they mainly all knew."

Sniping often followed. A young woman at another Kentucky settlement later recalled, "They used to quarrel—the women—a great deal." Rumors spread that Jemima's older sister, Susannah, who was married with children, was "a notorious prostitute." Stories meant to challenge women or tarnish their reputations predictably revolved around fidelity, sexuality, and paternity. Moreover, frontier women (Jemima and Rebecca included) were routinely cut off from learning to read and write and were thus deprived of the chance to project their own voices in correspondence, books, or pamphlets, while at the same time having less access to courts, another place where narratives, true or false, might crystallize and circulate in verdicts, testimony, and depositions. The dark side of rumors that might otherwise seem frivolous, like those about whether Daniel was Jemima's biological father, show how strong a young woman like Jemima had to be, to survive not just in hard physical terrains, but also in a social topography where whispers invisibly shaped reputations and opportunities.

GOVERNOR HENRY HAMILTON was in for a pleasant surprise. Underwriting tribal military missions already had begun to pay off for the leader of the British-controlled Fort Detroit, who was charged with neutralizing the settlers' presence on the frontier. Early in 1778, Hamilton was confident that America's infrastructure in Kentucky and its collective resolve were crumbling, bringing the inevitable demise of Boonesboro closer. "The alarm on the Ohio and the rivers which fall into it from the eastward has been very general," he reported to his superior, "and a large tract of country is deserted by the inhabitants—disagreements have arisen among themselves." Since the time his authority expanded, the Indian incursions also had begun to yield American prisoners, some of whom were brought to Hamilton at Fort Detroit. Hamilton kept a careful tally of these captives, as well as tokens of the rebels killed by Indians. "They have brought seventy-three prisoners alive, twenty of which they presented to me, and one hundred and twenty nine scalps." Even when his Indian allies suffered loss, he saw a silver lining in the chance to ratchet up their motivation. "The parties sent from hence have been in general successful," he noted on this point, "though the Indians have lost enough men to sharpen their resentment."

As winter turned to spring, prisoners continued to flow into Hamilton's fort. Some had more strategic value than others. In March, Mingoes brought a young settler whose father they had killed in a raid. In early April, Shawnee escorted four more rebel prisoners to Hamilton. Hamilton could use these prisoners for both leverage and intelligence. On April 5, two of Hamilton's men—the French operatives Charles Beaubien and Louis Lorimier—came to the British fort with Blackfish and other Shawnee. As soon as they arrived, they delivered a bombshell to Hamilton. The Shawnee raid on the Kentucky saltmakers—which Hamilton's operatives claimed credit for overseeing—had netted a grand prize. Daniel Boone. And now they had brought Boone to Hamilton.

As the "principal prisoner," Boone was placed in a room by himself. Whether it was a test or coincidence, the room contained sulfur, coal, and nitre (potassium nitrate)—all the ingredients needed to make gunpowder. Boone did just that, apparently just to show he could. When Hamilton discovered that Boone had turned raw materials into propellant for ammunition, he was taken aback by his skills, and it made the governor think twice about what "capabilities and resources" the unassuming Kentucky settlers really possessed. Boone may have made himself at home in other ways, and may have even entertained his captors. At another time when he was a prisoner, Boone sang songs for the British—reportedly singing quite well.

Hamilton brought Boone to his room. The meeting could easily have turned into a contest of wills or devolved into a hostile confrontation. Hamilton would have been seeing an exhausted and defeated woodsman who dared betray his loyalty to the king of England out of ungrateful demands for independence. On the other side of the room, Boone faced what appeared to be an overfed bu-

reaucrat manipulating tribes into trying to wipe out the hardwork-
ing frontier settlements for profit and power.

The governor and the prisoner played an intense game of chess
with pieces of information and intelligence. Hamilton asked the
prisoner about conditions on the frontier. "By Boone's account," as
Hamilton documented Boone's response, "the people on the frontiers have been incessantly harassed by parties of Indians they have
not been able to sow grain and at Kentucke will not have a morsel of
bread by the middle of June. Clothing is not to be had, nor do they
expect relief from the Congress." Hamilton also wanted to know
whether Boone had heard about British major general John Burgoyne, who led a campaign in New York that turned into a major
setback for the redcoats. "Yes," Boone replied, "it was well known
in Kentucky as a fact before I was taken, that Burgoyne and his
whole army have surrendered to General Gates." This was true. All
Boonesboro had celebrated that news when it reached them; they
had set a dry-cane bonfire.

Boone's polite answers were truthful but also shaped by strategy.
Emphasizing Boonesboro's deprivation and fragility could sway
Hamilton into believing that amassing forces against it would be
a misallocation of his resources. Making gunpowder (a rare skill),
in contrast, acted as a warning against underestimating the settlers
even at their weakest. Boone's banter about Burgoyne's defeat conveyed a grasp by the frontier of the larger movements of the Revolutionary War, despite their isolation and the choppy transmission of
news reports into Kentucky.

Hamilton had a choice to make. He could deal with Boone as a
prisoner or instead—at least on the surface—as a guest of the fort.
Some of the other saltmakers brought to Fort Detroit lamented being mistreated there, complaining that they had fared better with
the Indians. But Boone was influential, and Hamilton continued

to cultivate an advantage through a genteel rapport. The respectful reception by Hamilton likely blinded Boone to the fact that other saltmakers taken to Fort Detroit met with harsher realities. One of the other prisoners would later reflect that "he would carry the marks of his manacles when a prisoner with the British to his grave."

After Boone's comment about Burgoyne, Hamilton consulted with his private secretary, John Jay, who waited in an adjoining room. It's possible that Hamilton himself had incomplete information about Burgoyne's surrender, but more likely he wanted to compare notes with Jay about a potential morale problem. If the settlers knew about the recent British military setbacks, the Indians could learn about them, too, and their confidence in British prospects could weaken, in turn weakening their allegiance.

Trying his hand at propaganda, Hamilton returned to Boone and requested he not tell the Indians about Burgoyne. "You are too late, Governor," Boone replied. "I have already told them of it." Boone's son, Nathan, later recounted that Hamilton pressed Boone to manipulate the information. "The governor," Nathan said, "then desired that my father speak slightingly of the affair, as if it were mere vague report and was unworthy of belief—that he had jokingly spoken of it."

Boone likewise considered propaganda fair play to improve his position. By one account, Boone kept a leather bag around his neck that contained a commission from a British-appointed governor to mark his military service during Lord Dunmore's War, "ready to exhibit in emergency." He showed this commission to Hamilton. Possibly he wished to imply to Hamilton that he still harbored a latent loyalty to the crown and could be turned.

Hamilton offered the Indians a top price to "buy" Boone from them—100 pounds sterling according to Boone himself. This would transfer control of Boone to Fort Detroit. Though Blackfish sold other prisoners to Hamilton, including Jemima's brother-in-law James Callaway, the Shawnee chief refused to part with Boone even for the considerable sum. "Their affection for me was so great," said Boone, as relayed by his biographer, "that they utterly refused to leave me there with the others." To Blackfish, Boone's greatest value was as a new family member. Hamilton, ever the utilitarian, assumed the Shawnee wanted to keep Boone "expecting by his means to effect something." Hamilton did not consider the deeper connection Blackfish sought in Boone, bonded through the death of Catfish. Blocked from controlling Boone's fate outright, Hamilton planted seeds that might suggest to Boone to come back of his own volition—and in the process to abandon his role in the American insurrection.

The conspicuous gap between how Boone and others were treated increased. One saltmaker had untreated wounds from which he died. James Callaway was confined in the fort to a routine of quiet tedium and then assigned to work for a merchant. But when James refused to pledge loyalty to the crown, he was thrown into a prison. Cajah Callaway, James's brother, also faced hard times, and a Callaway relative later reported that, looking back with hindsight, the less fortunate saltmakers wished they had taken their chances by fighting their captors at the Lower Blue Licks: "They were treated so badly that they regretted they had not fought and resisted till they died." At the end of his time at Fort Detroit, Boone, in stark contrast, was invited by Hamilton to take possession of an old gray pony, with a saddle and bridle, and silver trinkets used as currency in the Indian towns. Boone, taking for granted that his natural poise and self-possession were traits easily accessed by everyone, believed that some of the saltmakers agitated their captors unnecessarily. Other prisoners took note of the relatively mild treatment received by Boone, and suspicions built up about the reasons. Hamilton actively sowed this discord as he plotted how and when to take Boonesboro.

Boone, meanwhile, hemmed and hawed before accepting the gifts. He had reason to delay his departure from Fort Detroit: he had a plot brewing back in Little Chillicothe.

BOONE'S SECRET IN the Shawnee village took the form of a kind of sleeper agent: an inconspicuous saltmaker named Andrew Johnson. Johnson was a short man who did not present as intimidating. Boone, early in captivity, advised Johnson to "play possum," that is, to pretend to be slow-witted. The tribe nicknamed him Pequolly, interpreted as meaning Little Shut His Eyes, referring to his apparent fear of weapons, or alternatively Little Duck. The Indians would set up a target on a tree and give him a gun. Johnson would intentionally miss the tree.

Like many of the saltmakers, Johnson was adopted into an Indian family. He nearly blew up his cover story, however, when he got into a fight with his Indian brothers. In the scuffle, a hint of his true physical prowess came out, and the family began to fear him. His Indian father reprimanded him and "threatened to sell him for his bad behavior."

But the Indians still believed they did not have to worry about Johnson trying to run away from the village. When they asked him which way to Kentucky, he would point in the wrong direction. He also acted afraid of leaving the grounds. To Boone, the tribe's underestimation of Johnson provided an ideal opportunity to get one of his men back to Boonesboro. As long as Blackfish and his traveling party—up to forty warriors—were occupied in Fort Detroit, fewer eyes were on Johnson. The Pequolly gambit throws new light on Boone's leisurely mind games with Henry Hamilton, which pro-longed Blackfish's stay.

A war dance was planned in anticipation of the return of this traveling party that included Blackfish and Boone. That night, Johnson's Indian father punished him for his earlier fight by sending him to bed and forbidding him from being part of the preparations. Johnson went to the house but then appeared at the celebration. He pleaded to be included. His father agreed that Johnson could dance for a short time. When Johnson readied to go, as a friend recalled him telling it, he "took his father's gun, tomahawk, knife, powder and lead, blanket coat." Johnson left the ceremony but didn't go back to the family's home. He just kept going—running right from the town into the wilderness.

When Blackfish arrived at his village, he was greeted with the distressing news of the escape not of a prisoner—that phase had passed—but an adopted member of the tribe, who was now val-ued as part of the community. Search parties hunted for three days without a trace of Johnson. Rather than being angry, they worried and grieved for him. "Pequolly, poor little fool," they said, "couldn't shoot and didn't know the way to Kentucky . . . he would die in the woods." Johnson's adoptive father blamed himself. The Shawnee consulted Boone.

"Boone! Think Pequolly found the way to Kentucky?"

Boone replied, "I don't know." Boone, according to family tradi-tion, explained to the tribe that Johnson "was mad, was of no sort of account anyhow, was no woodsman, that he had probably wandered off, and got lost."

BOONE'S STATUS IN the Shawnee community blossomed. The adoption process included various ceremonial steps that brought him closer symbolically and physically to the tribe. Boone was groomed, his hair "plucked," or thinned out in certain places on his head. An intense bathing process, according to Boone's grandson, was meant to "wash all the white blood out of him." He was renamed Sheltowee, meaning Big Turtle, probably for his top-heavy build and perhaps for his seeming indestructibility that Indians and settlers alike had long noticed. ("Quite appropriately named," one Boone family member commented later.) Outnumbered, outgunned, sometimes outmaneuvered, Boone made it through every predicament in his decades on the frontier, even when it seemed certain he was dead.

In contrast with Andrew Johnson's behavior, Boone showed his utility to the tribe, including by repairing gunlocks. But that did not mean an easy integration into the community. At first, Blackfish and his family overworked him as a kind of initiation or test of his commitment. In the fields, he was ordered to hoe corn. One Indian squaw whipped him and Boone pushed her to the ground. Blackfish patted Boone on the shoulder and called him a good warrior. Boone may have uncharacteristically lost his temper, or may have decided to test boundaries with Blackfish. For the squaws who insisted he work in the fields, Boone would handle the task so sloppily that the women eventually refused to allow him to hoe crops. Another time, Boone was assigned to cut down a tree and methodically carve out notches to hold salt for horses. Boone, showing blistered hands, complained that he was being treated as a slave rather than a son, a canny appeal to the familial structure into which they'd invited him, as well as an indirect insult to the enslaved men and women who built and protected Boonesboro. Blackfish agreed that Boone should not do what the settler considered menial labor.

Blackfish addressed Boone as "my son." Boone may have simply called Blackfish's wife Neegah (Mother) or Nikya (My Mother) and sometimes called her his "old mamma." He respected her as a Shawnee "queen" who protectively watched over him. By some accounts, one young member of Blackfish's family was a boy named Tecumsekeh, meaning Shooting Star, who was around ten years old. The child's father had been a Shawnee chief killed in Lord Dunmore's War, and some believed Tecumsekeh's mother had been a colonist long ago captured by tribes. Apparently Blackfish had taken in the child for a time. Tecumsekeh exhibited impressive character and skills even as a boy, and Boone's natural leadership may have had some influence on him: he later became a major tribal chief then called Tecumseh. Boone would sometimes talk about Jemima, about whom the Shawnee likely had many questions considering the impact of her kidnapping.

Two of Boone's very young sisters in his role as Sheltowee were Pommepesy, four or five, and Pimmepesy, a toddler. Boone would especially help take care of the younger one and spent silver trinkets given to him in Fort Detroit to buy the girls maple sugar as a treat. Affection was shown through food, some examples of which would strike the settler as odd. "To show old Blackfish's kindness, as well as to show an Indian's idea of taste," Boone's son Nathan explained, "many a lump of sugar old Blackfish . . . would lick awhile in his mouth, take it out and give to his son Boone." Boone was surprised at how readily the Indians shared their belongings, even with strangers, just as others had noticed about the bedraggled settlers at Boonesboro. Boone, failing to notice the similarity, called the tribe's habit "reckless generosity and hospitality, when they had any thing to bestow to traveling visitants."

Blackfish apparently invited Boone to participate in the spiritual practices of the tribal leaders, showing him a prized relic said to have come from the Great Spirit, which was thought to bring supernatural protection and power. Boone reportedly thought it was "a kind of ark." The Turtle, one of a range of animal identities assigned to members by Shawnee, was entrusted to carry the sacred bundle because that identity exhibited slow, careful traits. If Boone indeed was shown this relic, this privilege would reinforce the attributes of the name Big Turtle that had been granted him.

Though Boone did not play the fool as Johnson did, he did edit the skills he put on display. For target practice, Neegah advised him to make sure to miss sometimes because "the Indians would be angry with him if he beat them all the time." "I was careful not to exceed many of them in shooting," recalled Boone. He hoped this would sidestep any jealous feelings, "for no people are more envious than they in sport," and it also allowed him to keep some of his abilities in reserve in case he needed to count on the element of surprise later.

In other ways, Boone showed his usefulness freely. "He was perfectly trained in their ways," concluded a missionary who questioned Boone about his captivity, "could prepare their food, and perform any of their common domestic operations with the best of them." Blackfish's trust in him grew. The chief would draw maps in the dirt, showing his new son the locations of various Indian villages. Boone was permitted to hunt with the tribe and gradually to go hunting on his own. The village's food scarcity provided ample incentive to the tribe to expand Boone's liberties. "I frequently returned with the spoils of the woods," he recalled, "and as often presented somewhat of what I had taken to [Blackfish], expressive of my duty to my sovereign." Even as they entrusted him with responsibility, the Shawnee took precautions. Boone had to bring all of his ammunition back for inspection—any ammunition used had to be accounted for by an accompanying kill, such as a deer, so that he could not hoard ammunition to use against them.

In May, Blackfish was at a Shawnee sugar camp, making sugar

from maple sap in a laborious process, when they were fired upon. The unseen assailants vanished. Blackfish left some warriors behind to guard the camp and returned to the village to gather reinforcements, telling Boone he believed another tribe was trying to start a war. Returning to the sugar camp, Blackfish found two of his warriors dead and seven horses taken. He was on edge, as his enemies seemed to be everywhere while managing to remain invisible. Back in the village, Blackfish confessed to Boone that he could not figure out who the marauders had been. Then some Indians saw a group of settlers with the stolen horses—a group that included Andrew Johnson. The Indians reported to Blackfish.

Johnson had not gotten lost and died after running away during the war dance, as the tribe had assumed. He had found a raft to cross the river and reached Harrodsburg, a fort in Kentucky in as desperate circumstances as Boonesboro. The settlers at Harrodsburg told him Indians had taken some of their horses and now sought "retaliation." No longer Pequolly, Johnson became a leader. Using his knowledge gained while living in the Shawnee village, he guided four other men over fourteen miles and across the Ohio River to the sugar camp. The tribe's braves outnumbered them, so they decided to wait until morning to attack. During the night, however, the Shawnee's dogs sensed them and "forced us to fire," as one of the settlers involved in the raid recalled, leading them to engage in a gunfight before fully prepared. They killed a pair of Indians before escaping with horses. Their story of executing a successful mission gave other settlers a morale boost after so many setbacks on the frontier.

Blackfish now asked Boone if he knew who could have been behind the fatal raid on the sugar camp. Boone replied honestly, though he said he could not be certain, that it might have been Pequolly. Blackfish questioned how it was possible. Pequolly "was no fool," Boone admitted, according to his son Nathan, "but a man of good sense, and a fine woodsman."

"Then why did you not tell me so before?" Blackfish asked.

Boone answered, "Because you never asked me."

The truth had hit the village that "Pequolly was a little man, but a great rogue."

Johnson's success caused ripples throughout Little Chillicothe. Blackfish faced startling evidence that the Kentucky settlements once again could be a threat, even after being depleted of so many men. The Johnson raid also demonstrated to the tribe that the kidnapping of the saltmakers ultimately could prove to be destructive to the Indians because of the inside knowledge transferred to the settlers through escapees. Johnson had known precisely how and where to invade the sugar camp. The kidnappings, as Boone later mused, could end up disastrous for the Shawnee. But the taking of the saltmakers had been only a staging ground for weakening the frontier. The Shawnee—with Governor Hamilton supporting their position—had Boonesboro, the cornerstone of American settlement of Kentucky, in the crosshairs. Blackfish realized he had to accelerate his timetable.

Boone had the opposite agenda. He bided his time, collecting intelligence on Blackfish's war plans against Boonesboro. The longer he could remain with the Shawnee in a circle of trust, the more information he could uncover and the more skills he could appropriate. This particularly struck the missionary Timothy Flint, who interviewed Boone about captivity. "To make himself master of their language, and to become familiarly acquainted with their customs," Flint concluded of Boone, "he considered acquisitions of the highest utility." But the time had come to start accelerating the next move, too: an escape. He had to do this while he "carefully avoided their suspicions," as Boone said through his biographer.

Boone asked Blackfish if he could hobble the pony he'd brought back from Fort Detroit—that is, train it using restraints to graze on its own without running away. Blackfish stalled giving an answer before permitting Boone to try. As Boone trained the pony, he spotted warriors sent by Blackfish hiding flat in the grass with guns, watching to see if he would try to escape. "Boone pretended not to have seen them," recounted Nathan Boone, "turned out his pony and went to whistling as unconcernedly as if nothing had happened." After the routine repeated itself, Blackfish stopped sending spies.

A story arose about how Boone "proved" that he was not out to escape—a sleight of hand that played into the spiritual beliefs of the tribe he'd been learning so much about. While everyone slept, Boone collected the bullets out of all the rifles in camp. In the morning, he announced that he was leaving to go home. "If you attempt it," Blackfish reportedly said, "I'll shoot you." Boone started walking. Turning around after about forty feet, Boone told the braves they ought to try to shoot him. The dare tested Blackfish's honor, who gave what must have been a painful command to shoot his son. The braves opened fire, but they were firing blanks. Boone stealthily dropped the bullets he'd pilfered into his buckskin apron, then walked back and revealed them, as though they had all hit him and bounced down. "Take your bullets," he said. "Boone ain't going away." The witnesses believed that the Manitous, or spirit forces, had protected him. The tribe began to give him more leeway.

Boone also had to find a way to stockpile ammunition in spite of the fact that it was tallied by Blackfish's men. He had to harness all his skills to do this. Out hunting, Boone sighted two deer. Waiting for just the right moment, he shot and killed both deer with a single shot, "tucking away the extra ammunition he would have used" so that it would not be missed when examined in light of the game he brought in.

Blackfish, meanwhile, had begun to visit other tribes and chiefs to recruit warriors to march en masse against Boonesboro. He appealed to leaders of Mingoes and Delaware. As far as Chief Blackfish and Governor Hamilton were concerned, having Boone might actually allow them to avoid bloodshed. Boone could convince his settlement to surrender peaceably—just as he had with the saltmakers—and all the residents could be brought to Fort Detroit. The odds seemed to favor this outcome. Hamilton had shown Boone the relative comforts of the British fort compared with the crude backcountry settlements. Adoption into the Indian community had further estranged Boone from his past, and there were plenty of examples of settlers who refused to ever go back even when given the chance. Once Boonesboro was captured, the few other isolated settlers still in Kentucky could be removed without resistance.

JEMIMA BOONE'S LONG wait for any news of her father was finally rewarded—though the news itself was double-edged. Andrew "Pequolly" Johnson, one of the men taken at the Lower Blue Licks in February, was back in Kentucky. He was being lauded for "good success in the adventure" of taking horses from the sugar camp. Though he had not come home to Boonesboro, his story began to be shared and passed along. The saltmakers had not been murdered, Johnson revealed, but instead taken by the Shawnee. For Jemima, it was the first concrete—though not quite conclusive—evidence that her father could still be alive.

That was not all Johnson had reported. He had begrudged Boone the special place he received in Blackfish's family. Johnson's perspective resembled that of William Hancock, a fellow captive, who had stewed, watching Boone "whistling and contented" among, as Hancock put it, "dirty Indians." Boone himself admitted to "appearing as cheerful and satisfied as possible" so the tribe would continue to "put great confidence in me." Johnson also may have resented his own role as Little Shut His Eyes, the slow-witted man-child persona Boone had asked him to cultivate. Whether out of spite or genuine belief in wrongdoing, Johnson turned on Boone by the time he reached Kentucky again. "Boone was a Tory," went Johnson's tale, "and had surrendered them all up to the British, and taken the oath of allegiance to the British at Detroit."

This false narrative sounded farfetched but found a receptive audience in Richard Callaway, who had been grinding his ax more than ever. Already able to blame Boone's leadership for leading his two nephews into captivity, Callaway could now claim Boone betrayed the entire community.

Allies who usually would have stood up and defended Boone's name were scattered as the war against the British evolved. Simon Butler was now helping to lead a group of soldiers through the wilderness to rendezvous with their commander, George Rogers Clark, to move against a British fort in Kaskaskia, then part of Quebec, now in southern Illinois. This mission succeeded, and Butler was sent the very next day to gain intelligence on Fort Vincennes on the Wabash River. Butler recorded details of the dangerous operation: "We came and hid our hats and guns out in the commons, and then at night came back and walked the streets with the Indians and the French, with our blankets around us and tomahawks concealed under our blankets, for three nights." Though disturbed to hear of Boone's capture, Butler could do nothing about it. He had to finish his present assignment before being sent back to Kentucky.

Meanwhile, Callaway's dominance grew because most of the men of comparable military rank were far away on other endeavors. Rebecca Boone had squared off with Callaway during the militia mutiny before she left for North Carolina. Now fifteen-year-old

Jemima, the last remaining namesake of Boonesboro other than Squire Boone and his family, had to hold the family's ground on her own—and she, after all, was now a Callaway by marriage to Flanders. The unknown fate of Jemima's husband's brothers (James and Cajah) could tear apart the family she was building in the wake of such serious accusations against her father. Daniel Boone did not live a political life. Categories of Tories and Whigs, fluid to begin with on the frontier, would not have meant much to him. His integrity and his commitment to the settlement he helped define meant everything. Jemima now had reason to believe he was alive, but also had reason to fear that the family's standing in Kentucky was in imminent jeopardy.

URGENCY MOUNTED FOR Boone to escape Little Chillicothe in time to warn Boonesboro of the impending attack. Besides wanting to glean intelligence, Boone had intentionally delayed his exit so as to help the other saltmakers get situated safely. "I had many opportunities" to attempt escape, he'd say, but wanted to account for as many of the men as he could. Even so, he had managed to help get only Andrew Johnson out. Other escape attempts did not fare well. James Callaway and another captive, Samuel Brooks, made a break from Fort Detroit by canoe. Losing their way in fog, they came ashore on the bank of a stream that ran right through an Indian village. They tried to escape again, but because Callaway was hard of hearing, Brooks had to talk so loud that their captors overheard the plan.

Blackfish's family reportedly took in Benjamin Kelly, sixteen, one of the youngest saltmakers. Finding themselves in similar situations and in proximity to each other, Boone and Kelly had the opportunity to commiserate. Boone promised Kelly he would take him along when he escaped. He also told Cajah Callaway that he would try to bring him.

As Boone's escape plot came together, an obstacle presented itself: his gray pony vanished. Blackfish said he knew nothing about it. The area's Indians, according to settlers, by custom often "borrowed" from one another without asking permission, but it was considered bad form to confront the borrower. To search the village for the offending party could bring unwanted attention, but at the same time, as Nathan Boone related, Boone "feared lest [the pony] should not be brought back in time to aid him in his premeditated escape."

Another challenge developed, one even less expected. This challenge was emotional. Boone had grown to feel deep and genuine affection for his Indian family. "At Chelicothe I spent my time as comfortably as I could expect," Boone reflected, as conveyed later by his biographer. "[I] was adopted, according to their custom, into a family where I became a son, and had a great share in the affection of my new parents, brothers, sisters, and friends. I was exceedingly familiar and friendly with them." Of Blackfish, Boone felt proud that "the Shawnese king took great notice of me, and treated me with profound respect, and entire friendship." Boone helped his Indian mother, Neegah, hoe corn even after Blackfish told him he didn't have to. "My son," Blackfish said, "you need not work; your mother can easily raise enough for us all." Boone had been very affected by "the extraordinary love of his Indian mother manifested for him." He was said to become "as dear to his mother of adoption as her own son." They lived in close quarters. "My food and lodging was, in common, with them," according to Boone's account, "not so good as I could desire, but necessity made everything acceptable."

As Boone's bonds with Blackfish and Neegah grew, he had to weigh the potential for violence an attempted escape could bring if he was caught in the act—violence against him was one possibility, but another was that he would be forced to use violence against people he'd grown to care about, who had become an alternate family and community. The approach least likely to result in spilled blood rested on leveraging these emotional bonds.

It was announced that Boone would accompany an Indian mission to a salt spring in early June, coming full circle to a captivity that had begun during a saltmaking expedition. Just as it was for the colonists, salt was vital to the tribes to preserve meat and as balm for wounds. This salty creek, a tributary of the Scioto River, ran with a bluish tint. By one account, the salt spring was concealed by rocks carved to hide its location. Boone went out to hunt for meat for the Indian saltmakers. His hunting skill paid dividends, as he now had opportunity to stow away more ammunition for his own use.

Blackfish could beam with pride at the son he called Sheltowee. The patience and skills of this settler-turned-Shawnee surpassed expectations, and leaders from other tribes envied Blackfish. The chief could understand that Sheltowee would be torn up inside about having a role in the impending takeover of Boonesboro, which Blackfish had to try to keep from his adopted son. But in the mind of Blackfish, the outcome would be best for everyone involved. There were so many grounds to seek revenge, foremost among them the death of Catfish during the rescue of Jemima Boone and the Callaway sisters. But with Sheltowee, Blackfish felt he had found something better than vengeance: a son and a path forward.

HALF KING, OR DOWYENTET, was a leader of the Wyandot tribe in the Cumberland Valley who equally distrusted the British and the Americans in the Revolutionary War. He would come to

warn tribes in the region that "they were sitting between two powerful, angry gods, who, with their mouths wide open, were most
ferociously looking at each other . . . they were in danger of being
attacked and devoured; nay, even ground to powder, by the teeth
of one or the other of them, or perhaps by both at the same time!"
Half King wavered in picking the lesser of two evils before aligning himself in 1777 with the British, or more accurately aligning
himself *against* the ex-colonists. But he had no delusions about the
British protecting tribal interests in the long term.

Word spread fast about Fort Detroit backing Indian movements
against settlers' outposts, so Half King had a perfect opportunity to
actively protect native lands. Winter having thawed, Half King set
his sights on Fort Randolph, possibly in response to Cornstalk's murder there. Though Cornstalk had been Shawnee, the murder outraged all tribes. Despite American gestures at meting out justice for
Cornstalk, results remained mixed. A $200 reward was offered for
the soldiers responsible. Captain Arbuckle and others gave depositions against the offenders. On April 7, one of the soldiers accused of
killing Cornstalk and the other Indian prisoners was placed on trial
in Virginia. A legend developed that Rockbridge County was formed
in Virginia for the sole purpose of giving this accused soldier a more
favorable jurisdiction for the trial to be held. The witnesses who were
called never showed up to court. Three other men were also tried for
the murders in late April and mid-May. All four were acquitted.

With the futile court proceedings exhausted, the Wyandot warriors, apparently joined by Mingoes, approached Fort Randolph on
May 16, 1778, with advantages in their favor. Matthew Arbuckle
was away from the fort visiting his long-suffering wife and family
in nearby Greenbrier, leaving one of his officers, William McKee,
in command. (This McKee does not appear to have been closely
related, if at all, to Alexander McKee, the interpreter and British

sympathizer who was romantically connected with Nonhelema, Cornstalk's sister residing at the fort.) One of the officers stationed at Fort Randolph captured a panoramic moment of reckoning as the sea of Indian troops came into view: "Their whole army rose up at once in sight of the fort, extending across the point from the banks of the Ohio to the banks of the Kanawha" River. The garrison was surrounded. Captain McKee sent out Nonhelema to speak to the approaching troops. "Grenadier Squaw," Fort Randolph's secret weapon, reported the number of Indian warriors at three hundred, though other information set the number closer to a hundred. She also discovered that the move against Fort Randolph was a feint, that the troops were really targeting Greenbrier's other military outposts. Her information was borne out. After minor exchanges of gunfire and vague talk of peace at Fort Randolph, the braves moved on.

Armed with Nonhelema's intelligence, Captain McKee sent out runners to Greenbrier from the fort painted and dressed as Indians. The runners reached Greenbrier just days before the Indian troops and spread the word of the oncoming attack. At sunrise on May 29, the Wyandots massed against Donnally's Fort, a residence turned into a garrison a few years before. Only twenty-five men were at the fort. Indians burrowed underneath it and wounded a man by shooting through the floor. The inhabitants moved floorboards and shot downward into the earth. Matthew Arbuckle, already in Greenbrier, helped round up soldiers and arrived to spell the fort with approximately sixty-eight men. The battle continued into the night, with an estimated seventeen Indians killed and four casualties among the soldiers in both forts.

The Indians spent part of that night dragging off and burying their dead and were left to assess a miscalculated strategy.

BOONE CONTINUED TO hunt and help the Shawnee saltmaking expedition at the Scioto Licks as he weighed his best move and when to make it. In early June, Half King, retreating from the failed raid against Forts Randolph and Donnally, arrived at the same salt licks with his warriors. The arrival of Half King signified two recent changes: One, the destabilization of relations between the frontier settlers and Indians had taken another turn into warfare. And two, stinging from defeat, Half King was primed to join Blackfish in a campaign against Boonesboro. Safe to say, Boone pondered these dangers, as he "repeatedly cast a jealous eye upon them." In addition, Half King's troops came with a bounty of arms.

Blackfish did not notice Boone's special interest in the new arrivals. The chief again showed off his new son, having him hunt and prepare guns. The message was clear: Sheltowee was one of them, not to be harassed or harmed.

A man named Jimmy Rogers visited them, a meeting that, if a coincidence, was an instructive one—a mirror into what could be Boone's future. A former Virginian who had been kidnapped as a child, Rogers had been adopted by Blackfish to replace yet another lost son of the war chief. Rogers grew up in the Shawnee community and became, for all intents and purposes, a chief. He married Blackfish's daughter and was considered wealthy. (Rumors persist that Boone, too, was offered or even took a squaw for himself during captivity.) For Blackfish's purposes, Rogers could show Sheltowee an example of a bright, enviable destiny in the Shawnee villages. Any conversation between Rogers and Boone in this meeting has been lost to history, and Rogers was said to speak broken English by this point in his life. But Boone complied with Rogers's request to repair one of his guns. Hamilton had been amazed at Fort Detroit when Boone made gunpowder, and now the archetypal frontiersman attracted a crowd of Indians as he rebuilt guns. Like most tribes, the Shawnee had long ago become dependent on European-style weaponry.

Boone was asked to repair another Indian's rifle, which probably had been damaged during the unsuccessful Half King raids, with the challenge of making it shoot into the circle of a dollar from a hundred yards away. Boone agreed to do this in return for six charges—or shots—of ammunition, to test the weapon before returning it to the owner. Boone was given the rifle and tied the requested powder and balls in a shirt flap.

After ten days at the licks, Boone was sent back on an errand to Little Chillicothe. While there, he caught sight of something Blackfish would not have wanted him to see. "Four hundred and fifty Indians," Boone recalled through his biographer, "of their choicest warriors, painted and armed in a fearful manner." This was no ceremony, no drill. The warriors were readying to take Boonesboro. Time was up. Boone knew what he had to do. "I determined to escape the first opportunity."

He set out to find a way to flee "in the most secret manner." By this point, Boone's pony had been returned. But the animal had been "badly used" and now had a sore back. He began nursing the pony back to health to ready it for what could be an ordeal.

Back at the salt springs about a week later, Blackfish and a group of warriors started back toward Little Chillicothe. One morning before sunrise, they spotted a flock of turkeys. Blackfish entrusted Boone to protect the women and children while the chief and other braves pursued the game on foot—possibly to provide meat for the imminent journey to Boonesboro. Boone had a difficult decision to make. He saw his chance to get away, but would not be able to retrieve fellow captives Benjamin Kelly and Cajah Callaway as he had promised to do. If he did not leave immediately, the window of opportunity would close. Boone removed a knife and began to cut down the kettles and supplies that were tied to the group's horses.

Neegah knew something was wrong.

"My son, what are you going to do?" she asked.

Boone had learned enough Shawnee that he no longer had to rely on Pompey to interpret. "I am going to see my squaw and pappooses and I must have the horse to ride."

"Blackfish would be angry." She warned that Boone would be killed.

"They couldn't catch me," Boone promised. He added, "I can't help it. I must go and see my family." By one account, he promised her he would be back. In "a moon and a half," he said, he would bring his wife and family to live among the Indians.

"But how can you go? You have no ammunition." She rattled off the risks. "It is too far . . . you would starve," she said of being in the woods without a way to hunt or defend himself. He showed her his stash of ammunition. By revealing to her he had swiped supplies and risking her spreading an alarm on the spot, he showed how much he trusted her.

Neegah's desire to keep him safe combined with the power of his appeal to see his family. As Boone continued to rush preparations, Neegah and her sisters decided to help. They stole more gunpowder for him, an act that put them at risk and revealed the degree to which they cared about him. "Well, if you will go, child, you must take something to eat," Neegah said. They brought him ash pone, or ashcake, a staple made mostly of cornmeal and water. Boone mounted the old gray pony and readied his whip.

Even with more supplies, the journey would encompass 160 miles back to Boonesboro, and a betrayed Blackfish could unleash his resources to hunt him down. This may have been on Neegah's mind as she cried out: "Wait!"

Boone, feeling deeply sorry, later remembered he turned his horse so he could see his adoptive mother one last time, then rode out of sight. No longer able to protect him, the women had to protect themselves from blame and raised the alarm.

BOOK III

THE
RECKONING

Chapter
8

RISEN

DANIEL BOONE WAS DEAD. For the second time in six months, another family, this time Shawnee, had reason to reach this conclusion about him. With only a pony, a rifle, and a trifling amount of food, surviving a 160-mile journey was unlikely. True, Andrew Johnson had escaped back to Kentucky—but no one had been chasing him. Unlike Johnson, who had fooled the tribe long enough as Pequolly that they believed he had to be lost, Boone would have some of the finest warriors on the frontier tracking him almost immediately. He wouldn't be able to pause to catch his breath, much less to hunt or sleep, heightening the risk of injury and death in dark, unforgiving woods. Boone's brother-in-law and dear friend, John Stuart, had once concealed himself in a hollow sycamore tree while hiding from Indians and was never seen again; his skeletal remains were found by Boone inside the tree five years later, in 1775, identified by the initials engraved on his powder horn and horse tack.

Blackfish had a choice to make. He could take Boone's death as a given and not squander resources by deploying his braves on a demanding search mission so soon before the planned attack against Boonesboro. But Blackfish had come to know Boone, and he knew better than to underestimate him. Plus, Boone was still Sheltowee to him. He was his son. Family or not, though, Blackfish could not take any chances that he could warn Boonesboro. Too much rested on the impending campaign. The tribes needed to regain Kentucky to save their way of life, and this was their best chance.

Jimmy Rogers, the captive-turned-chief, was called in to join Blackfish's search expedition and raced into the woods with other braves. They came upon the tracks of Boone's pony. After following these into the next afternoon, they came to the Ohio River, "swollen from bank to bank" and impossible to cross without a vessel. Boone's bridle and saddle were spotted hanging in a tree. Rogers later recalled the next incredible clue. "We found where [Boone] had cut a grapevine, the top of which was fast to the top of a tree on the opposite side, with which [he] swang [himself] across."

The search party held a meeting at the river. The consensus was to let Boone go, that he would starve to death before getting home on foot. Giving up the chase, Shawnee messengers went to Fort Detroit to inform Henry Hamilton that Boone had escaped. Meanwhile, Rogers disagreed with the conclusion that Boone was a goner. As a former captive himself, Rogers may have felt a special insight into Boone, and he later recalled telling the council that the fugitive would get home going "as straight as a leather string." One of the captive saltmakers recalls other Indians returning from the unsuccessful pursuit, buzzing with speculation on Boone's fate.

Upon departing from his "old mamma," Boone had been traveling as fast as the pony would go, relishing the fact that his instrument of escape had been provided by Henry Hamilton and the British. Boone reportedly "rode hard" through the night and into the next morning. He stopped for a moment and found that the animal's legs had stiffened to the point where they couldn't move. Boone hung up the saddle and horse tack in the tree, leaving the pony behind to recover. Boone did not swing across the river on a vine, though the fact that Rogers and the search party believed this shows how highly they thought of Boone's skills. The clue provided by a cut grapevine, though, had indeed related to the manner in which Boone actually crossed. He used "a couple of dry logs (very likely a standing dry sapling, nearly rotted at the roots) tied together with a grape-vine," his son Nathan later explained. "[He] placed gun and clothes upon it, and swam over pushing his raft before him."

Having crossed on his makeshift raft, Boone now covered his tracks. He reversed the position he had found himself in when searching for Jemima two summers earlier, when he had desperately looked for any sign of her tracks; now he needed to leave as few traces as possible of his path. He changed course frequently. He ran atop fallen trees to leave fewer footprints and rode on logs along streams. He did not want to fire his rifle and risk the noise giving away his position, so he did his best to keep up his strength without hunting by eating the food he had brought from Neegah—food that could only last so long.

That night, exhaustion caught up with him, and he took a risk by stopping to rest. Covering himself with his blanket, he removed his moccasins and slept heavily. During the night, something woke him up "seizing one of his toes." His thoughts turned to having been caught by his pursuers. "He jumped," recalled Nathan Boone, but did not see anybody. He "judged it was a wolf or a fox, by the noise it made in scampering off."

The journey took its toll. Boone could no longer move at high speeds, and constant moisture on the bottom of his feet had produced scalding, thick layers of skin peeling off and exposing the soles to tremendous pain. He would not be able to go on without treating his wounds, and to do so would mean having to slow down even more. He peeled and smashed oak bark that produced ooze in which he soaked his feet. Now running out of the food carried with him, he had to rely on roots and berries. Once he passed the Blue Licks, he judged that he finally could take a chance by using his weapon to hunt. The rifle was the one he had promised to repair for one of Half King's men, for which Boone had tied ammunition in his shirt. There was a problem. He had not had time to actually repair the rifle prior to his escape. Now he had no supplies, but all around him he had what always answered his needs: nature. Cutting a sapling with his knife and using some tugs (or strings) that had attached his bundle to his back, he constructed a new stock for the weapon.

He shot an American buffalo and roasted the meat. He always remembered the time and place where he had the one real meal of his journey, later describing it as the "open place of ground at a buffalo road and the forks of three branches of the waters of Johnson's fork," a spot on the Licking River. Using the makeshift gun kept him going. "You can depend upon it," he said later, "I felt proud of my rifle." He saved the tongue of the buffalo to give to his youngest son, Daniel, who now was ten years old. With one more day's journey ahead of him, Boone envisioned a happy reunion with his family.

SINCE THE SHAWNEE had departed from Fort Detroit holding their prized prisoner Daniel Boone, Detroit's British governor Henry Hamilton had been busy. He facilitated several American operatives to defect to the British side, including Alexander McKee, the interpreter who had a romantic relationship with Cornstalk's sister and American ally, Nonhelema. McKee had been held prisoner by Americans and, after being released, fled the American fort. Hamilton also continued to negotiate and strengthen alliances with those he called "our savages," although challenges accumulated there. "'Tis easy to foresee numberless difficulties," Hamilton wrote to another British officer, "which must arise in satisfying the Indians at a Peace." Tribal representatives made clear that they expected to be rewarded with land left behind by vanquished settlers, were the British to triumph in the Revolutionary War—a promise Hamilton did not have the power (nor necessarily the desire) to offer. All the while, Hamilton had to expend energy to stock arms and provisions for his "inroads upon the Frontier" against the Americans.

At the same time that Boone was riding his pony to the breaking point in the wilderness, Hamilton convened representatives from at least eleven tribes to Fort Detroit for one of his "councils." Alexander McKee had arrived to serve as interpreter, as had Simon Girty, the onetime captive and later adoptee of the Senecas, who had fled the American ranks alongside McKee. Hamilton used his usual paternalistic, oracular rhetoric to motivate his audience by drawing on past defeats. "Children! Listen!" he called out, as he handed out symbolic belts, "with these belts which I present to each nation, I efface from your memories every disagreeable thought, I cleanse your hearts, and wipe the tears from your eyes which are brought into them by the deaths of your friends and relations."

Around the very moment that Boone abandoned his pony and crossed the river, Hamilton was accepting two American scalps from visiting warriors of the Delaware tribe—a faction of Delaware far removed in philosophy from the staunch American ally from that same tribe, Chief White Eyes, who had clashed with Hamilton. Governor Hamilton then passed each scalp to a representative of one of the other tribes, to be used to rally their followers.

While Boone was shooting a buffalo with his jury-rigged rifle—and in the process testing whether he really had managed to elude his pursuers after his improbable escape—Hamilton was divvying up ammunition, clothes, and other supplies among the tribes. "I have often told you," Hamilton addressed those gathered there, "that what you receive does not come from me but from the king who has thought of you, though at a great distance," while also appealing to their spiritual beliefs by thanking "the Great Spirit for giving us clear skies and good weather" for their assembly.

By the time a runner from the Shawnee tribe tracked down Hamilton to tell him urgent news, yet another gathering had begun between Hamilton and newly arrived tribal leaders. In addition to Simon Girty, Charles Beaubien, the French agent who had helped lead the Shawnee to capture Boone at the Lower Blue Licks, now acted as interpreter. Beaubien had a personal connection to the tribes, having married Taucumwah, a woman of high stature in the Miami tribe. Beaubien had fought to extricate Taucumwah from her physically abusive marriage to another trader.

At this latest Fort Detroit gathering, Hamilton presented an ax to a tribal war chief, urging both fierceness and mercy, "with the recommendation of sparing the blood of the aged, women and children." The runner broke the news to Hamilton: Boone had escaped. The Shawnee requested his "further orders." Boone's timing had been uncanny as usual. Just as Hamilton had not wanted Boone to inform the Indians about British losses in the Revolutionary War, Hamilton would not want the news about Boone's escape to spread to the tribes. How delicious it would have been for Boone—had he been able to witness it for himself—to have seen the faces of Hamilton and Beaubien, who had been brought so high by his capture, now blindsided in front of a tribal audience.

In many ways, Daniel Boone *was* Kentucky at this time, as far as the British were concerned. Boonesboro was Kentucky's strongest presence by settlers. The territory formed part of an all-important western boundary for the rebel nation, and if it collapsed—as it was coming within a wisp of doing—the British could seize a foothold in a game-changing theater of the Revolutionary War. The transition from *declaring* and *realizing* independence rested in part with Kentucky. Now the British plan to swoop in and take down Boonesboro had been turned on its head with Boone's escape.

Even though some among the tribes believed Boone would never survive the harsh woods, Hamilton could recall his astonishment as Boone made gunpowder from scratch at Fort Detroit. If anyone would make it through the wilderness back to Boonesboro, it was Daniel Boone. And if Boone made it back to his fort, he would bring with him all the intelligence he'd gathered from Fort Detroit and from his captivity among the Shawnee. The British-and-Shawnee-led attack plan could no longer take anything for granted. They needed to summon an undeniable force as quickly as possible.

DANIEL BOONE, "EMACIATED and starving," took his first steps back into Boonesboro on June 20, 1778. Settlers reacted to the sight with disbelief. They greeted him, as one nineteenth-century magazine profile recounted, "like one risen from the dead." Residents repeated exclamations of astonishment such as "Bless your soul!" Boone's hand was grabbed and shaken so many times, it felt numb. He asked for Rebecca. One of the residents tried to tell him as gently as possible. "She put into the settlements long ago. She thought you was dead, Daniel, and packed up, and was off to Carolina."

Hearing that his family had gone dealt a heavy blow to Boone, whose desire to return to them had fueled his odyssey across the wilderness. He went to his cabin, where he soon found the family's cat, who had been gone for a long time but returned shortly after Boone did. The cat jumped into his lap. Jemima must have been occupied when he first appeared in the fort, but as soon as she heard the news, she would have run as fast as she could. She burst through the cabin door and they embraced. The earliest full-length study of Boonesboro suggested that Boone was tempted to set off at once to follow Rebecca and the others to North Carolina, but that he could not bring himself to abandon the settlement. Jemima's perseverance, despite the overwhelming gloom from almost everyone else about his fate, provided an inspiration to stand his ground at Boonesboro in the face of long odds.

Boone came armed with what a fellow settler characterized as an "abundance of news." The headline, of course, was that Blackfish had amassed an army, with the full backing of Fort Detroit's commander Henry Hamilton, to overwhelm Boonesboro. If the settlers had been shocked to see Boone walk through the gates of the fort, the fort itself had shocked Boone. It was in poor shape. Its dwindling population had been insufficient—or unmotivated under the severe leadership of Richard Callaway—to complete unfinished fortifications and carry out repairs after the battering of a hard winter.

"I found our fortress in a bad state of defense," recalled Boone through his biographer. The alarming tidings he brought with him from Little Chillicothe, along with his focused, task-based leadership style, propelled the settlers into action. An enemy could have easily overtaken the fort in its present condition. "We proceeded immediately to repair our flanks," continued Boone, "strengthen our gates and posterns, and form double bastions, which we completed in ten days." The bastions, corner structures that provided strategic perches from which sharpshooters could fire, were raised. They expanded the footprint of the fort to the east. They stocked up on powder and lead for ammunition and began to dig a well to provide enough water in case they were besieged. A sense of urgency was palpable. They expected the Indian army any day.

As thrilled as Jemima and her father were to be reunited, she had news of her own to break to him. Jemima knew of the serious complications to Boone's leadership that he himself had no idea about when he stepped onto the fort's grounds. The complication had come in the form of Andrew Johnson. He still had not returned to Boonesboro, but ever since his escape, his explosive claims had taken on a life of their own. Boone was a traitor and a British conspirator. When Boone heard about Johnson's accusations, he fumed, pointing to the British recruitment of the tribes against them. "Goddamn them," the usually stoic Boone responded, "they had set the Indians on us." At the same time, Boone genuinely cared about his adoptive Indian family, feelings he had to guard from those already casting suspicion on his motives.

Richard Callaway found himself in a familiar position—one repeated since his arrival at the settlement and the kidnapping of his girls—with his place as leader thrown into limbo by Boone's presence. But this time, Boone would be isolated, with young Jemima as his primary ally, and Callaway was armed with damning allegations courtesy of Johnson. He was about to add to his arsenal.

WILLIAM HANCOCK, one of the other kidnapped saltmakers, also lived with an influential member of the tribe, Will Emery, or Captain Will, the one who had warned Boone to forget about Kentucky long before the establishment of Boonesboro. Captain Will had lost a son in battle, and adopting a settler added to his family in compensation, as Boone did for Blackfish. When Captain Will asked his newly adopted son his name, the settler answered, "William Hancock." The chief said the name was too long—"Will was enough," he said. The chief, known for his humor, spoke English, but may have been amused to give his adopted son the same nickname he had.

Hancock, forty, had lived in Boonesboro for about a year, after first visiting Kentucky in 1775. The veteran of militia fighting had served under William Byrd in the French and Indian War when Byrd led a mission against the Cherokee. The operation stalled and became an infamous failure that caused Byrd to resign, tagging all those who participated with embarrassment. On New Year's Day 1777, Byrd, an inveterate gambler in heavy debt, died by suicide. By the time Boone led Hancock at the Blue Licks, Hancock felt justified in resenting Indians as well as his own military superiors.

In contrast to how Boone ingratiated himself with Blackfish's family, Hancock was confrontational with his adoptive family. One instance of this had to do with a horse. When he was living in Boonesboro, Hancock had a gray mare that went missing. Now in the Shawnee village, Hancock saw what he insisted was the same horse. Indians and settlers regularly would steal horses from each other, in part to slow down their counterparts. Captain Will approached and asked Hancock why he was looking at the mare. "She's mine," Hancock replied, "you stole her from me at Boonesboro." The Shawnee replied: "All the men and all the horses at Boonesboro belong to me." The argument over the horse revealed irreconcilable worldviews. To Hancock, Captain Will's words confirmed the Indians' thievery. To Captain Will, the appropriation of Indian lands by settlers rendered the entire settlement and everything on it illegitimate.

Though Hancock admitted that his captors "treated him well" while nursing him through illness, distrust grew on both sides. His adoptive Indian family would take his clothing each night to prevent him from trying to escape. After Boone escaped, Hancock was on high alert trying to gather intelligence. He witnessed the aftermath of Boone's getaway among the Shawnee. On July 5, Hancock was present when multiple Indian chiefs came together in a Grand Council. A Frenchman had traveled from Fort Detroit—this may have been Charles Beaubien, whom Henry Hamilton dispatched so often to deal with tribes. The chiefs informed Hamilton's operative of their plans to attack Boonesboro with 200 braves. But Hamilton, having heard of Boone's escape, had other ideas. Hamilton's agent told them to be "400 strong" instead. The chiefs were also promised four swivel guns, small cannons on rotating stands. Most important, Hancock was able to overhear the Indians' proposed timeline for the attack.

After the council, Captain Will apparently informed Hancock that when their army reached Boonesboro, if the residents refused to surrender, they would kill the men and take the women as prisoners. Captain Will actually presented this as good news for Hancock—it meant, the Shawnee chief said, that Hancock would be reunited with his wife, Molly, and their children, who would become prisoners alongside him. But in addition to Hancock's immediate family, his brother, Stephen, was also in Boonesboro, and if Captain Will was right, Stephen soon would be in mortal danger. Hancock faced a crossroads. Though some derided him as a mediocre woodsman, he decided to follow Boone's footsteps in an escape.

To prepare, Hancock squirreled away three pints of corn. That night, Captain Will kept watch on Hancock, who pretended to be asleep. Finally, the Shawnee chief fell asleep, with his head lodged against the door, blocking Hancock's exit. Little by little, Hancock pulled the door against his adoptive father's head until he could slip out. Running from Captain Will's home, Hancock got tangled up in the fastening of a horse, slowing him down until he finally freed himself. Just as Boone had done during his escape, Hancock rode the horse until it collapsed—150 miles to the Ohio River, by which point he had already used all the corn he had brought along. He tied logs together and rode on the river, where his makeshift raft knotted up with driftwood, veering him off course.

He became increasingly disoriented. Back on dry land, he wandered without direction. The weather darkened with his prospects. Boone had reached Boonesboro in under four days; Hancock now had been traveling for almost nine. He was "lost, weak and hungr[y]." He lay down, resigning himself that he was "never to arise" again. But when he woke, his eyes landed on a carving in a tree. In what seemed to be a miracle, it was his brother Stephen's name. Stephen had cut it into the bark when the two of them had hunted in the area. With that sight, the will to live returned. He now knew just where Boonesboro was—only four miles away.

ON JULY 17, inside the fort at Boonesboro, people stopped what they were doing when a familiar voice rang out. It came from across the river and belonged to William Hancock. People ran out of the fort. After nearly a week and a half in the wilderness, Hancock was in dire condition. For three days, Boone, Richard Callaway, and William's brother, Stephen, tended to him, hoping to nurse him back to health.

Despite Hancock's frail condition, Callaway, as an official of Boonesboro, interviewed Hancock for a deposition the same day he arrived. Callaway wanted to know all that Hancock witnessed leading up to his escape. Hancock reported what he had learned from the council of tribal leaders and what he had learned separately from Captain Will. After Boone escaped, he explained, the Shawnee had rushed the news to Henry Hamilton. Based on Hamilton's advice, the invading army determined to increase their arsenal of weapons and recruit more braves, and in doing so delayed the attack plan by three weeks. By the time Hancock recounted all this to Callaway, the settlers could count on only twelve more days to prepare.

Boone composed his own account of the situation faced by Boonesboro, writing that they "intend to fight hard." Boone's letter and Hancock's deposition were rushed to Virginia to ask for military reinforcements, with similar requests delivered to the only remaining Kentucky forts of significance, Harrodsburg and Logan's Fort. Reading through those materials, a Virginia military officer, in an understated and somewhat cold-blooded fashion, reported that "it will be unfortunate for the western frontier" if the British-backed attack plan against Boonesboro was carried out. As was increasingly common, Henry Hamilton figured as the central villain to the frontier cause. "By the accounts of the prisoners," the officer wrote, "the Commandant at Detroit has effectually set against us the most vindictive Indian Tribes, & no doubt he profits much in a private way by the plunder of our frontier." Despite this declaration, the officials could not yet send soldiers to Boonesboro, as war stretched military resources thinner in every direction.

In addition to gathering intelligence while it was fresh in Hancock's memory, Richard Callaway had another motive for losing no time deposing Hancock. On the heels of Andrew Johnson's allegations, which reached Boonesboro secondhand, Hancock could provide Callaway directly with additional incriminating details about Boone. Though Hancock's family, reflecting on the situation years later, claimed Hancock did not blame Boone for the capture of the saltmakers, other surviving evidence suggests that Hancock resented Boone's actions and played into Callaway's vendetta.

Boone had little patience for what he considered petty infighting and personal attacks, especially when every minute counted to prepare their defense. But with suspicions against him snowballing, the Boones needed to build their coalition, and they soon added supporters to their side. Simon Butler, who had first come into the Kentucky interior after hearing about Jemima's kidnapping, had completed his risky mission at Fort Vincennes for military phenom Lieutenant Colonel George Rogers Clark. His next assignment was to bring intelligence reports to the frontier. Valuable information had to be prevented from falling into enemy hands, so Simon memorized and then destroyed the documents containing the latest reports. After reciting his reports to key officials, he then made his way back to Boonesboro, where he found out that Boone recently returned from captivity. Butler remained loyal to Boone due to their past encounters, including the April 1777 battle outside the fort. William Bailey Smith, a Boone ally since the days of Jemima's rescue, also returned to Boonesboro after being away on assignment for Lieutenant Colonel Clark. Smith, ordered by superiors to help protect "the most important settlement in Kentucky," threw himself into Boone's preparations against an attack. Another asset to the fort was John South, who had brought along a large family with him. South was a strapping man—"fat and fleshy," Squire Boone's son called him—whose dark complexion led some in the settlement to wonder if he was of mixed racial heritage (common enough on the frontier, but still never failing to be a source of speculation and gossip). The hefty military figure could be glimpsed somewhat incongruously at rather delicate domestic chores. Wearing a hemp outfit, he would sit in his cabin in the shade by the window, using a small wheel to spin tow (flax fibers), as he occasionally sipped from a tickler, a cup with a small amount of alcohol in it.

Meanwhile, the settlement was being watched. "The Indians had spies out," Boone told his biographer, "and were greatly alarmed with our increase in number and fortifications." The sense of increased numbers would have been bolstered by the reappearances of Boone, Hancock, Smith, and Butler. In addition, Logan's Fort had sent fifteen men north to Boonesboro to help secure it. As noted by Boone, and possibly discovered by the settlers' own network of scouts, "the grand councils of the [Indian] nations were held frequently, and with more deliberation than usual." Shawnee and British planners readjusted, once again delaying their attack plan.

Boone, too, changed his tactics. Rather than entrenching themselves and waiting for the attack, he and his allies—Simon Butler and Billy Smith included—decided on a raid against a nearby Indian camp, Paint Creek. The planners' specific goals and rationales remain shrouded in mystery to this day. Evidence points to various possible objectives: to gather intelligence through observation, to take a hostage who could provide information on attack plans, to swipe horses either to slow down Indian movements or to replace horses taken from Boonesboro, or maybe a combination of these. Boone may also have wanted to defuse the accusations of Johnson by showing his willingness to risk everything for the sake of Boonesboro.

Richard Callaway fumed when he heard about the proposed strike and "opposed the plan with all his might." Boone, so recently returned, had already slipped the reins of command away from his rival. Power struggles aside, Callaway had legitimate objections. Risks abounded in the mission. If the settlers miscalculated the timing, the Indian army could arrive at Boonesboro while Boone and the others were absent, depriving their already small force of leaders and riflemen when they would be needed most. Likewise, if the men suffered casualties on their raid, the mission could end up harming rather than helping the ultimate defense of the settlement.

In preparing to depart from the settlement, Boone also took a big political risk by leaving behind Callaway and William Hancock unfettered in Boonesboro. As the only other captive to return to Boonesboro, Hancock was afforded a degree of authority and deference to his knowledge of what had happened among the Shawnee.

At the moment, Callaway strongly shaped that narrative. He was poised to stoke Hancock's resentment against Boone. The colonel's grudges against Boone had room to grow, worsened by details of Boone promising to take Callaway's nephew Cajah with him in an escape and then failing to do so. The fact that Cajah and James were Flanders's brothers meant that Callaway also could drive a wedge within the Boone family. If Flanders Callaway caught his uncle's distrust of Boone, Jemima would have to choose sides between her father and her husband.

BEFORE THE THUNDER

BOONE ROUNDED UP TWENTY-NINE MEN to be in his party. But their eagerness dissipated once they reached the Blue Licks at the Licking River. Association of the Licks with the catastrophic capture of the saltmakers—some two dozen of whom were still captive, assuming they were alive—was unavoidable. It had become "a place of evil omen to Kentucky," in the words of one writer who interviewed Boone. Eleven of the men in the raiding party decided to head back to the safety of the fort, judging the mission unsound. Seeds of doubt had been sowed before they left by the vocal protests of Richard Callaway. Remaining with Boone was John Holder, Fanny Callaway's husband, who had increasingly taken on a leadership role in the fort. Billy Smith, the consummate bachelor, pinned the partial retreat on the "irresolution" of men overly anxious about leaving their families unprotected in the fort. Smith believed those who remained committed to the cause would be "animated by the reflection that the glory of success would be increased by the diminution of their number"—a romantic sentiment similar to Henry V's questionable exhortation to his outnumbered men ("the fewer men, the greater share of honour") as dramatized by Shakespeare, whose plays were among the books at Boonesboro.

Shaky unity, vague goals, and high risk were uncharacteristic of a Daniel Boone–led mission, harking back to when he "appeared void of fear of consequence" in the initial journey to settle Boonesboro, which produced several casualties. One settler, recognizing the apparent foolishness of this latest plan, begged his brother not to go "on such a mission. . . . If anything would happen to you, how could I ever see our mother?" Possibly Boone's usual steady impulses caved to a desire for revenge for his own kidnapping— echoing his angry demand to "allow me two [Indians]" while hunting for Jemima's kidnappers. The raid's rationale—whatever it was at the time—may have been obscured by this drive for retaliation. Machismo was another frequent and often destructive motivation in frontier life: men demonstrating their courage for its own sake, a desire that could be manipulated by others and to which Boone was susceptible.

One big difference in this mission was the presence of Simon Butler. As in his original flight from justice that led him into Kentucky, Butler's activities on the frontier and on military missions projected a stealthy, heedless quality, including his use of his alias and, in his spy-craft, disguises. The Paint Creek mission may well have been shaped as much by Butler as by Boone. One member of the party noted that Butler was "our best pilot and well acquainted with this part of the country." Butler's influence also revealed itself after more than a third of their men retreated. The remaining party painted themselves in the style of Indians before building rafts and crossing the Ohio River. The paint could help camouflage them and also symbolized being on the warpath.

Butler moved ahead of the party as they came within four miles of Paint Creek, serving as a scout and advance man. He spotted two Indians riding a single horse. One of these riders, it turned out, was the son of Moluntha, a Shawnee chief. In a chilling moment later recounted by Butler, he watched the riders laughing with each other before he decided to shoot at them. As his son later put it, "Without really thinking what he was doing or really intending to do it," Butler aimed and shot twice, sending both Indians tumbling to the ground. Both bullets hit one rider, killing him. They passed through his body and hit the man's companion, wounding him in his flank and his wrist. Its riders displaced, the horse galloped off. Reinforcements from the Indian camp burst through the thick cane, firing at Butler. Others followed on horseback, between thirty and forty braves. Overmatched, Butler ducked behind a tree.

Just then, Boone, Smith, and the others arrived, firing from all sides to give Butler cover and push back their opponents. "A smart fight," as Boone called it, went on for a while until the Indian warriors retreated. From what Boone observed, he believed that the warriors with whom they had traded gunfire were preparing to join the larger campaign against Boonesboro.

Left behind in the retreat was the Indian whom Butler had shot off a horse. Butler now went to the murdered man and scalped him. It was an uncharacteristic moment of bloodthirsty violence for a Boone-led operation, both another indication that Butler may have been steering their course and a sign that Butler's time as George Rogers Clark's secret weapon had hardened him. This killing was reported without comment when the excursion was summarized in a Virginia newspaper months later: "Captain Boone, the famous partisan, has lately crossed the Ohio with a small detachment of men, and near the Shawanese Towns repulsed a party of the enemy, and brought in one scalp, without any loss on his side." Like the face paint, the scalping was also a call to war.

Further evidence of Butler's leadership role accumulates. When Boone and nearly all the other members of the raiding party elected to turn around to go back to their settlement, Butler decided to keep going to the Paint Creek town to finish their operation. Only one other man, Alexander Montgomery, opted to join him. Butler, family tradition had it, "could not find it in his heart to go back without some evidence of victory." As Butler and Montgomery approached the town and hid themselves among pumpkin vines, Indian children passed through the cornfields close enough for them to touch. Butler was later asked if he considered attacking the children. "No!" he answered. "I would not have hurt them for the world."

On the way back toward Boonesboro, Boone and his group felt eyes on them. "We were hard pressed by the Indians who were pursuing us," recounted one member of the party, detailing their wearisome path through coarse vegetation. Once the party reached the Lower Blue Licks, Boone witnessed a contingent of Indians congregating in proximity—a huge number of warriors preparing for the attack on nearby Boonesboro. The worst-case scenario had come to pass. Boonesboro was on the cusp of an onslaught, with Jemima and their loved ones inside, while Boone and many able-bodied fighters were blocked from returning.

BLACKFISH'S COMMAND OF the army of 440 marching to Boonesboro was at once a culmination of his place as war chief and a testament to lessons learned from the regime of his murdered peer, Cornstalk. The fact was, Blackfish's present mission did not *have* to claim casualties from either side, just as Blackfish had captured the saltmakers without shedding a drop of blood. The British wanted Boonesboro wiped off the face of the earth, at which point the redcoats would gain control of that westernmost frontier. Given the small number of residents at Boonesboro, reduced significantly by

the loss of the saltmakers, there was no realistic chance for Boonesboro to withstand an onslaught from the British. Henry Hamilton's
intelligence confirmed that the Kentucky settlements were "in the
utmost distress for clothing and other necessaries . . . they are wea-
ried out and unable to support the war any longer." Boonesboro's
downfall had become a matter of time.

After Boone's escape, Hamilton had worked diligently to ensure
the campaign against Boonesboro would be at maximum strength.
But though he sent surrogates to accompany Blackfish's troops, the
governor of Fort Detroit would not be present on the battlefield.
Blackfish, by leading the campaign personally, could try to convince Sheltowee, whom he still considered a son, to persuade the
settlers in Boonesboro to surrender en masse and peaceably submit
to Fort Detroit. Those settlers willing to pledge an allegiance to the
British crown could live a comfortable existence at Detroit; others
could join the Indians and become part of their families. Blackfish's
goal reflected a vision that could be considered truly groundbreaking. Rather than absorbing a settler here and there (such as Jimmy
Rogers or Simon Girty and Mary Jemison with the Senecas), an
entire community of settlers could be welcomed and integrated.
Instead of a map divided up by disputed treaty boundaries that
inevitably led to conflict, they could combine the tribal and settler communities with benefit for all. (Captain Will had shared a
similar vision with William Hancock before his escape, when the
tribal chief excitedly spoke of the Boonesboro expedition allowing
them to integrate Hancock's wife and children into the Shawnee
villages.) The outcome could be revolutionary—in a very different
way than the American war with the British.

Some among the tribes would never move beyond the many
outrages, losses, and tragedies of the frontier. Blackfish finally had
in his grasp an outcome that left behind cycles of retribution once

and for all. Among those present he had ideal partners for this. Young Shawnee leaders Blackbeard and Blackhoof were among the troops, as was the elder chief based in Paint Creek, Moluntha, and Captain Will. Both of the latter were Maquachakes, the branch of the tribe that had produced Cornstalk (Moluntha was Cornstalk's brother-in-law) and traditionally prized diplomatic rather than military engagement. Blackbird, a Chippewa chief, also held a high position among the troops.

If the settlers refused the overture for their surrender, the tribal army would overrun the fort. But Blackfish had faith in Sheltowee to do what was right.

At Fort Detroit, Hamilton eagerly awaited news of the operation. In correspondence with other British officers, he sometimes attributed the march to Boonesboro to the Shawnee's "jealous[y]" over land encroachments. In fact, Hamilton viewed the mission as his to control and assigned Captain Antoine Dagnieau DeQuindre to represent Fort Detroit. DeQuindre was said to be the first child ever born in Fort Detroit, loyalty to the military base running in his blood. Also present were French traders Pierre Drouillard and Charles Beaubien, the Hamilton ally who had married into the Miami tribe and had been credited by many for the capture of Daniel Boone at the Lower Blue Licks. Whatever Blackfish believed, Hamilton had convinced himself that his own operatives would be the real leaders in what looked to be the pivotal frontier showdown of the Revolutionary War.

WHEN SIMON BUTLER and Alexander Montgomery finally entered the Indian village of Paint Creek, the sight awaiting them made their hearts drop—not what was there, but what was not. The warriors of the town had gone. Those braves were on the way to Boonesboro and the two settlers had no chance of reaching the settlement before the Indian army.

There was irony in the situation. The successes of earlier wartime missions Butler carried out for George Rogers Clark—such as helping to secure Fort Vincennes for the revolutionaries—had put added pressure on the British, prompting Henry Hamilton to more aggressively push the tribes into their campaign against Boonesboro. Now locked out from Boonesboro by battle lines, Butler could only wait on the periphery.

Meanwhile, at Boone's position near the Licking River, things went from bad to worse when John Holder's strength gave out. Holder was immobilized right when Boone's group needed to move swiftly to get to the fort before the Indian troops. A plan formed for one man, reportedly Pemberton Rollins, to stay behind with Holder until he was able to walk again.

Boone and the others had to devise an out-of-the-way route that circumvented the Indian troops while racing to the fort. Boone plotted a course. After a series of starts and stops, they finally arrived in sight of the fort gates. They could breathe a sigh of relief to see that they reached home before the braves. With Boone and the others announcing the imminent attack, the settlers flew into last-minute preparations. They would not have time to finish digging the well they had started, which meant a prolonged battle could leave them without enough water.

In a space designated as his "gunsmith shop," Squire Boone worked on building a cannon from black gum, a tree native to Kentucky with especially thick bark. Squire had been fascinated with weapons from a young age, at one point apprenticing with a relative who was a gunsmith. Squire banded the cannon with iron. But when he tested it, it cracked. He started again, and when he finished building, his latest test succeeded without incident.

With Butler, Montgomery, Holder, and Rollins still in the wilderness, they were even more shorthanded than expected. Michael Stoner, close Boone ally in so many journeys and battles, was also away from the fort without time to return. William Patton, a respected Boonesboro resident, was out hunting. One witness considered only forty of the men present "efficient" and skilled soldiers. Between twenty and thirty women and children also remained inside the fort. The women, as always, would have to play vital roles in every facet of the defense even when overlooked by the men.

Fanny Holder (née Callaway), meanwhile, faced the prospect of her husband being trapped behind enemy lines, which gave her father, Richard Callaway, yet another loss that he could pin on Boone. But with Pemberton Rollins's help, John Holder reached the fort mere hours before the Indian troops were anticipated. Jemima's brother-in-law, William Hays, who had left with his wife, Susannah, and Rebecca Boone to go to North Carolina, had also returned. Hays had a strong dynamic with his father-in-law, having tutored Boone in writing and helped with the family's financial accounts. Hays apparently had heard about the impending arrival of Indian troops and rushed back from North Carolina in time to aid Boonesboro's defense.

Boone was standing outside the fort when the approaching army came into earshot. Moses and Isaiah, Squire Boone's young children, could hear riders on horseback in the distance. The children, as well as others at the fort, believed the sounds came from the Virginia reinforcements that Boonesboro had requested, and they prepared to greet them. Daniel—whether by the sounds, by calculating distance or direction of the incoming troops, or by instinct—knew it was the Indian army he'd seen at the Licks. "Run in!" he told his nephews. Rifle in hand, he rounded up everyone who was outside.

The Indian army marched under the flags of both British and French, as though the whole world were turning on Boonesboro. Blackfish stopped about 150 yards from the fort. With a white flag posted to signify peace, Pompey called out for Sheltowee. Boone identified himself from inside the fort. Blackfish asked that he come to him. Boone walked out "unconcernedly," as a witness put it, to a tree stump 60 yards away from the fort. He and Blackfish took each other's hands warmly. One account suggests Jimmy Rogers was also present. As a settler who was once kidnapped and adopted by Blackfish—and who now stood a full-fledged and acculturated leader of the tribe—Rogers represented Boone through the looking glass, if Blackfish's plans came to pass.

Boone and Blackfish sat together on a log. After his time in cap-tivity, Boone spoke Shawnee with ease. Some inside the fort bristled that Boone would engage in private conversation with the leader of the enemy force, the man who had kidnapped him and so many of their companions. The exchange was as personal as it was political.

"My son," Blackfish said to Boone, "what made you leave us in the manner you did?"

Boone told him what he'd told his tribal mother, Neegah. "I wanted to see my wife and children." Blackfish insisted that he would have helped Boone in returning "if you had but let me know you want[ed] to see your wife."

Blackfish handed over letters from Henry Hamilton addressed to Boone. The letters have been lost, but Nathan Boone later sum-marized the contents: "[Hamilton] advised Captain Boone to sur-render the fort, inasmuch as it was impossible to defend themselves against such a force as was then going against them; that if they attempted any defense, men[,] women and children would probably all be massacred. That if they surrendered the fort, none should be hurt—all should be safely conveyed to Detroit; that any of their property that they lost by the surrender, should be made good to them. Those who held office should have the same rank under the British government."

Blackfish also brought wampum, colored beads used for currency and as ornaments. He laid these out in lines. Hamilton always prided himself on participating in and adding to tribal rituals, and to that end Hamilton had given Blackfish specific instructions about the wampum's symbolism. Blackfish explained that one end of the wampum represented Fort Detroit and the other end represented Boonesboro. The lines were white, black, and red, representing, respectively, peace, trouble, and war. The wampum provided a message parallel to the one conveyed in the letters. The settlers had a choice, Blackfish said, and had to pick their destiny.

"If you will surrender," Blackfish said, "I will take you all to Chillicothe, and you shall be treated well." He made clear that he had given thought to the settlers' safety and comfort. "I have brought forty horses and mares for the old people and women and children to ride." By one account, Blackfish balanced out this reassurance with a threat that if the settlers did not comply, the saltmakers still held in tribal towns would be killed.

Boone used the very real power struggle inside the fort to his advantage. He explained to Blackfish that while he had been in captivity, another commander had taken his place as leader of the fort: "All the power [is] not now in [my] hands." He said the most he could do was consult with Boonesboro's other leaders, and he asked that Blackfish grant them two days to come to a decision about surrendering. Blackfish, whether in deference to Sheltowee or as part of a strategy to solidify his positions surrounding the fort, agreed. But the war chief pointed out that the warriors outside did not have enough to eat. Boone gestured around them. "There you see aplenty of cattle—kill what you need and take what corn you want, but don't let any be wasted." The braves cheered Boone's instructions and reciprocated his gentility by expressing hope that the firing of guns would not alarm the women in the fort.

Moluntha, the chief from Paint Creek, had a less favorable reaction to Boone. "You killed my son the other day," the chief said, "over the Ohio river."

"No, I have not been there," answered Boone.

"It was you," replied Moluntha. "I tracked you here to this place."

Boone's diplomatic integrity clashed with his half-truths. Given the likelihood that Moluntha's son was one of the riders on horseback whom Simon Butler killed, Boone was technically honest when saying he had not committed the violence, but lied about not being near Paint Creek. His answer may also reflect his regret and embarrassment at the futile mission he had organized in defiance of Richard Callaway.

Like Blackfish, Captain Will also desired to know the fate of the man he considered his adopted son. The venerable chief found some high ground on which to stand and called out toward the fort, asking if "Will had reached there," meaning William Hancock. From inside, Hancock replied that he had made it, but did not engage on a personal level the way Boone had with Blackfish. Hancock had never experienced the bonds Boone had made with his Indian family; Hancock, who evidence suggests had been swayed into Richard Callaway's anti-Boone camp, reinforced the difference between him and Boone to the rest of the settlement by snubbing Captain Will.

Inside the fort, Boone lost no time. "It was now a critical period with us," reflected Boone, as related by his biographer. No voices rose to advocate surrender, despite the long odds of 70 settlers facing 440 soldiers. The sentiment of the fort became "Death is preferable to captivity." "Well, well," Boone remarked to the others when the consensus became clear, "I'll die with the rest." Callaway reportedly had a more aggressive statement of their position, phrased in his punitive manner. He swore "he would kill the first man who proposed a surrender."

They had two more days to prepare the fort for siege. They filled any container they could find with water. "We immediately proceeded to collect what we could of our horses," explained Boone through his biographer, "and other cattle, and bring them through the posterns [secondary doors] into the fort." When Blackfish's troops heard that the "white squaws" were frightened to come outside to help, the Indians helped round up the cattle into the fort. Included among the livestock was Squire Boone's much-loved cow, Old Spot. Squire's family believed Old Spot could sense danger and give warning before an attack.

When the two-day deadline arrived, Boone exited through the front gates again. This time, he emerged with William Bailey Smith at his side. Smith wore a dark red coat and an elaborate hat with a feather in it. Smith's military uniform allowed him to pose as Boone's superior, lending a face and persona to Boone's tale about answering to a higher authority. (Smith's pompous garb also may have been a sly mocking of Boone's actual rival, the dictatorial Richard Callaway, who waited inside.) The Indians spread a panther skin to sit on. Smith played his part, listing many objections to surrender. One account had Boone ultimately telling Blackfish there would never be surrender, "not as long as a man of us is alive."

Taken aback by what he heard from Smith and Boone, Blackfish said, "Governor Hamilton would be very much disappointed, as he expected [surrender]." Still, they were under orders, Blackfish explained, "not to massacre them" if surrender could not be agreed upon. Blackfish made symbolic gestures toward peace. The Indians gifted Boone and Smith with dried buffalo tongue to give to the women. Though suspicions swirled that the food could be poisoned, it turned out to be safe and was a welcome addition to the meager larder.

Blackfish suggested that the fort send eight men into the Indians' encampment to form a council with tribal leaders in order to discuss terms for peace (by Nathan Boone's account, it was his father who suggested the number of settlers who could come out). Returning inside the fort, Boone proposed to the other leaders that they accept Blackfish's offer, arguing they should be grateful for the possibility that "they could make peace." Some settlers were particularly encouraged by recent reports of a successful treaty between Indians and George Rogers Clark. Richard Callaway argued against holding discussions outside, saying if the Indians wanted to talk, they should come inside the fort, where the settlers could protect against treachery. As had happened so many times before, fault lines widened between Boone and Callaway when it came to decision time.

Eventually the leaders among the Indians and settlers agreed to a neutral zone in front of the fort where no one would be armed. The settlers believed that agreeing to the meeting proved they were not afraid. At the appointed time, Boone, his brother Squire, Richard Callaway, Flanders Callaway, William Smith, Stephen Hancock, John South, and Jacob Stearns (a relative of South's) emerged from the fort without weapons. Meanwhile, Jemima and the other women decided to make "a great show of strength." The women put on men's hats and coats, spoke in deep masculine tones, and marched with rifles back and forth near the open gates.

Additional clothes were spun, and even children were dressed like soldiers. The goal was to make the Indians believe there were more soldiers. (Accounts of women disguising themselves in masculine clothing to participate in war go back to Epipole, who did so to fight alongside the Greek men in the Trojan War—who stoned her to death for her trouble.)

Samuel South, a boy at the time, carried water out to the negotiators. Multiple meetings among the representatives were held under a cluster of large trees. First came a legalistic discussion. "Brethren," said Blackfish, "by what authority did you come and settle this place?" The settlers retold the narrative of Boonesboro's formation and the now-defunct Transylvania Colony, going back to the Richard Henderson–led negotiations at Sycamore Shoals with the Cherokees that included Hanging Maw. Blackfish seemed skeptical. But then, by one account, the chief brought over a Cherokee who was among the Indian troops and asked whether the Cherokees really had agreed to the transaction, a question that reflected the confusing patchwork of treaties between settlers and the various tribes. "Yes, we did," the Cherokee answered.

"Friends and brothers," Blackfish then reportedly said to the settlers, "as you have purchased this land from the Cherokee and paid them for it, it entirely alters the case. You must keep it and we must live like friends and brothers. Hereafter you must allow us to hunt on your ground and you must hunt on our side of the river, thus we are willing to make a peace with you as long as wood grows and water runs."

With this groundwork, a treaty conference between the sides was arranged to finalize terms. Blackfish explained that Indians from twenty-four different towns would be brought over in order to make the treaty binding, showing the incredible diversity of tribal representatives among the troops. At this meeting under the "divine elm" that served as an outdoor chapel, each of the eight settlers had two Indians seated on either side. On September 9, 1778, conditions of peace, including boundaries at the river, were discussed and agreed upon. The terms included a withdrawal by the Indian troops and the settlers' gradual abandonment of Boonesboro over a six-week period, after which they would turn themselves over to Governor Hamilton at Fort Detroit. They would return Kentucky to its former status as a hunting ground for everyone.

An elaborate meal, relative to the fort's resources, came out on pewter dishes. They likely used utensils with handles made of bone, decorated with crosshatching, but probably did not introduce any of the fort's knives, which were kept sharpened on whetstone and could be used as weapons. Meat was cooked. Isaiah Boone later recalled carrying out a chair for one of the adults. The feast conveyed a message: the fort had plenty of provisions if necessary with which to outlast any siege.

"Brethren," Blackfish said to the group, "we have made a long and lasting treaty." Blackfish impressed observers with his "fine voice . . . and eloquent oration." A hybrid pipe-tomahawk—symbolizing a wary peace and the joining of cultures—was brought out and, by some accounts, smoked by men from both sides. Blackfish said that "one thing remained to be done" and instructed everyone to rise to shake hands in a way that brought one another "as near the heart as they could." As they did, two Indians gripped each settler in an elaborate gesture. "One Indian," as Nathan Boone described it, "locking his right arm with a white man's left, and with his left hand, shaking the white man's left; and the other Indian in the same manner on the white man's right." Blackfish and the Indian who had held the pipe-tomahawk took Boone's hands. Callaway objected to the whole ritual and struggled against the Indians shaking his hands.

Theodore Roosevelt would later marvel at what happened next, which he categorized as a "curious mixture of barbarian cunning and barbarian childishness" shown by both sides, with the events coming off "as if it were a page of Graeco-Trojan diplomacy."

According to the accounts of settlers, the Indians had contrived the handshake as a way to drag the settlers away behind an embankment to kidnap or kill them. Suspicions also spiked over the apparent attendance at the treaty of young, strong Indians who were clearly soldiers rather than chiefs. Blackfish's men had concealed tomahawks and guns amid a perimeter of Indians surrounding the treaty conference. By the description of one witness, "an Indian at a little distance rose up and fired into the air a signal gun, which he had secreted under his blanket." Some settlers suspected that even Blackfish's loud, clear voice announcing peace was itself a signal. Reports also indicated that in the days leading up to the treaty, settlers witnessed the Indians holding a war dance at the bottom of the hill, which convinced Boone that the treaty and its rituals were all a facade to launch an attack.

In hindsight many of these assumptions appear dubious. Some of the features of the Indians' handshakes are documented as rituals in other peace treaties, and the specific conditions of the treaty, rather than seeming to be improvised for show, methodically satisfied the goals evidenced in Henry Hamilton's correspondence and in accounts of Blackfish's aspirations. If Nathan Boone was right about his father choosing the number of settlers who would be delegates to the treaty talk, a master plan by Blackfish to have Indians outnumber the settlers at the treaty also becomes less likely. And if the Indians really had a secret attack plan all along, the settlers certainly did, too. The morning of the treaty meeting, went family tradition, "Boone had given orders that all the men in the fort should be on the watch, seated at every convenient place with his rifle in his hand pointed and cocked, his finger at the trigger." The fact is, both sides remained distrustful and had plans to fight if necessary. And with both sides waiting for a sign or signal, the ceremony of peace was poised to become violent with a single twitch—the unfamiliar Indian handshake may have triggered the first strike from a settler, or Callaway's struggle against his Indian counterpart may have caused the Indians to open fire, or both may have happened at the same time. Either way, everything fell apart.

Chapter 10

THE LAST SIEGE

MARKSMEN ON THE HIGH PLATFORMS inside the fort and in concealed positions throughout the garrison unleashed a hail of gunfire "like claps of thunder." The settlers at the treaty council wrestled to free themselves from the grip of the Indians, who lunged for their hidden weapons. A "dreadful scuffle" ensued. John South pulled down the two Indians who gripped him. William Bailey Smith later claimed that both of the Indians holding him were instantly shot dead by the fort's marksmen. Stearns yanked himself free, then pushed down and leaped over a second Indian. No doubt with some hyperbole, Squire Boone later claimed he threw down three attempted captors as if they had been "so many little children."

Daniel Boone also struggled free. Boone "throwing Blackfish flat on the ground" (as Nathan Boone recounted) conjured an evocative tableau of the adopted son standing over the fallen father. The second Indian near Boone reached for the pipe-tomahawk and tried to bring it down on him. At the last moment, Boone dodged, the blunt handle catching the back of his head and the blade landing between his shoulders. As Flanders Callaway fled, he was shot in the left hand. South got shot in the heel as he ran. About fifteen paces from the meeting ground, Squire Boone took a bullet in his shoulder.

Settlers would long assume that Flanders, John, and Squire were hit by Indian gunfire, but circumstances suggest that friendly fire from the riflemen in the fort is equally probable; they were shooting from fifty feet away, and Boone already had told his men that they would be only somewhat more likely to hit an Indian than a settler from that distance, as they would be intermingled.

Inside the fort, chaos spread. Dogs barked and livestock scurried in what a witness called "wild confusion." One of those firing from the fort into the assembly outside was Ambrose Coffee, the Irish immigrant who had come over to Boonesboro from Harrodsburg to lend a hand after Boone and the saltmakers had been taken. Coffee lay flat on part of the southeast bastion with his weapon. David Gass (uncle of the young hero of Jemima's rescue operation, John Gass) had warned Coffee to lower his body in case the Indians fired on the fort. Now, before he could heed Gass's advice, a flurry of gunfire came Coffee's way. He tumbled from the bastion down to the ground floor of the fort, landing uninjured—remarkable, considering his clothes were riddled with more than a dozen bullet holes.

Outside, Boone staggered from the injury he had received from the pipe-tomahawk. Daniel and Squire Boone, Callaway, and the others who had been at the treaty meeting hid behind logs and trees and along a protective ridge. From the fort, Jemima watched as treaty participants began to dash toward safety. She rushed to open the gates. One by one, they ran inside. As Jemima manned the entrance, a bullet fired from the other side of the river hit the gate, ricocheted, and struck her, knocking her to the ground. Though alarming, the bullet had only grazed her, and those inside managed to close the gates.

Squire was unable to reach the front gates, but he squeezed in through a cabin's outside door before it was sealed. The men who had gone outside to the meeting had hidden their weapons inside the fort, which now permitted the wounded Squire to grab his gun and find a position inside from which to shoot. Daniel was the last one into the fort, making sure that everyone else got inside first. All the while, Indians continued to unleash heavy fire.

Squire fired, but his shoulder caused him so much pain he couldn't reload. He called for help. Another settler, likely one of the women, helped him place the bullet into position. Though Squire was as loath as his brother to leave a battle behind, he entered his cabin to find his wife, Jane. She was Squire's "childhood sweetheart." She studied the wound. Jane concluded it was shallow, so Squire went back into action in the fort.

William Patton, the settler who had been on a long hunt, had started back to Boonesboro. He saw the Indian troops from a distance. Braves had surrounded the fort on all sides. Careful not to be spotted, Patton went back into the woods.

Behind the fort walls, William Hancock, the former captive of the Shawnee, ran up and down to portholes firing at the Indian troops with a vengeance. Molly, his wife, was casting bullets for him, working to the point of collapse. "She fell asleep," according to a friend of the Hancocks, "holding her hands to her face, and her elbows on her knees, and though asleep exclaimed: 'Pour it to them, Billy.'" In the first round of firing, a bullet broke through the protective fencing, hitting Pemberton Rollins above the elbow and breaking his arm.

At first, Boone sensed that timidity had swept through some of the settlers inside Boonesboro. When a potter refused to fight, Richard Callaway picked up a tomahawk, probably collected from an earlier battle with Indians, and chased him with it.

Squire continued to struggle with searing pain from his gunshot wound. At a break in the action, he went to his brother. Boone examined him and, unlike Jane, judged the wound serious. In taking a closer look, he discovered the ball, still in Squire's shoulder. As reported by Squire's son, who witnessed these events as a child, Daniel "cut a gash of an inch or more" into Squire's flesh and carefully removed the ball. Despite Squire's eagerness to participate, he had to remain in a cabin to recover from the wound and the impromptu surgery, so the fort was another man down. Squire's frustration with his circumstance becomes easy to imagine when paired with his reputation for fiercely defending his property and family. Squire planned not to let anything stop him from being with his family, even death. When he got around to thinking about his own end, he instructed his family to bury him in a cave and for them to camp out near the mouth of the cave so that he could communicate to them as a spirit.

A pattern began in which daytime battles alternated with nights spent regrouping. During the day, gunfire rained so thick against every part of the fort, especially near the portholes, that the bullets would "strike against each other" and fall down. The bastion on the side of the river ended up embedded with a hundred pounds of lead. After nightfall, Jemima and the other women would search the ground outside for used ammunition, crawling around on the ground to "scrape the bullets in their aprons" by the handful. In the fort, Jemima worked to mold the warped bullets into shape to be used the next day. As they came out of the molds burning hot, Jemima would carry them to the riflemen by once again using her apron. During the siege, observed Nathan Boone, "[Jemima] was fearless and seemed to expose herself more than the other females."

The tribal army faced scarcities as well. The Indians did not have the swivel guns promised by Fort Detroit, though the reason has been lost to history. In one peculiar exchange, Pompey tried to engineer a swap with the settlers, wanting to trade an old pony—possibly the same one Boone had left behind in his escape from the Shawnee village—for a gun, but nobody in the fort agreed. Resentment toward Pompey ran high, as some likely blamed him for having served as an interpreter at the Lower Blue Licks when the Boonesboro group had been captured. In reality, Pompey had voted to spare the captives' lives, but such nuances remained obscured among the settlers. An escaped slave who held an allegiance to Indians was inherently a traitor in the eyes of some settlers. No doubt some projected onto Pompey their lingering anger about Grampus, who had escaped enslavement and defied efforts to capture him. Some of the men vowed that if Pompey approached the fort again, they would shoot him on the spot.

In the meantime, settlers began to hear sounds of roots being cut. They couldn't trace the sounds but grew concerned that the Indians were attempting to undermine the fort in some way.

With Squire now confined to his cabin, the other settlers brought out the cannon he had built. Richard Callaway fired a two-pound ball more than two hundred yards. The weapon proved its power, but it cracked in the process. Some Indians deduced that the settlers had problems with what had been intended as a fearsome display. "Fire your wooden gun again!" one taunted. Without Squire, they would not be able to fix it. In a less technological experiment in warfare, John Holder, a relative giant of a man, heaved large stones over the wall and down the hill.

The British and Indian forces had a choice of strategic positions from which to fire, with a particularly clear shot from the opposite bank of the Kentucky River. On the closer shore, a sycamore tree gave cover for one Indian sharpshooter who got a bead on some of the fort's portholes. To the south of the fort, a hill offered another ideal spot for marksmen.

The settlers had raised an American flag in the center of the fort, with a wooden gun carved by Squire Boone atop as a weathervane; the display became a target. Bullets severed the fifty-foot-tall flagstaff, sending the flag careening down. On September 11, David Bundrin, one of several men called Dutchman by the settlers, was looking through a porthole in the fort in the southwest bastion when a bullet struck him in the forehead. He was found alive but in dire condition.

Pompey reportedly got into a habit of concealing himself behind a log. By one account, a man named William Collins inside the fort targeted Pompey's position, possibly with a long-range Jaeger rifle. He took aim squarely at Pompey's head, killing him. Pompey's role as interpreter and strategist had been highly valued by Blackfish and the Shawnee, and signs point to Pompey's death demoralizing the tribal army. The settlers' grudges against Pompey contributed to warping the story of his demise. Over time, legend turned the death into personal vengeance in a fabricated story that Pompey was an enslaved man in Boonesboro who deserted to the Indian side midway through the siege.

Provisions in the fort ran extremely low; the Indian troops' earlier plan to starve them out could come to pass. The settlers ground corn by hand. Jemima and other young women would dart out of the fort some two hundred yards to a spring to collect fresh drinking water. As they ran back into the fort, bullets flew from Indian marksmen, likely aimed not at the women but rather into the gates as they opened.

The settlers caught rainwater for the livestock. As days passed, the cattle "became extremely gaunt" from lack of food. The Indian leaders knew that as resources diminished, the more urgency settlers would feel. When shooting into the fort, horses and cows became targets. A ball struck and injured Old Spot, Squire Boone's cow. A gray mare belonging to Richard Callaway was killed by a stray bullet. The South family's cattle that they had brought from Virginia to Boonesboro all died during the siege. The settlers, archaeological evidence now suggests, may have dug a pit near the center of the fort to dispose of the horses and other animals while movement was restricted to the garrison.

The volleys of gunfire seemed to continue around the clock, what the settlers called "a hot engagement." During lulls in battle, verbal exchanges, parlays, and conversations occurred between the sides. Blackfish asked to see Jemima, by one account explaining that two squaws who accompanied the Indians' war party wished to get a glimpse of her and possibly other "squaws" from the fort. The request was argued back and forth among all parties. We do not have records of the discussions inside the fort or whatever input came from Jemima. Boone, coming outside, eventually agreed, and presumably so did Jemima. She stepped out near the front gates (if other women emerged they likely included the other two kidnapping survivors, Betsy and Fanny). Some of the ten warriors arrayed around Blackfish moved toward Jemima.

The moment was charged. Jemima, Daniel, and Blackfish formed a triangular standoff. It was another indelible tableau that epitomized the larger saga. The kidnapping of the three girls, the death of Blackfish's son during their rescue, the return of Daniel after his own kidnapping and escape—Jemima had been at the center of all of it. During Daniel's captivity, the Indians had asked him about Jemima—no surprise their curiosity was still so intense. Her hair—so admired by Hanging Maw during her kidnapping—continued to inspire special interest, and Indian observers around the fort called for her to take her combs out. Jemima removed the combs and let her "bountiful" dark hair fall over her shoulders. The Indians seemed interested in touching her hair or, some more cynical settlers suspected, in grabbing her to "use her to extort surrender of the fort." Richard Callaway remained behind her, lowering his rifle and warning everyone: "Back off." This combination of ritual, performance, and stratagem ended when Jemima returned through the gates into the fort.

From inside, Boone examined the river below, observing that it had become muddier. A cedar stick lodged in the ground near the water trembled. The clues confirmed that the earlier sounds of roots being cut signified a larger scheme. The troops outside were digging underground, cutting a passage four to five feet on each side. They tunneled from the "low water mark" of the river as far as twenty-five feet toward the fort. Settlers scrambled to decipher the troops' plan. One possibility was to invade through the tunnel; another was to blow up the fort from below.

Indeed, the invading force prepared poles wrapped in bark and flax that could set the garrison's structures on fire if the underground passage reached close enough. This subterranean scheme was attributed to DeQuindre, the troops' "French engineer." The goal was supposedly yelled out by a brave taunting the settlers that the besiegers would "blow you all to hell."

To counter the tactic, Boone ordered thirty feet of trenches, ten feet deep and two feet wide, to be dug on the river side of the fort. An armed sentinel in them would be able to fire as soon as the tunnelers got close enough. The Indian troops noticed the dirt thrown from the ditches the settlers were digging, and the two projects became a race. Inside their respective passages, the settlers and Indians heard digging from the other side.

London, the enslaved man who had come to Boonesboro with Nathaniel Henderson and remained when Henderson left, was assigned the vital role of keeping watch by crawling into an underground passage. London lay on his stomach with his rifle at the ready.

Blackfish's troops stepped up direct assaults. Braves would fling flaming sticks toward the roofs. A torch was also tossed to an out-side door of one cabin; the fire spread, reaching the housetop. John Holder brought out a bucket and poured water over the torch, cursing as he did. Margaret Callaway, Richard Callaway's wife and Holder's mother-in-law, scolded him for cursing instead of praying. Holder, recalled a witness, "said he had then no time to pray," or in another version, "I've no time to pray, goddamnit!" The Indi-ans spread flax across a fence that ran into the fort before setting the fibrous material aflame. The settlers passed through the under-ground trench and pulled down the fence, stopping the fire from spreading farther, then slipped back inside the fort.

Inside a cabin, Bundrin continued to suffer from his head wound. "Rocking his body the while with his elbow upon his knees, in a sitting posture," Nathan Boone recounted, Bundrin "never spoke a word." Still, his pious wife remained optimistic.

The settlers scrambled to improve their shelter and reinforce mo-rale. New doors were built between cabins to provide safe passages away from gunfire that penetrated into the center of the fort. The settlers replaced the American flag and cheered as they raised the new one up the flagpole. The riflemen formed platoons to coor-dinate their firing from the fort. With ammunition running low, the defenders had to limit themselves to high-probability shots. The women formed their own united band, gathering in a cabin at the center of the fort where they would huddle with the children. Jemima and the other women melted down their jewelry to make more bullets. Pewter dishes and spoons also were melted and mixed with lead and turned into ammunition.

William Patton, still confining himself to the woods nearby, observed the fort while remaining out of sight at strategic points on hills. At night, he crept closer to learn as much as possible about the siege under the cover of darkness.

While on watch at night in the underground passage at the corner of the garrison, London saw the flash of an Indian's gun coming toward the fort. London fired back. When he did so, he inadvertently exposed his position with the light from his gun. The Indians fired on London and shot him in the neck, killing him.

The campaign to burn the settlers out of the fort intensified. From behind the large trees surrounding the fort, braves would shoot flaming arrows wrapped with combustibles and powder. The arrows sometimes would land on a roof of one of the fort's cabins. A witness described a moment when "the powder flashed and set the adjoining shingles on fire." Settlers, including Jemima, scrambled to put out the flames, sometimes climbing on the roofs.

As days passed, residents found themselves in a terrifying position. They were running low on water, and the more water they had to use to put out fires, the less they'd have for future flames. Climbing on the roofs to try to stamp out the flames, they were easy targets. Every outcome could be fatal. "The fort seemed doomed," wrote nineteenth-century Boonesboro historian George Ranck, "and for a few terrible moments all was black despair within it." Huddling together, the residents waited for the end, expecting the fort to burn down around them.

Flaws in construction turned out to limit damage. Because the shingles were attached to the roof only by wooden pins, they could be loosened from inside the cabins, and then they'd slide to the ground. Squire Boone repurposed extra musket barrels to hold and discharge water, which were wielded by the women of the fort to put out flaming material. Rainfall at night also helped moisten the roofs of the cabins, making them less flammable. The arrows' flames were dying. "Boonesboro," wrote Ranck, "had escaped by the skin of its teeth."

The Indians continued excavating their tunnel, extending from the river toward the fort for 120 feet. But heavy rain showers fell nightly. The tunnels caved in. The rain also helped extinguish fires and replenished the water supply.

Still, casualties mounted. David Bundrin died. Squire remained confined. As recalled by his son, Squire "had to keep to his house but had a light broad-axe placed beside the door, declaring he would use [it] as long as he could, in case the Indians should scale the fort." With bullets flying, Daniel Boone was also hit. He found Jemima and asked her to take a look at his neck, assuring her that although it "smart[ed]" he was certain it was a "slight flesh wound." But as Jemima removed his stock, or neckcloth, blood poured out. Jemima was "alarm[ed]." She insisted that her father lie down in his cabin, despite his urgency to return to action. Meanwhile, braves outside called out, "We know we have killed Captain Boone!" Jemima examined her father's wound and bandaged it. With no surgeons at Boonesboro and with basic supplies scarce, each wound was a race against the clock.

By this time, the young women of the fort did not limit themselves to molding and running bullets, but also took up the guns themselves to defend the garrison. Jemima had gone full circle to the day years earlier when Rebecca had handed her a rifle to fire in the air to compensate for the men missing from the fort. The sight of Jemima, Betsy, and Fanny aiming rifles would have startled and amazed all who saw it—their former kidnappers and former rescuers alike.

At one point as Jemima rushed between the cabins carrying ammunition, a bullet splintered as it entered the garrison and hit the gate. The split bullet struck Jemima from behind, knocking her down. The wound received by her husband, Flanders Callaway, during the treaty gunfire had already taken a toll. He lost the little finger on his left hand.

The night of September 17 was the Indians' biggest onslaught. In the darkness, the incoming troops held torches as they stormed the fort. Between the torches and the gunfire, what a witness described as "vivid flash after flash," the entire fort was illuminated "even to a pin," as Squire's son recalled.

At the same time, under the protection of the night, William Patton had positioned himself closer to the fort. He was shocked by what he witnessed. In the braves' all-out attack they stormed the fort with torches "and made the dreadfullest screams and [hollering] that could be imagined." Then Patton heard other noises, the implications of which were undeniable: heart-wrenching screams. Patton ran into the woods, this time with no intention of turning back. He would head for Logan's Fort. Boonesboro, he now knew, was gone.

PATTON REACHED LOGAN'S FORT with his bleak tidings. He described to the group at Logan's what he had witnessed and the outcome that had made him flee. "They took it by storm," he said of Boonesboro. He had dared to move so close to the fort that he had heard the Indians slaughtering the Boonesboro settlers. Patton described, as relayed later by a witness, how he "heard the woman and children and men also screaming when the Indians was killing them."

After leaving Paint Creek, Simon Butler and Alexander Montgomery, his companion in the senseless preemptive attack against the nearby Indian village, now approached Boonesboro through a foggy night. They identified the tracks of the Indian troops. Confirming their belief that the braves were already massed in Boonesboro in great numbers, Butler and Montgomery instead rode south.

Butler and Montgomery arrived at Logan's Fort not long after Patton. They heard Patton's distressing though unsurprising news: the fort at Boonesboro had been overtaken and the settlers killed. The range of emotions coursing through Butler could be imagined. Having spearheaded the mission to Paint Creek that had ultimately prevented him from returning to Boonesboro, Butler had taken himself out of position to help defend the fort. Butler and Montgomery determined to ride to Boonesboro, which would give them the chance to survey anything left of the fort and search for survivors.

Benjamin Logan also absorbed the news about the neighboring fort. Logan, thirty-five, was, like Boone, a natural leader, though with a markedly different style. Logan was over six feet tall, and his presence and manner intimidated as much as they inspired. Logan and his wife had a young son and, like the Boones, surrounded themselves with extended family. Their fort, near an area originally staked out by John Floyd known under the name St. Asaph, was completed shortly after Jemima Boone's kidnapping, presenting an alternative to Boonesboro. Like Boonesboro, the settlement boasted a series of cabins, blockhouses, and gates in a rectangular layout. One improvement came in its access to water, a problem for Boonesboro that had become a key factor during the "big siege." As Logan and his fellow settlers constructed their fort, they created a tunnel to a spring that could be safely accessed during battles to retrieve fresh water. A gristmill was built to allow residents to make bread, another resource always in short supply at Boonesboro. For many, the identity of Logan's Fort continued to be defined in relation to Boonesboro. "The people in this fort," wrote one traveler of Logan's Fort, "lived here much better than at [Boonesboro] fort."

Hearing that Boonesboro was wiped out was a personal blow to many at Logan's Fort—they had sent fifteen of their own men to Boonesboro after Boone and Hancock had returned from captivity. Patton's news meant those fifteen friends and relatives were dead, causing "great distress" among those left behind at Logan's. The story of Boonesboro's fall was also foreboding to Logan and the other inhabitants. They had "little doubt" the Indian army would come for Logan's Fort next, putting them in what they felt to be a "great predicament." At present, the fort had only 24 men, far fewer than had tried and failed to defend Boonesboro. "If the Indians took Boonesboro with 75 men," the settlers feared, "what will become of us with only 24?" The absence of Butler and Montgomery, two skilled soldiers who had come and gone, further depleted their chances. The fort inventoried their total number of guns, which added up to 21. They would have to rest their hopes on the fort's superior design. Logan gave orders to lock down the garrison. The residents collected corn and other crops and filled their water vessels, "as industrious as I ever saw people in my life," according to one settler who helped prepare the fort for their desperate last stand.

Logan gathered a squad of men to venture out and bring cattle from near the river back to the fort. As the group started to leave, Logan rushed after them. "Stop!" he called out, according to one of the men who had prepared to go. "I am afraid for you to go. I will go by my self. Go back in the fort. I will hunt the cattle and Indians alone."

An air of martyrdom attached to Logan on his ride. He mounted a white horse and traveled through the tall cane to conceal himself from Indians. As courageous and imposing a leader as he was, he lacked the ability to blend into the setting that came naturally to Boone. Shortly after he left the fort, Logan was spotted. As many as ten braves appeared around the narrow path and fired at him.

Several bullets struck him, shattering his arm. He rode as fast as he could back toward the fort. His disabled arm repeatedly got caught in the cane, so he had to put his thumb between his teeth to keep the arm raised.

By the time Logan reached the fort, his white horse was drenched in his blood. The fort's leader was brought inside to a man named Benjamin Pettit, considered the settlement's surgeon because he had learned healing skills from the Cherokee tribe, with whom he had been a trader. Pettit used the bark of slippery elm to try to treat Logan's wounds. Indian methods of medicine—as well as agricultural techniques and warcraft—were appreciated as more advanced by many settlers on the frontier.

Logan, whose injuries proved serious, was confined to a room. The fort now had lost its commander at a critical time. From his bedside, Logan would call in his men and encourage them. "It is certain," Logan said to one of his officers, "if the Indians take the fort they will kill me and all the sick and wounded and perhaps won't spare any." Logan urged the residents that they would have to hope for reinforcements and in the meantime "to fight until the last man was killed and try to kill as many of them as possible."

The residents were in a state of excruciating uncertainty as they waited to share in Boonesboro's fate. "They was a courageous people," reflected Daniel Trabue, the fort's young quartermaster sergeant, "but yet I will say they all looked very wild. You might frequently see the woman [*sic*] a walking around the fort looking and peeping about, seeming that they did not know what they was about, but would try to encourage one another and hope for the best." They calculated how long it would take before the victorious Indian troops would arrive from Boonesboro. They saw braves in every shadow as they expected the attack to commence. "About half the men stood all night at their posts," wrote Trabue, "and so would relieve on[e] another."

After the agonizing wait, it came almost as a relief when the oncoming troops were announced by Logan's sentinels the next morning as coming from the direction of Boonesboro. "Yes, yes, the Indians is a-coming" was called out. The invaders were three hundred yards away and closing in. The men took positions in the bastions, guns aimed, praying for a miracle. Several of their wives would be ready to take up arms when, as they all expected, the men began to fall to the onslaught. "Damn you! Come on!" cried out the men, unable to stand the suspense. The riflemen called out to each other to confirm they had clear shots. "Look sharp!" the quartermaster sergeant cried out. All the women of the fort had run to look out through portholes.

It was the women who first realized what was happening. "It is our boys," they said. The soldiers who were walking single file toward them were not Indians at all. They were the settlers previously sent to Boonesboro and assumed dead. With a mixture of laughing and crying, the men and women in Logan's Fort couldn't believe their eyes as "their brother, husband, or relation" gradually came closer. "Are you alive? Are you all here?" Some headed right for the bedridden Logan, who smiled for the first time since before he'd been shot.

Another startling realization dawned on them: Boonesboro, the anchor of the frontier, had never been taken after all.

SIMON BUTLER AND Alexander Montgomery came to that same shocking and energizing revelation on the morning they reached Boonesboro. They had expected to find a gruesome scene. Instead, friends greeted them. No one who had been in Boonesboro was surprised to hear that William Patton had insisted the fort had been taken. The final night of the siege had seemed apocalyptic, filled with flashes of fire and screams. But the chaos prevented both sides from having a clear view of the battle, and the shouts of settlers Patton had heard were those of defiance, not defeat. The eerie illumination of the Indians' gunfire and torches actually helped the settlers quickly locate their weapons and choose defensive positions.

How a couple dozen settlers ultimately withstood this final barrage of an army of hundreds remains unclear. In line with national teleological rhetoric that the creation of America was sanctioned from on high, Daniel Boone and other settlers on the ground voiced a belief that divine intervention delivered them from death. As with the other nine days of warfare, the Indian troops did not end up penetrating beyond the gates of the fort that final night. By sunrise, only a few could be seen outside the fort. The Indians and their allies were gone. From the perspective of the settlers, the invading force seemed to have vanished into the air. Traces of blood were found outside, but no bodies. The settlers, who were often as curious as they were hostile toward Indian culture, speculated that the Indians had carried off their dead according to custom, possibly placing some bodies in the river and in caves. Boone estimated Indian casualties at thirty-seven, with exaggeration-prone Billy Smith giving a count of enemy deaths of two hundred. What was clear was that by successfully defending Boonesboro, the British plan to crush the western edges of America had been beaten back.

Indications suggest that, more than any single factor, the torrential rain foiled the primary tactics of the invasion: setting the fort on fire and tunneling into the garrison. The wet wood of the fort weakened flames, and the downpours had caused the tunnels to collapse. One account suggests Blackfish also pulled back in order to help tribal communities in danger elsewhere. Two Indian messengers on horseback reportedly had galloped into Blackfish's encampment outside the fort and brought news that settlers targeted several Indian towns, which required their troops to return.

Settlers almost instantly turned their stand at Boonesboro into legend: forty soldiers against four hundred. Boonesboro may have been founded "before the very existence of the Americans as States," as a spokesperson later recalled, but now it had become a test case for the United States. Outlawed by the British powers and even having its legal title challenged by the new government, the rebellious settlement had refused to fold, equating the settlers' "defending their property at a vast expense, trouble and danger" with vested rights in the land, a kind of frontier version of the Declaration of Independence. The manner by which Boonesboro settlers pushed against external controls reflected the new nation's larger search for freedom. Independence was a complex political process, but freedom was visceral, a state of mind. Moral costs included consistent reliance on slave labor and trampling the tribes' long-standing access to Kentucky's natural resources.

Though history of the era sometimes treats the tribes as puppets of the British, Blackfish's autonomous military and political goals profoundly affected what happened in September 1778 at Boonesboro. The British, helmed in regional strategy by Henry Hamilton, wanted the American population of the frontier eradicated or imprisoned. Though Blackfish did not shy away from violence, his paramount goal was different. He wanted to move the settlers out of Boonesboro, not to kill them. Questions have been raised about the Indians' choice not to construct ladders to enter the fort—indeed, the immobilized Squire Boone waited with his ax in his cabin, fully expecting the Indian troops to scale the walls. The Indians' failure to do this could have been a tactical oversight, as has been assumed, or a conscious decision. It should not be discounted that even if Hamilton indeed had ordered a "massacre" in absence of surrender, as Hamilton's letter to Boone apparently indicated, Blackfish may have resisted those orders. Simon Butler had explained, "I would not have hurt them for the world," when asked about the Indian children he saw outside Paint Creek. We do not possess such glosses from Blackfish on his decisions at Boonesboro, but a reluctance to hurt women and children may have been just as important to him as to Butler, not to mention Blackfish's strong paternal feelings toward Boone. That the settlers' antagonists nurtured a degree of sympathy for them—and perhaps admiration for the fortitude shown at Boonesboro—is further suggested by the fact that two leaders present, Charles Beaubien and Chippewa leader Blackbird, soon after the siege appeared to turn against Hamilton in siding with or assisting Americans.

Only an hour after the last Indian troops disappeared from the area of the fort, settlers ventured out to take cabbage from the garden for the "half starved" cattle. Old Spot, the injured cow, healed up, remaining a beloved part of Squire's family for years to come. Gunshot wounds were treated. Both Boone brothers' injuries healed over time. The bullet that struck Jemima lodged in her petticoat, making it easy to remove. Wearing the restrictive undergarments of a frontier woman may have saved her life.

Jemima would always remember how happy she was finally stepping outside, where she felt "she could be free." She relished how she could go into the garden to explore outside the fort again and would "not have to be shut up in the garrison." With relative tranquility came time for her to reflect on her own journey. In the last two and a half years, Jemima had transformed in the eyes of the community from a child into a leader, from a daughter to a woman starting her own family amid dire circumstances, from a kidnap survivor to a combatant. "It was joyful times," she said when she came out the other side.

The Boones could have been tempted to bask in the glory of such a victory against all odds. Then word came that indicated Richard Callaway was not content challenging Boone for leadership of their settlement or indirectly undermining his rival. Callaway traveled to Logan's Fort to execute his next move. He was charging Boone with treason.

AFTERSHOCKS

THE BOONES WERE IN THE fight of their lives, and this time not because the British bankrolled a siege or tribal warriors set fire to walls. Richard Callaway accused Boone of conspiring with Blackfish to capture the settlers and aiding the Indian troops and the British powers against Boonesboro. Once again, Boone allies and supporters were neutralized at a time he needed them most. Simon Butler and Alexander Montgomery, who had returned to Boonesboro after the siege, were called away on another military mission for George Rogers Clark; William Bailey Smith reportedly was struck with a fever and confined to a cabin after the siege ended; Rebecca Boone and the rest of their family were still in North Carolina.

The injured Benjamin Logan now qualified as the highest-ranking military officer in Kentucky, which meant he would preside over a court-martial, the format for military trials that colonists had brought over from England. Courts-martial had begun to be used to target anyone in the Continental Army and its affiliated militias with allegiance—perceived or actual—to the British cause.

On the way to Logan's Fort, thick woods gave way to a strong-flowing stream, which pushed the gristmill. The fort's primary structures having been completed only a year before, there had been less time than in Boonesboro for wear and tear. Boone would have no chance to savor the view or the amenities, including relatively plentiful provisions. Summoned to face charges so soon after the British-backed tribal army fled Boonesboro, Boone came out of the ashes to enter a fire. Jemima and Squire were among the last people at Boonesboro whom he could trust unequivocally, and he had to scramble to prepare his legal defense, far out of his comfort zones of the wilderness and battlefields.

Logan's Fort became a makeshift courthouse, possibly Kentucky's first. Benjamin Logan made an ideal ally for Callaway. Apparently already convinced that Boone had solicited the Indian invasion, Logan blamed him for the gunshot wounds he'd received while on horseback trying to prepare his own fort to withstand an expected attack by the same Indians who had targeted Boonesboro. Like Callaway, Logan had lived in Boone's shadow for a long time. Despite his overall acclaim as a frontiersman and founder of Kentucky, Boone could not expect goodwill from those in charge of the court; the Boones could not be faulted for having a feeling that they were walking into a trap.

A decade before Kentucky's first newspaper, word of the trial spread fast. Settlers crowded into Logan's settlement to witness the proceeding. Many sympathized with Boone, but that did not change the gravity of a wartime court-martial, especially one engineered by formidable and well-respected adversaries. Guidelines for military justice had been formalized by the Continental Congress in 1775 and then refined the following year. British rules informed the basic tenets. Punishments for convictions ranged from thirty lashes and running the gauntlet to firing squads and hanging. Two of the Articles of War updated on September 20, 1776, laid the groundwork that would have supported Callaway's charges:

> *If any commander of any garrison, fortress, or post, shall be compelled by the officers or soldiers under his command, to give up to the enemy, or to abandon it, the commissioned officers, non-commissioned officers, or soldiers, who shall be convicted of having so offended, shall suffer death, or such other punishment as shall be inflicted upon them by the sentence of a court-martial.*

> *Whosoever shall be convicted of holding correspondence with, or giving intelligence to the enemy, either directly or indirectly, shall suffer death, or such other punishment as by a court-martial shall be indicted.*

Charges less serious than the ones against Boone had been punished by death over the course of the war. Tribal warriors had nearly struck Boone down hundreds of times, including at close range during the rescue of Jemima and at the siege at the fort. But the enemy with the most power against him proved to be the enemy within. Even if he avoided a death sentence, Boone faced prospects of being stripped of rank and status, barred from future military service, and branded a disgrace. If convicted, he faced oblivion, one way or the other.

LOGAN HAD TO preside over the court proceeding from his bed. The members of the court-martial panel—not named in the surviving records, but in all likelihood men who knew Boone personally—would decide the verdict. As Boone was arraigned, official charges were given. The accusation of collusion with the enemy involved two key points. First, that Boone conspired with the Shawnee in their capture of the saltmakers at Blue Licks and secretly became allies with the tribal powers to the detriment of the other captives; second, that he conspired with the British in the tribal attack on Boonesboro, intentionally weakening the defenses and leaving the residents vulnerable.

"Boone was in favor of the British government," the enraged Callaway said of his longtime colleague, and "all his conduct proved it."

For Jemima, the courtroom drama was personal, not only because it was her father accused. Though Callaway had been stockpiling reasons for resenting Boone, including the fact that his nephews taken at Blue Licks remained prisoners, there was no mystery about the origins of Callaway's bitterness. The turning point went back to the kidnapping of Jemima and the Callaway girls. Callaway could never forgive Boone for taking charge of the rescue and upstaging him by saving his daughters, depriving Callaway of a moment of familial triumph that could never be equaled, in an era that elevated heroic acts above almost all else. Callaway even spread a fabricated version of the events in which Boone did not rescue the girls. In essence, the entire series of events in the two and a half years since that moment Jemima was taken was now at issue and on trial. No attempts at persuasion by Jemima or Flanders dissuaded Richard Callaway from trying to take down Boone once and for all. Nor could Callaway succeed in displacing the loyalty toward Boone shown by Jemima and her husband, his own nephew. Moreover, even as the fissure within the Callaway family deepened, neither Betsy nor Fanny Callaway took their father's side against him.

With all the dangers that came with conviction, defendants in those early days of courts-martial often brought up technical objections to the proceedings or attempted to stall. But Boone made clear he would fight head-on with two words: *Not guilty*.

AS HIS FIRST charge against Boone, Callaway recounted his version of the capture of the saltmakers at the Lower Blue Licks. Boone—so Callaway explained to the court—was ten miles from the saltmakers when the Shawnee found him. "They were not going towards these men," Callaway insisted. Boone himself told the Indian chiefs about the saltmakers and volunteered to bring the Indians to them. Callaway presumed to quote Boone's speech to the saltmakers at the Licks: "'You are surrounded with Indians and I have agreed with these Indians that you are to be used well; and you are to be prisoners of war and will be given up to the British officers at Detroit, where you will be treated well.' And these men against their consent had to go with the Indians to Detroit."

Depicting Boone's captivity as part of the larger conspiracy, Callaway alleged that Boone carried over his plot when he arrived at Fort Detroit as Blackfish's prisoner. Here, Callaway told the court-martial panel, Boone made a deal with Henry Hamilton to "give up all the people at Boonesboro" to the British. Callaway's details clearly drew from the account of William Hancock and possibly that of Andrew Johnson, and some surmise Hancock and Johnson actually testified during the court-martial. Hancock, as recalled by another settler, would tell others, "Daniel Boone was at Detroit and had agreed with the British officers that he would come with the Indians, and that the fort should be given up, and that the people should be taken to Detroit and live under the jurisdiction of his gracious Majesty King George III." Though surviving materials do not reveal all of the proceedings, courts-martial were a legal venue where women's testimony was regularly heard, since cases often involved family members as witnesses. Jemima, her father's greatest advocate, would have been poised to add her voice to the defense to attest to his unwavering loyalty to the settlement.

Callaway also introduced the fact that Boone led the ill-fated mission of Boonesboro troops to attack the Indian town at Paint Creek, a decision Callaway had vehemently opposed. This was the strongest part of his case against Boone. Callaway made clear the operation had been irresponsible, tantamount to abandoning the fort, and nearly spelled disaster. "Our men hurried back with all their might," Callaway said, "and they only got to the fort a few hours before the Indian army got there." Finally, Callaway described how Boone was willing to try to make peace with the Indian leaders "out of sight" of the fort, recalling the argument over where the treaty discussions would occur during the siege. Among Callaway partisans, the fact that Boone seemed to go out of the fort at Blackfish's beck and call was suspicious. For skeptics of Boone's good faith, the private conversation between Boone and his Indian father outside the fort—which nobody else could hear—could have been devious. With this line of argument, Boone's courtroom opponents sought a general condemnation of attempts to find common ground with Indians. The more specific bottom line was clear: "Boone was willing and wished to surrender," and if not for Richard Callaway himself, the fort would have been lost.

Rather than mounting a defense using witness testimony, Boone, in typical fashion, took on the allegations directly. He defended himself by telling the court that when it came to countering the British-Indian alliance, "[I] thought I would use stratagem," a jab at Callaway's black-and-white approach to battles (and to life) that went back to Callaway's desire to rush in against the captors of their daughters during their kidnapping crisis. Considering that Boone, Jemima, and Squire all had been shot in the siege, the allegation that

Boone had invited the Indian incursion stood out as particularly insulting and illogical.

As for the events at the Lower Blue Licks, Boone explained that he felt he had no choice but to broker the surrender of the saltmakers. The Indians had indicated they had their sights set on Boonesboro, and Boone had to find a way to distract them. With Boone and the other saltmakers away from the fort, "the Indians would take it easy." By diverting Blackfish, Boone tried to give the settlers time to strengthen their defenses and bring in more soldiers. When Boone met with Henry Hamilton at Fort Detroit, he led Hamilton to believe that he would cooperate with the British, again as a means of blunting them. If the British thought they didn't need to harness military might against Boonesboro, they would conserve resources. Boone also tried to convince Hamilton that the fort was weak, which would lessen the urgency to mount an attack, and Hamilton's letters confirm that Boone successfully duped him. Boone explained to the court that he "told them all these tales to fool them."

When the court-martial panel announced their decision, it was not only decisive; it was resounding. The panel acquitted Boone and simultaneously promoted him from his rank of captain to major. The message was clear, directed as much against the accusers as in favor of the accused. Callaway and Logan stewed over the defeat—one understated observer wrote that they were "not pleased about it." Though a burden had been lifted from the Boones, something had been robbed from life in Boonesboro for its namesake family. It could never be the same. Soon after, Daniel and Jemima left it behind and reunited with Rebecca and the rest of the family in North Carolina.

EVEN AS THE court vindicated Boone, most of the saltmakers remained in captivity, some in grim circumstances. Several tried to escape over the next months and years, but most failed.

The divergent experiences of Jemima's brothers-in-law Cajah and James Callaway represented the range of outcomes for those salt-makers. Cajah Callaway, seventeen years old when adopted by the Shawnee, became well integrated into the Indian community. He learned the language and came to serve as an interpreter. The strapping young man—six two and more than two hundred pounds according to a family member—also became a warrior fighting alongside Shawnee braves, labeled by one witness from an American regiment "the worst savage amongst them!"

In contrast, the Shawnee apparently refused to bring James Calla-way into a tribal town because his behavior had been so difficult to control on the march from the Lower Blue Licks. Sold to Henry Hamilton at Fort Detroit, James refused to be a laborer. As a result, he remained imprisoned. James tried multiple times to escape. Then, as Hamilton prepared to leave on a military campaign, he worried what would happen if James tried again. Hamilton knew that if the young man managed to get free, he could pass along damaging intelligence about Fort Detroit. Hamilton ordered James taken away from the region entirely. He was transported under lock and key on a series of ships to Montréal and then Québec, where he remained imprisoned for years.

While Hamilton was away on a series of military maneuvers, Fort Detroit added to its ledger another prisoner connected to Boones-boro: Simon Butler. After Butler and Alexander Montgomery had discovered to their astonishment that Boonesboro had withstood the "big siege," the duo set off almost immediately on what Butler called a mission of "discovery"—that is, espionage—to the Shaw-nee town of Chillicothe on behalf of George Rogers Clark. While exploring on his own, Butler was surrounded by armed Shawnee warriors. Montgomery approached, firing at the Indians to try to free Butler, but the braves pursued Montgomery, shooting and killing him. Taken by the Shawnee, Butler may have been viewed as a replacement for their escaped prisoner Daniel Boone. An unforgiving brave named Bonah took charge of Butler, framing Butler's fate as punishment for ruining the tribe's way of life, focused on lost hunting grounds and resources: "Indians," Bonah said, "have got no cattle about their doors like white people—the buffalo are our cattle, but you come here and kill them; you have no business to kill Indians' cattle." Blackfish, who was returning from the Boonesboro siege, questioned Butler. Interestingly, Blackfish made an effort to tie Butler's presence to Boone, asking whether Boone had directed Butler to carry out his latest mission. As had happened when Boone had been a prisoner, a tribal council met to decide on Butler's fate, likely around the very same time as Boone underwent his court-martial. With Butler's reputation for ferocity in battles against Indians, and the tribe's lingering regret for losing Boone, the result may have been inevitable: Simon Butler was sentenced to death.

After a failed escape attempt and increasingly violent treatment by his captors, Butler had lost hope until he encountered Simon Girty, with whom he had crossed paths years before during Lord Dunmore's War. Girty, the Indian captive–turned–interpreter, threw his arms around Butler in an embrace, expressing regret for the deterioration of relations among the tribes and the Americans hastened by the Revolutionary War. Girty's brothers had voted for clemency toward Boone at the Lower Blue Licks, and Girty now expressed his willingness to help his "ancient comrade" Butler. But Girty's attempts ultimately only stalled the tribe's decision to carry out a death sentence. As braves prepared to burn Butler at the stake, a clear sky opened up—according to dramatized accounts that became part of family lore—pouring rain down, extinguishing the fire, and providing a reason to believe in divine intervention.

Mingo chief Logan (no connection to Benjamin Logan of Logan's Fort), whose family had been slaughtered by Daniel Greathouse years earlier in the lead-up to Lord Dunmore's War, had come upon Butler and his captors. This well-respected tribal leader, who had a reputation for compassion for enemies even in the heat of wartime, rushed out a message to Fort Detroit, which dispatched a trusted operative, Pierre Drouillard, who had been part of the leadership at the siege against Boonesboro. Arriving in the Shawnee town, Drouillard made it clear to the tribe that the British needed to extract intelligence from Butler. He negotiated with tribal leaders to allow him to take Butler into his custody and bring the prisoner to Fort Detroit, overriding—or at least staving off—his execution.

Rather than being placed in the prison cell that until recently had held James Callaway, Butler was given liberty in and around the fort with boundaries he could not cross. Among the other Americans held at Fort Detroit, Butler bonded with two of the former saltmakers who had been captured with Boone, Jesse Copher and Nathaniel Bullock. As Butler healed from a variety of injuries, including a shattered collarbone and a broken arm, he began to plan an escape.

While Butler was in Fort Detroit, Henry Hamilton led a British expedition to retake Fort Vincennes (also known as Fort Sackville)—a stronghold in present-day Indiana that Butler recently had helped George Rogers Clark secure. Hamilton's force succeeded in taking back the fort, but after a series of miscalculations by the British, Clark reseized it for America. Now Hamilton became a prisoner of the forces he had fought so long to put down. Clark made his personal animosity to the British officer clear, emphasizing that

Hamilton's history of deploying tribes against Americans justified harsh treatment. On April 22, 1779, as Hamilton and his fellow prisoners were transported by troops through Kentucky toward Virginia, they were handed off to Richard Callaway, who was tasked with their oversight.

Seven months removed from his debacle of a court-martial against Boone, Callaway had another chance to prove his leadership in front of a crowd. Hamilton, himself a rather showy leader, was taken aback by Callaway's style as he "made a great display of military abilities" and talked of grand maneuvers. When it rained, Callaway grew comically frustrated. Callaway's orders seemed to exhaust his own troops. Hamilton, coming full circle to his earliest engagements with the frontier, would sit and sketch the scenery as his place in the world crumbled.

That June, Hamilton, in shackles, entered a prison cell in Williamsburg, even as Simon Butler escaped his loosely monitored captivity at Fort Detroit. Butler brought with him the two saltmakers, Bullock and Copher. Leaving the immediate perimeter of the British-controlled area presented few challenges, but a thirty-day journey through isolated and unforgiving woods took a toll. Copher wanted to surrender himself to the first Indian they came across. Butler, according to later accounts by his son, promised Copher he "would not hesitate to shoot him first" if he tried to surrender. The point became moot, as Butler guided them to safety.

But Butler's true liberation came soon after. Before 1779 was over, Butler ran across someone from his home region of Virginia, and in the course of an exchange of news and information, Butler learned that William Leachman—Butler's onetime romantic rival whom he had believed for so many years he had killed in a fight—was alive and well. Butler's entire reason for flight, his haunting drive to get away from home that had led him into Kentucky and Boonesboro and into so many death-defying military missions, had rested on a case of mistaken information. (More dramatic versions of Butler's realization suggested that Copher, a Virginian, told Butler all this during their arduous flight from Fort Detroit, or that Butler became superstitious that he was about to be caught for Leachman's murder and went to Virginia to surrender himself.) As it turned out, after Butler had fled following his fight with Leachman in the woods, Leachman actually had regained consciousness and found help. Ironically, when Butler disappeared, his own family believed for years that Leachman had murdered Butler and hidden the body. With his shocking new intelligence, Simon Butler became Simon Kenton again, adding a dramatic story of redemption to frontier lore.

Henry Hamilton found himself in what he called a "dungeon" in Williamsburg. He estimated his fetters weighed eighteen pounds and lamented the tiny cell he shared with other prisoners as an affront to his high rank and stature. Under these conditions, Hamilton received word of an unexpected party who arrived in Williamsburg on his behalf: Daniel Boone, Hamilton's former adversary and prisoner. According to Hamilton, Boone was there "to remonstrate against the injustice and inhumanity [to] the Governor and Council of Virginia." The fallen governor of Fort Detroit was touched by Boone's generosity. In sharp contrast to Richard Callaway, Boone sought to cultivate charity and empathy for former enemies.

After spending part of 1779 in Virginia as a legislator, Richard Callaway returned to Kentucky, where he planned to start a Kentucky River ferry service to Boonesboro. On March 8, 1780, Callaway oversaw the construction of the ferry with Pemberton Rollins, the Boonesboro resident who had helped John Holder reach the fort in the hours before the big siege (and who had then been shot during the siege itself). Rollins was by this point engaged to one of Callaway's younger daughters. Callaway watched as enslaved men labored on the project. Then, from across the river, shots rang out. A group of Indian warriors shot at Callaway and Rollins, killing them both. A story passed down in the Callaway family claimed Callaway's enslaved men risked their lives to retrieve his body. However, those details strike an implausible chord. In a more reliable version, Callaway's body was recovered only later, "the worst barbecued man I ever saw," according to a witness, who found that the attackers had "cut his head bones up. They stripped him stark naked, and rolled him in a mud-hole . . . there was not a bone as big as your hand." If the killing seemed more personal than most, there may have been a reason. Cajah Callaway, so deeply integrated into his tribal community by this point, was said to be one of the warriors who maimed and killed his uncle. According to these reports, the manner of death was linked to Richard Callaway beating Cajah in Boonesboro over a trivial infraction shortly before the saltmakers had been taken. "He had threatened revenge on his uncle," some of the other captive saltmakers had recalled.

In a chilling moment, another former saltmaker who became part of the Shawnee community recognized the scalp brought back by Shawnee warriors as belonging to Callaway by its telltale salt-and-pepper hair.

Two years later, Richard Callaway's seven-year-old son, Jack, was taken by a Shawnee warrior, and when he returned to Boonesboro years later, other residents observed he had forgotten his name and acted as "quite an Indian." Multiple members of the family of the "veteran Indian fighter" had taken on Indian identities.

AFTER THE SIEGE at Boonesboro, Blackfish returned to Chillicothe to face ever intensifying pressures on his leadership as the Revolutionary War stretched into its fourth year. The British pushed the Shawnee to increase strikes against American forces, while the Americans redoubled efforts to weaken the Shawnee's alliance with the British. The capture of Henry Hamilton left support for the Shawnee from Fort Detroit in shambles. American authorities could pivot into diplomacy to try to bring tribes to their cause, or they could strike against the Shawnee with military power. Emboldened, they chose the latter. The American military set its sights on Chillicothe, one of the tribe's key towns. Led by several Kentucky settlers, including Benjamin Logan and John Holder, nearly three hundred American troops invaded. The timing proved fateful. Most of the braves were away in other military engagements, so Blackfish had to mount a defense with a handful of warriors. The town's structures and crops were burned, but the Indians managed to save their all-important council house. Blackfish was shot in the leg. He tried to negotiate terms to be brought to American doctors but failed. Within two months, he died of his wound.

Even tribal leaders who had risked their lives to help Americans found themselves in harm's way from scorched-earth political and military policies. Benjamin Logan captured Nonhelema, sister of the murdered Shawnee chief Cornstalk, during a raid. She was held prisoner despite the many years of documented help she had provided to Americans as informant and interpreter. Daniel Boone successfully negotiated her release, once again clashing with Logan, onetime overseer of his court-martial. However, that didn't mean she had received the gratitude of a nation that she deserved. She later petitioned for her long service to America to be compensated with land, to which she hoped to bring her relatives, including several settlers who had been adopted into the tribe—reminiscent of Blackfish's earlier vision of a community of mixed heritage. Her request was refused. Faring even worse was White Eyes, the Delaware chief bullied out of Fort Detroit by Hamilton for supporting

Americans. Months after the siege of Boonesboro, White Eyes, "at the moment of his greatest exertions to serve the United States" (in the words of an American officer), was murdered under unknown circumstances. The American government attributed the killing to smallpox. His death echoed the senseless killing of Cornstalk exactly when they needed the Shawnee's friendship the most. Meanwhile, Captain Matthew Arbuckle, who had tried but failed to stop Cornstalk's murder, stepped back from his military role and sought funding to improve safe travels through the frontier. In June 1781, he was crushed and killed by a tree during a fierce storm.

Hanging Maw, who carried out the kidnapping of Jemima Boone, continued to hold an elevated status among the Cherokee in opposition to the militant Dragging Canoe. Years later, as Hanging Maw traveled to a peace conference, a rogue detachment of American soldiers attacked his party and killed his wife. The ringleader of the massacre, an officer named John Beard, was tried by an American court but not convicted. In contrast, when a Cherokee killed an American farmer in Tennessee the following year, Hanging Maw spearheaded a tribal search party that caught the renegade and turned him over to the Americans. He was executed, but the murderer of Hanging Maw's wife was never held accountable.

THEODORE ROOSEVELT LATER posited that if the siege on Boonesboro in the fall of 1778 had succeeded, the small population of settlers in Kentucky would have been swept out. This statement ought to be extended. The girls' kidnapping, the retaliatory actions that pulled Boone into tribal life, and the battle over Boonesboro together constituted a turning point in a variety of ways.

Dragging Canoe had triggered a kidnapping to leverage settlers out of Kentucky, and Henry Hamilton believed he could enhance conflicts between settlers and tribes, harden the enmity between them, and thus entrench Britain's position in the Revolutionary War. Both instigators underestimated the role of personal loyalties and emotional complexities that transcended military tactics. Hanging Maw ultimately sought to protect Jemima, and Daniel Boone and Blackfish felt the pull of family ties across cultural boundaries—a link that ironically began with the death of Blackfish's son in the rescue of Jemima. That web of relationships defused Hamilton's push to destroy Boonesboro. Meanwhile, the bond of loyalty between Jemima and her father came through the other side of the kidnapping saga intact and solidified, contributing not only to the defense of Boonesboro, but also to the defense of Boone against personal vendettas. The climactic military victory at Boonesboro allowed the Kentucky settlements to survive; the Boones' victory in the closely watched court-martial provided reason to believe Kentucky could move beyond settlers' survival and stabilize into an era of laws.

The 1778 siege, in retrospect, was the last realistic chance to dislodge the settlers from Kentucky. Had Hamilton captured Boonesboro—had Blackfish, whom he tried to treat as a puppet, massacred its inhabitants as he could have—Hamilton would have crippled a base of operations on the frontier and initiated his own. The loss by Hamilton forced him into other ill-conceived escapades, resulting in short order in his capture. With Hamilton out of power, the frontier raids by Indian troops diminished (though scattered violence continued in waves). Farmland was expanded and cultivated; a school was begun at Boonesboro. Squire Boone, his gunshot wound healed, left Boonesboro and established his own "station," a small-scale fort. Transport routes were set up, and industry gradually expanded. In addition to Richard Callaway's involvement in a ferry line, former Boonesboro resident William Bailey Smith swapped military missions for the chance to launch a shipping service on the Kentucky River. John Floyd, one of the rescuers during the kidnapping, returned to Kentucky and became a judge, but on his first day after court, he was struck by a bullet from an Indian soldier, dying of his injury soon after.

The future of Kentucky remained clouded, but what had been avoided was clearer. Had Boonesboro collapsed in the period after the three girls vanished on the Kentucky River, the frontier's border would have receded east. Hamilton would have been emboldened.

What never would have happened was restoration of tribal rights to Kentucky. No matter which side tribes aligned themselves with (or against) during the Revolutionary War, British or American, Indian interests were left behind. Blackfish proposed a true revolution—a conceptual one—building on the legacy of Cornstalk, to turn the frontier into an integrated, shared space. Evidence suggests elements of this appealed to Boone, too. Instead, the Kentucky settlements became a bulwark against a British western front in the war and a testing ground of an American doctrine of expansion by force, framed as divine entitlement that justified warfare in the pursuit of land, which in turn involved relying ever more on enslaved labor.

The Boones continued to move around, including for stretches of years back in Kentucky, although for the most part away from Boonesboro, with its increasingly unfamiliar faces and its growing enterprises. Relatives described Boone as too unselfish to focus on commerce, while others viewed him as a poor businessman. "I've opened the way for others to make fortunes," Boone would say, indirectly acknowledging both of these interpretations and evoking earlier speculators such as George Washington and Patrick Henry, "but a fortune for myself was not what I was after." The family's economic profile grew more conventional over the decades, and more ethically compromised: tax records indicate that the Boones eventually claimed ownership of slaves.

Saving Boonesboro and preserving the frontier—as Daniel and Jemima Boone had been instrumental in doing—allowed the United States of America to keep pushing westward, ultimately to the Pacific Ocean, monetizing land to pay war debts and fund economic development, with progressively catastrophic consequences for American Indian tribes. Boone, as characterized by family tradition, "had no vague idea of empire, or rule, or profit." Writers who introduced Boone into the public consciousness identified his removal from concerns of capitalism and commerce as key to his contentment and greatness. In his epic poem *Don Juan*, Lord Byron remarks that among the luckiest of great men:

> *The General Boon, back-woodsman of Kentucky,*
> *Was happiest amongst mortals anywhere;*
> *For killing nothing but a bear or buck, he*
> *Enjoy'd the lonely, vigorous, harmless days*
> *Of his old age in wilds of deepest maze.*

Boone indeed treasured solitude, one reason why, after he had helped establish a community, he felt compelled to move along. He did enjoy occasionally running across reminders of those formative years in Boonesboro—Indians and settlers alike. His adoptive Shawnee sister remembered him with great affection and eagerly greeted members of the Boone family passing through her village. After relocating to Missouri, Boone was visited by William Hancock, the saltmaker who escaped from Captain Will, and whose anger toward Boone had helped fuel Richard Callaway in his court-martial. Together they rehashed the capture of the saltmakers, Hancock complaining about what he viewed as Boone forcing their surrender. "They would all have been killed," Boone insisted. "The Indians were four to [our] one and they came in the midst of winter." Finally, after reliving the events, Hancock admitted that Boone "really acted wisely."

Nineteen years after the kidnapping of Jemima, Boone visited the site of the rescue and walked to the very spot where the party rested for the night. But Kentucky, a few years into its official statehood, was no longer a place of Boone's dreams. The cutthroat race for land and money, the suspicions by narrow-minded people of genuine bonds formed with Indians, the quick slide into violence by so many—including on occasion by him and those he led—had soured him. Trails of discovery left trails of blood. When invited to return to Kentucky some years after he left, Boone said he had "the intention of never stepping his feet upon Kentucky soil again, and if he was compelled to lose his head on the block, or revisit Kentucky, he would not hesitate to choose the former." Squire Boone followed his brother to Missouri but may have later wished he had adopted his brother's attitude before returning to Kentucky, where he ended up imprisoned for debt; when released, Squire settled in Indiana, where he christened his home Traveler's Rest. The Boones' experiences as "travelers" into Kentucky had influenced the path of the nation, but they had also pushed the family away almost completely in the post–Revolutionary War era.

Familiar faces would visit Boone when passing through Missouri. Michael Stoner, partner in so many early journeys into Kentucky, called on Boone in the early 1800s. "I haven't seen Boone so long," Stoner reportedly said. "I would rather see him than any brother I had." The two men, Stoner in his sixties and Boone in his seventies, planned a long hunting trip up the Missouri River, though Stoner ended up going alone, possibly due to an illness holding Boone back. Simon Kenton, who had been known for so long as Simon Butler, also visited the Boone home in Missouri in the early 1800s. Rebecca Boone, then in her sixties, was inside their house that evening, while Daniel was outside chopping wood or skinning a buck. Kenton inquired if they had an extra bed for a traveler, which Rebecca said they did not.

"I think you would, if you knew who I am," the newcomer said. She studied him.

"Would you know Simon Butler?" he asked.

"Yes," replied Rebecca, "but you are not him."

Kenton smiled, showing his facial features more clearly in the dim cabin. "Yes, I am!" he said. Rebecca embraced him, and Boone ran inside. Kenton had brought along one of his sons, John. In the course of his travels, Kenton had become friends with Bonah, his former Indian captor. Kenton had Indian families living on his land, and when some neighbors had threatened to kill them, he took down his gun and promised that he would have to be killed first and he would take as many assailants with him as possible. Kenton and the Boones reminisced all night about the Boonesboro days and all their "ancient companions."

Boone came across as a stoic man in these later years. One young traveler passing through the area recorded his impression that Boone's poise still seemed to project an optical illusion of great height: "Seeing a tall slender old gentleman sitting in the shade of the house, I inquired if that was Colonel Boone. He answered 'Yes, what is left of him.'" Sometimes, Boone's reticence thawed. When a snake bit a young relative, he rushed to help. The boy later remembered that Boone, as he tended to the wound, distracted him with stories. "This reminds [me] of . . ." Boone would begin, then bring the boy with him back in time to stories of being a captive and other memories.

Rebecca Boone passed away at seventy-four at the home of Jemima and Flanders in the spring of 1813, and several years later Daniel fell ill while at the home of one of his other children, Nathan. The eighty-five-year-old turned away medicine, insisting he had no fear of death. Jemima rushed to her brother's house to be with her father, who passed away minutes after Jemima's arrival while holding her hand, as though he had held on to life until she could be with him. In yet another pivotal moment, they fought against time and odds to be together.

When James Fenimore Cooper's *The Last of the Mohicans* was published in 1826, Jemima in all likelihood could not read it; like many frontier women, she had not been taught to read in her youth and no evidence suggests she learned later in life. Still, she surely would have known of the immensely popular novel that was viewed as a kind of dramatized Boone family biography. The "taking" of Jemima Boone occurred not only in her actual kidnapping but by being "taken" out of the historical narrative, her name blurred by Cora Munro, her proxy in *The Last of the Mohicans*; the complex but doomed literary character's fate is determined by a web of political and military decision-making by men. Cooper in his preface actually warns away female readers altogether, because they were liable to be shocked by the realism of his story. Marketing gimmick or not, between that warning and her lack of literacy, Jemima was locked out of the most popular version of her own story.

When her life was memorialized, Jemima was generally presented as a victim rather than the fighter, survivor, and leader she was. Her story was warped and sensationalized. The kidnapping and rescue became a story of courtship and romance (exemplified by the insertion into the narrative of John Holder, Fanny Callaway's future husband, as a rescuer) rather than one of the perseverance of strong young women amid volatile geopolitics. Sometimes the sensational veered into simple fabrication. One older man in Indiana in the early nineteenth century actually claimed to be the deceased

Colonel Callaway, telling his own faux first-person stories of the girls' kidnapping. Well-known mid-nineteenth-century paintings by Charles Wimar called *The Abduction of Daniel Boone's Daughter* depicted Jemima as a becalmed, praying figure as Indians control her, editing out the Callaway girls altogether, and even erasing Jemima's name from the title, defining her through her father. In the early twentieth century, a gathering at Jamestown, Kentucky, reenacted the kidnapping of the Boonesboro girls, "faithfully reproduced to the great interest and delight of a goodly throng which assembled to witness the exercises." The leadership role Jemima would take on her path from the kidnapping to the last siege of Boonesboro rarely broke through the popular narrative.

Jemima did dictate her stories in her own words to be preserved. The manuscript pages, however, were lost among the cargo of a wrecked vessel on the river, and no copies had been made. On August 30, 1834, Jemima passed away in Marthasville, Missouri, at seventy-one. She had never stopped telling her story in her own way. At their comfortable Federal-style log home built by Flanders, she would be surrounded by children (she was a mother to nine) and then grandchildren, plus endless delegations of nieces and nephews. They would beg to hear about the kidnapping and rescue, stories they in turn passed on to their own children. When Jemima described the scene of searching for lice in Hanging Maw's hair, one niece objected to her Aunt Mima, "I wouldn't have done it." When Betsy Callaway would retell similar tales to her family, her son came to fear imaginary lurking warriors around every corner. But Jemima tried to restore complexities that had been wiped out by dramatizations and simplifications—those nuanced personal relationships between Hanging Maw and Jemima, between Blackfish and his son who was killed by Boone during the girls' rescue, between Boone and his adoptive Indian parents, between Matthew Arbuckle and

Cornstalk's sister, Nonhelema, between Jemima and her father, between Boone and Richard Callaway, all of which underscored the sweeping drama of the frontier and altered its course.

"Oh yes, you would," Jemima replied to her niece. "For the Indians were really kind to us, as much as they well could have been, as their circumstances permitted."

Months before her death, Jemima was still sharing the story. One relative remembered sitting with Jemima as she vividly retold the whole narrative of her kidnapping, slowing down to detail that moment when her father, crawling on his stomach on the ground, motioned his hand at them through the trees, a signal of hope frozen in time.

AUTHOR'S NOTE

FOR BOTH THE TRIBES AND the settlers involved in this story, excavating experiences from an era of cultural divides, uneven documentation, and limited literacy is a complex task for researchers and writers. I have leaned on primary sources whenever possible. Nineteenth-century enthusiasts Lyman C. Draper and John D. Shane conducted and collected a remarkable number of interviews with people connected to the frontier. Materials from these Draper manuscripts (now at the State Historical Society of Wisconsin), a collection that eventually absorbed Shane's papers, provide vital details of both sweeping events and day-to-day routines. Documents from the Draper Manuscript Collection are cited throughout the notes as DM with its access number in that repository's idiosyncratic organization.

If a quote is specified as representing written text, the original capitalization, spelling, and punctuation are preserved, but for other quotes these have been normalized, especially when representing dialogue. The term "American Indians" or "Indians" is chosen instead of "Native Americans" in the text, following the latest standards in the United States articulated by institutions including the National Museum of the American Indian. As the story told here takes place during the Revolutionary War, "America" and "Americans" designate a country or country-in-the-making and its people, but carry rhetorical flaws by suggesting an inherently separate category from American Indians. Such terminology remains imperfect and tangled.

We cannot lose sight of the fact that tribal experiences were often documented by outsiders and it is essential to consider layers of context in order to judge reliability, which I have endeavored to do throughout, especially when quoting dialogue. The spelling and presentation of American Indian names have many variants, both in tribal tradition and in Anglicized versions.

Early biographers who interviewed Daniel Boone, namely John Filson and Timothy Flint, had unprecedented access but also sometimes succumbed to dramatization. I have used these sources selectively, evaluating reliability piece by piece, and have specified whenever possible within the text when quotes reached us through such intercessors.

Harry G. Enoch, Boone and frontier expert, and Colin G. Calloway, scholar of the American Indian experience, both graciously and patiently fielded my inquiries, as did Carlton Larson on the subject of courts-martial. There are many comprehensive and insightful publications, some cited here, on Boone's life and times, including those by John Mack Faragher, Michael A. Lofaro, Robert Morgan, and Meredith Mason Brown. Ted Franklin Belue edited and annotated an invaluable edition of Lyman Draper's writing on Boone, *The Life of Daniel Boone*, complementing a variety of important publications by Belue. Works by Enoch, Anne Crabb, and Neal O. Hammon have expanded frontier scholarship, as has Nancy O'Malley's unique archaeological work and scholarship. In citations, I have tried to point to publications that reproduce original documents, including George W. Ranck's *Boonesborough*, multiple books by Reuben Gold Thwaites and Louise Phelps Kellogg, and more recent works such as Crabb's *And the Battle Began Like Claps of Thunder*. Like Professor Calloway's books and articles on Indian life, John Sugden's scholarship provides a standard of excellence for examining tribal history. Limitations here and in endnotes necessitate leaving out many worthy publications, past and present, on these subjects.

ACKNOWLEDGMENTS

THIS BOOK OWES EVERYTHING TO the faith and the efforts of my tireless and generous agent and editor, Suzanne Gluck and Sara Nelson, respectively. Many thanks also to the hard work and dedication of the team at WME Agency, including Andrea Blatt and Hilary Zaitz Michael; and at HarperCollins, Jonathan Burnham, Robin Bilardello, and Mary Gaule.

I am lucky to receive regular doses of moral and writing support from Kevin Birmingham, Benjamin Cavell, Gabriella Gage, Greg Nichols, and Scott Weinger. Always, I am grateful for the support of my parents, Susan and Warren Pearl, and my mother-in-law, Marsha Selley. Never failing to inspire and advise is my wife, Tobey Pearl. Finally, Cooper, Graham, and Lulu light up our home with laughter and wonder, with credit to Cooper, my research assistant and fellow Kentucky explorer.

NOTES

Prologue

1 Rebecca Boone noticed: Martha McCorkle (as "Mrs. Samuel Scott"), 1840s, Draper Manuscript Collection (DM) 11CC225–226, State Historical Society of Wisconsin, Madison, WI.

2 Jemima carried the lesson: Theodore Roosevelt, *The Winning of the West*, vol. 1 (New York: Putnam, 1889), 326; Stephen Railton, introduction to *The Last of the Mohicans*, by James Fenimore Cooper (New York: Barnes & Noble Classics, 2004), xii; John Alexander McClung, *Sketches of Western Adventure* (Cincinnati: U. P. James, 1839), 40.

Chapter 1: Duck

7 Jemima strolled the banks: Will. M. Bransford, "The Capture and the Rescue, Part 1," *Southern Lady's Companion* 2, no. 8 (Nov. 1848): 170 (though a romanticized account, this contains information provided by the Callaway family); George W. Ranck, *Boonesborough* (Louisville: John P. Morton, 1901), 41.

8 Late the previous year: Harry G. Enoch and Anne Crabb, *African Americans at Fort Boonesborough, 1775–1784* (Richmond, KY: Fort Boonesborough Foundation, 2019), 30–31.

8 With summer blazing: Eudocia Estill, 1852, DM 24C31; Richard French, 1840s, DM 12CC203; Nathan and Olive Boone, 1851, DM 6S94; Daniel Boone Bryan, 1844, DM 22C14(10).

9 The Boones had led: Jerry E. Clark, *The Shawnee* (Lexington: University Press of Kentucky, 2015), 52–53.

9 "Now, brothers": Lyman C. Draper, *The Life of Daniel Boone*, ed. Ted Franklin Belue (Mechanicsburg, PA: Stackpole Books, 1998), 216; Maureen Hancock Ward, *The Hancock Brothers from Virginia* (Richfield, ID: Hancock Family Organization, 1992), 11.

10 Boone's early, temporary excursions: John Mack Faragher, *Daniel Boone: The Life and Legend of an American Pioneer* (New York: Henry Holt, 1993), 83; Anna M. Cartlidge, "Colonel John Floyd: Reluctant Adventurer," *Register of the Kentucky Historical Society* 66, no. 4 (1968): 326; Neal O. Hammon, "The Fincastle Surveyors in the Bluegrass, 1774," *Register of the Kentucky Historical Society* 70, no. 4 (Oct. 1972): 283, 286, 292.

11 Fanciful notions: John Filson, *The Discovery, Settlement and Present State of Kentucke* (Wilmington, KY: James Adams, 1784), 46; Felix Walker, "Narrative of an Adventure in Kentucky in the Year 1775," *DeBow's Review* 16, no. 2 (Feb. 1854): 150–55; William Pitt Palmer, ed., *Calendar of Virginia State Papers and Other Manuscripts, 1652–1781*, vol. 1 (Richmond: R. F. Walker, 1875), 282ff; Ranck, ix; Joseph McCormick, 1870, DM 30C110–113.

12   Another pioneer: (Richard Callaway's birth year has been in dispute. Possibilities include 1717, 1722, and 1724.) Charles W. Bryan Jr., "Richard Callaway, Kentucky Pioneer," *Filson Club History Quarterly* 9 (Jan. 1935): 35–50.

13   The settlers took pains to appear fair: Stan Hoig, *The Cherokees and Their Chiefs: In the Wake of Empire* (Fayetteville: University of Arkansas Press, 1998), 58; Palmer, ed., 282.

13   Dragging Canoe, part of the: Neal O. Hammon and Richard Taylor, *Virginia's Western War, 1775–1786* (Mechanicsburg, PA: Stackpole Books, 2002), 3; Palmer, ed., 283, 292.

13   Years earlier, the British had forbidden: "Proclamation Respecting New Governments in America," *Gentleman's Magazine* 33 (1763): 479; Ranck, 149, 181.

14   Such brewing controversies: Draper, *Life*, 363, note t; Delinda Boone Craig, 1866, DM 30C47; Faragher, 91.

15   Before beginning her own journey: Draper, *Life*, 363, note s; Ranck, 5.

16   Boone's thirty-person advance party: Neal O. Hammon, "The First Trip to Boonesborough," *Filson Club History Quarterly* 45 (July 1971): 249–63; Ranck, 192.

16   "Delightful beyond conception": Willard Rouse Jillson, *Tales of the Dark and Bloody Ground* (Louisville: C. T. Dearing, 1930), 73; Ranck, 166.

17   "A new sky and strange earth": Walker, 152; Harry G. Enoch, *Pioneer Voices* (Winchester, KY: 2012), 3.

17   Conceiving of themselves as versions of Columbus: Draper, *Life*, 337–38; Hammon and Taylor, *Virginia's Western War*, 7.

18   Boone wrote weeks later: Walker, 154; Ranck, 169, 183.

18   Into these combustible circumstances: Sidney Lee, ed., *Dictionary of National Biography*, vol. 55 (New York: Macmillan, 1898), 102–3; John Ferdinand Smyth, *A Tour in the United States*, vol. 1 (London: G. Robinson, 1784), 331; Ranck, 32–33; Wilbur H. Siebert, "Kentucky's Struggle with Its Loyalist Proprietors," *Mississippi Valley Historical Review* 7, no. 2 (Sept. 1920): 114–15.

19   The far bank of the Kentucky River: Stephen Hempstead, 1863, DM 16C76; Moses Boone, c. 1846, DM 19C48; S. Paul Jones, 1889, DM 21C8(3); William Phelps, 1868, DM 24C57; Willis A. Bush, 1853, DM 24C59(4); Estill, DM 24C31; Samuel Dixon, 1852, DM 24C30; Evisa Coshow, 1885, DM 21C28; Daniel Boone Bryan, DM 22C14(10).

20   Changes had swept the region: Ranck, 31–32.

20   A figure thrashed: French, DM 12CC204; Ranck, 180; Enoch and Crabb, *African Americans at Fort Boonesborough*, 62–63.

21   "Simon! How you scared me!": Nathaniel Hart Jr., c. 1843, DM 17CC192; Daniel Boone Bryan, 1843, DM 22C5(9); Bush, DM 24C59(4); Nathan and Olive Boone, DM 6S94; Craig, DM 30C47.

Chapter 2: Bloody Ground

22   During that same era: Henry Timberlake, *The Memoirs of Lieut. Henry Timberlake* (London: J. Ridley, 1765), 33, 112.

23   Most of their exchange: Robert S. Allen, *His Majesty's Indian Allies* (Toronto: Dundurn, 1993), 41; Delinda Boone Craig, 1866, DM 30C78.

24   That pattern played itself out: Reuben Gold Thwaites and Louise Phelps Kellogg, eds., *Documentary History of Dunmore's War, 1774* (Madison: Wisconsin Historical Society, 1905), 12; Robert G. Parkinson, "From Indian Killer to Worthy Citizen: The Revolutionary Transformation of Michael Cresap," *William and Mary Quarterly* 63, no. 1 (Jan. 2006): 100–101; Henry Rowe Schoolcraft, *Historical and*

Statistical Information Respecting the History, Condition and Prospects of the Indian Tribes of the United States, part 4 (Philadelphia: Lippincott, Grambo & Co., 1854), 624; Richard White, *The Middle Ground: Indians, Empires, and Republics in the Great Lakes Region, 1650–1815* (New York: Cambridge University Press, 2011), 357.

25   Soon after that: Peter C. Mancall, "'The Bewitching Tyranny of Custom': The Social Costs of Indian Drinking in Colonial America" in *American Encounters: Natives and Newcomers from European Contact to Indian Removal, 1500–1850,* eds. Peter C. Mancall and James H. Merrell (New York: Routledge, 2000), 194–215; James H. Perkins, *Annals of the West* (St. Louis: James R. Albach, 1851), 142.

26   According to one account: Colin G. Calloway, *The Shawnees and the War for America* (New York: Viking, 2007), 51.

26   When the dust settled: Thwaites and Kellogg, *Documentary History,* 433; Jerry E. Clark, *The Shawnee* (Lexington: University Press of Kentucky, 2015), 56–57; Samuel Hazard, ed., *Pennsylvania Archives,* vol. 4 (Philadelphia: Joseph Severns, 1853), 497.

27   Whatever resistance Cornstalk put up: Joseph C. Jefferds, *Captain Matthew Arbuckle: A Documentary Biography* (Charleston, WV: Education Foundation, 1981), 62; Harry G. Enoch, *Captain Billy Bush and the Bush Settlement* (Winchester, KY: 2015), 14; Edward Eggleston and Lillie Eggleston Seelye, *Tecumseh and the Shawnee Prophet* (New York: Dodd, Mead & Co., 1878), 37.

28   In contrast to the conventional narrative: Neal O. Hammon, ed., *John Floyd: The Life and Letters of a Frontier Surveyor* (Louisville: Butler Books, 2013), 63–64; Eggleston and Seelye, 37.

28   Cornstalk ended up leading treaty talks: Calloway, *Shawnees,* 62.

29   From a non-native perspective: Joe Nickell, "Uncovered—the Fabulous Silver Mines of Swift and Filson," *Filson Club History Quarterly* 54 (Oct. 1980): 324–45; John Filson, *The Discovery, Settlement and Present State of Kentucke* (Wilmington, KY: James Adams, 1784), 73.

29   The confused fable: John Ferdinand Smyth, *A Tour in the United States,* vol. 1 (London: G. Robinson, 1784), 337; Lewis H. Kilpatrick, "The Journal of William Calk, Kentucky Pioneer," *Mississippi Valley Historical Review* 7, no. 4 (Mar. 1921): 369; Clark, 39–40.

30   When colonists protested: Alan Leander MacGregor, "Tammany: The Indian as Rhetorical Surrogate," *American Quarterly* 35, no. 4 (Autumn 1983): 396–97.

31   The visitors reported to the Cherokee leaders: William L. Saunders, ed., *The Colonial Records of North Carolina,* vol. 1 (Raleigh, NC: Josephus Daniels, 1890), 773, 778.

32   "to take a look at the white people": George W. Ranck, *Boonesborough* (Louisville: John P. Morton, 1901), 38.

32   Not far from Boonesboro: E. Polk Johnson, *A History of Kentucky and Kentuckians,* vol. 3 (Chicago: Lewis Pub. Co., 1912), 1445–46; John Floyd, 1776, DM 33S300–303.

33   As he stepped out: Clark, 45–46; J. P. Hale, "Daniel Boone, Some Facts and Incidents Not Hitherto Published," *West Virginia School Journal* 2, no. 4 (Feb. 1882): 85–86; Craig, DM 30C46; Nathan and Olive Boone, 1851, DM 6S95.

Chapter 3: The Plan

34   From her vantage point at the fort: George Soelle diary, Apr. 12, 1771, Archibald Henderson Collection, North Carolina Collection, University of North Carolina; George W. Ranck, *Boonesborough* (Louisville: John P. Morton, 1901), 40.

34   Rebecca married Daniel: Nathan and Olive Boone, 1851, DM 6S40.

35   As she glanced down: Nathan Reid, n.d., DM 31C2(25); S. Paul Jones, 1889,

DM 21C8(3); John Gass, 1844, DM 24C73; Eudocia Estill, 1852, DM 24C31; Samuel Dixon, 1852, DM 24C30(3); Nathan and Olive Boone, DM 6S96.

35   In one of the cabins, Daniel: Nathan and Olive Boone, DM 6S96; Ranck, 177; Evisa Coshow, 1885, DM 21C28.

36   Nathan Reid had forgotten: Reid, DM 31C2(25); Anna M. Cartlidge, "Colonel John Floyd: Reluctant Adventurer," *Register of the Kentucky Historical Society* 66, no. 4 (1968): 320, 337.

36   Samuel had been out hunting: Richard French, 1840s, DM 12CC204.

37   John Gass volunteered: Lyman C. Draper, *The Life of Daniel Boone*, ed. Ted Franklin Belue (Mechanicsburg, PA: Stackpole Books, 1998), 367.

37   Richard Henderson had commented: Ranck, 191.

37   Some of these settlers: Anthony Camp, "John Ferdinand Smyth: Loyalist and Liar," *Genealogists' Magazine* 31, no. 11 (Sept. 2015): 404–14; Sidney Lee, ed., *Dictionary of National Biography*, vol. 55 (New York: Macmillan, 1898), 103.

38   In the case of John Floyd: Cartlidge, 319–21; Neal O. Hammon, ed., *John Floyd: The Life and Letters of a Frontier Surveyor* (Louisville: Butler Books, 2013), 58; Ranck, 171, 173, 188; John Gass, 1840s, DM 11CC11.

38   Also rushing to the spot: Lowell H. Harrison and James C. Klotter, *A New History of Kentucky* (Lexington: University Press of Kentucky, 1997), 28; "Richard Callaway," in *The Kentucky Encyclopedia*, ed. John E. Kleber (Lexington: University of Kentucky Press), 152.

39   Herculean legends: Michael A. Lofaro, "Tracking Daniel Boone: The Changing Frontier in American Life," *Register of the Kentucky Historical Society* 82 (1984): 327–28; Josiah Collins, 1840s, DM 12CC74; Nathan and Olive Boone, DM 6S43; Reuben Gold Thwaites and Louise Phelps Kellogg, *Documentary History of Dunmore's War* (Madison, WI: Wisconsin Historical Society, 1905), 89.

39   Not that Boone's missions always succeeded: Harry G. Enoch, *Captain Billy Bush and the Bush Settlement* (Winchester, KY: 2015), 4; Nathan and Olive Boone, DM 6S83, 6S42.

39   In their long history of hunting: Jerry E. Clark, *The Shawnee* (Lexington: University Press of Kentucky, 2015), 31.

40   James Boone's group: Ranck, 229; William Goodell, *Slavery and Anti-Slavery*, vol. 2 (New York: William Harned, 1852), 75; William Waller Hening, ed., *The Statutes at Large; Being a Collection of All the Laws of Virginia from the First Session of the Legislature, in the Year 1619*, vol. 4 (Richmond, VA: R. & W. & G. Bartow, 1823), 131.

41   One of the enslaved men: Delinda Boone Craig, 1866, DM 30C45.

41   Informed of what happened: Soelle, Archibald Henderson Collection; George Bryan, 1844, DM 22C16(2).

41   Rebecca gave her husband blankets: Craig, DM 30C45; Nathan and Olive Boone, DM 6S83; *Rind's Virginia Gazette*, Dec. 23, 1773; Thwaites and Kellogg, *Documentary History*, 39; Arthur Campbell, Oct. 16, 1774, DM 3QQ124.

42   One of the few: Robert M. Addington, *History of Scott County, Virginia* (Johnson City, TN: Overmountain Press, 1992), 16–17; Robert L. Kincaid, "Boone and Russell Graves in Lee County, Virginia," *Virginia Magazine of History and Biography* 60, no. 1 (Jan. 1952): 174.

42   When the Indian warrior towed: The girls' experiences in this section are drawn from Gass, DM 11CC11; Pleasant Henderson, n.d., DM 24C36(4); Coshow, DM 21C28, 21C43; Willis A. Bush, 1853, DM 24C59(4); William Phelps, 1868, DM 24C57; Nathan and Olive Boone, DM 6S95; Ranck, 190.

45   As captors and captives: James E. Seaver, *A Narrative of the Life of Mrs. Mary Jemison* (New York: G. P. Putnam's, 1898), 45; for background and context on Jemison, Susan Walsh, "'With Them Was My Home': Native American Autobiography and *A Narrative of the Life of Mrs. Mary Jemison*," *American Literature* 64, no. 1 (Mar. 1992): 49–70.

45   Boone ordered the rescue party to split into two: Reid, DM 31C2(25).

46   Floyd's trio identified the captors' initial trail: Will. M. Bransford, "The Capture and the Rescue, Part 1," *Southern Lady's Companion* 2, no. 8 (Nov. 1848): 173; Nathan and Olive Boone, DM 6S97.

46   Boone hatched a strategic plan: Gass, DM 24C73; Ranck, 190; Henderson, DM 24C36(5); Nathan and Olive Boone, DM 6S97; John Filson, *The Discovery, Settlement and Present State of Kentucke* (Wilmington, KY: James Adams, 1784), 47.

47   Daylight faded: Willard Rouse Jillson, *Tales of the Dark and Bloody Ground* (Louisville: C. T. Dearing, 1930), 73; Hammon, ed., *John Floyd*, 107.

47   The British were launching fronts: Harry G. Enoch and Anne Crabb, *African Americans at Fort Boonesborough, 1775–1784* (Richmond, KY: Fort Boonesborough Foundation, 2019), 57, 58; Elizabeth A. Perkins, *Border Life* (Chapel Hill: University of North Carolina Press, 1998), 115; Marion B. Lucas, *A History of Blacks in Kentucky: From Slavery to Segregation, 1760–1891* (Frankfort: Kentucky Historical Society, 2003), xiv. Hines also appears with spelling variants that include Hinde, Hine, Hind, Hinds.

48   Young John Gass: Reid, DM 31C2(26).

48   By break of day: George Bryan, DM 22C16(14); Ranck, 14.

49   The experience and circumstances: Nathan and Olive Boone, DM 6S83.

49   Daniel's striking descriptions: Nathan and Olive Boone, DM 6S83; Craig, DM 30C45–46.

50   In the improvised team: Ranck, 12.

50   At six feet, Smith stood: Draper, *Life*, 525 n12.

50   the mission to find Jemima: Draper, *Life*, 3; Charles H. Ambler, *The Life and Diary of John Floyd* (Richmond, VA: Richmond Press, 1918), 11–12, 20; Cartlidge, 317–20.

51   Floyd married young: Cartlidge, 319; Ambler, 13, 18.

51   Some members of the rescue party: Hazel Atterbury Spraker, ed., *The Boone Family: A Genealogical History* (Rutland, VT: Tuttle Company, 1922), 119, 123; Joseph Scholl, 1868, DM 24S209; Stephen Hempstead, 1862, DM 16C75.

52   The girls' thoughts: French, DM 12CC204.

53   Legal consequences: Thwaites and Kellogg, *Documentary History*, 39, 78; LaVelda R. Faull, *Isaac Crabtree: Portrait of an American Frontiersman and His Family* (Glasgow, KY: L. R. Faull, 1993), 29; Addington, 16–17.

54   The girls' minds raced: Josiah Collins, DM 12CC75; David Henry, n.d., DM 31C40; Ranck, 32–33; John Ferdinand Smyth, *A Tour in the United States*, vol. 1 (London: G. Robinson, 1784), 330; Camp, 404–14.

54   The captors informed the girls: Hammon, ed., *John Floyd*, 108.

55   The next day: Estill, DM 24C31(2); Bush, DM 24C59(4); Jacob Boone, 1890, DM 14C84; Craig, DM 30C47.

55   Some of this escaped: Moses Boone, 1846, DM 19C48; Jones, DM 21C8(5); Nathan and Olive Boone, DM 6S96; Daniel Boone Bryan, 1843, DM 22C5(9); George Bryan, 22C14(10); Gass, DM 24C73(20); Bransford, 193 (romanticized account but containing information provided by the Callaway family).

55   The Cherokee culture: Clark, 31, 36.

56   Jemima urged the other girls: Coshow, DM 21C28, 21C37.

Chapter 4: Ends of the Earth

57   Boone's party: Neal O. Hammon, ed., *John Floyd: The Life and Letters of a Frontier Surveyor* (Louisville: Butler Books, 2013), 107; John Gass, 1844, DM 24C73(20); Theodore Roosevelt, *The Winning of the West*, vol. 1 (New York: Putnam, 1889), 326n1; Nathan Reid, n.d., DM 31C2(26).

58   Boone had decades of experience: Robert Wickliffe, 1849, DM 5C51(8–9); George W. Ranck, *Boonesborough* (Louisville: John P. Morton, 1901), 237–38.

58   "It would never do to follow": Nathan Reid, DM 31C2(26–27).

59   Continuing through the sweltering heat: Ralph Clayton, 1877, DM 7C43(1–5); William B. Smith, "Adventure with the Indians" in *The Museum of Perilous Adventures and Daring Exploits* (New York: G. & F. Bill, 1859), 420; Nathan and Olive Boone, 1851, DM 6S97–98.

60   A renowned hunter: Ranck, 206.

60   To Boone, the buffalo: Nathan and Olive Boone, DM 6S98; Jerry E. Clark, *The Shawnee* (Lexington: The University Press of Kentucky, 2015), 39; Nathan Reid, DM 31C2(27–28).

60   Callaway family legend: Will. M. Bransford, "The Capture and the Rescue, Part 2," *Southern Lady's Companion* 2, no. 8 (Dec. 1848): 197.

61   Even those members: S. Paul Jones, 1885, DM 21C15(5); Ranck, 22–23, 188.

62   Boone stopped again: Nathan and Olive Boone, DM 6S98; Nathan Reid, DM 31C(27–28).

62   Boone directed the group: Nathan and Olive Boone, DM 6S98; Jones, 1889, DM 21C8(2–6); Joseph Scholl, 1868, DM 24S209.

62   They discovered items on the ground: Nathan Reid, DM 24C2(27); Gass, 1840s, DM 11CC12; Smith, 420.

63   For the hostages: Colin G. Calloway, *The Shawnees and the War for America* (New York: Viking, 2007), 55–56.

63   The Girtys were four Pennsylvania-born brothers: George W. Ranck, "Girty, the White Indian," *Magazine of American History* 15 (Mar. 1886): 256–60; Colin Calloway, "Simon Girty" in *Being and Becoming Indian*, ed. James A. Clifton (Chicago: Dorsey Press, 1989), 43–44.

64   As the war progressed: James E. Seaver, *A Narrative of the Life of Mrs. Mary Jemison* (New York: G. P. Putnam's, 1898), 117–18.

65   News about the Boone and Callaway girls: Joseph C. Jefferds, *Captain Matthew Arbuckle: A Documentary Biography* (Charleston, WV: Education Foundation, 1981), 80.

65   Arbuckle had been a key commander: Jefferds, 15, 40.

66   Fort Randolph was recognized: Jefferds, 46.

66   Right around his thirty-fifth birthday: Jefferds, 80; Matthew Arbuckle, 1776, DM 7C17(1).

66   "The girls were caressed": David Henry, n.d., DM 31C2(40); John Sugden, *Blue Jacket: Warrior of the Shawnees* (Lincoln: University of Nebraska Press, 2000), 31; Smith, 419; Daniel Boone Bryan, *The Mountain Muse* (Harrisonburg, VA: Davidson & Bourne, 1813), 164–65.

67   Hanging Maw admired: Jones, 1885, DM 21C15(6); Moses Boone, 1846, DM 19C48; Nathan and Olive Boone, DM 6S100; Delinda Boone Craig, 1866, DM 30C49; Lyman C. Draper, *The Life of Daniel Boone*, ed. Ted Franklin Belue (Mechanicsburg, PA: Stackpole Books, 1998), 415.

67   The Cherokee warrior's difficult position: Arbuckle, DM 7C17(1); Jefferds, 19–20.

68 To help them: Craig, DM 30C47; Nathan and Olive Boone, DM 6S95; Evisa Coshow, 1885 DM 21C37.
68 At one point, all three: Coshow, DM 21C28, 21C37, 21C40(1); Gass, DM 24C73(21); Josiah Collins, 1840s, DM 12CC75; Nathan and Olive Boone, DM 6S96; Eudocia Estill, 1852, DM 24C31(2).
69 When they reached a place by a stream: Coshow, DM 21C48; Craig, DM 30C48–49.
69 She also had reason: Jacob Boone, 1890, DM 14C84.
69 Hanging Maw insisted: Coshow, DM 21C28; Joseph Haven, *Mental Philosophy: Including the Intellect, Sensibilities, and Will* (Boston: Gould and Lincoln, 1862), 73–74; United States War Department, "Railroad Line East from White Clay Creek" in *Reports of Explorations and Surveys, to Ascertain the Most Practicable and Economical Route for a Railroad from the Mississippi River to the Pacific Ocean* (Washington, DC: A.O.P. Nicholson, 1855–1860), 15.
70 With Hanging Maw on his errand: Josiah Collins, DM 12CC75; Frances Lamme, 1851, DM 6S305–306.
70 "There the girls were": Coshow, DM 21C28; Gass, DM 24C73(20); Estill, DM 24C31(2); Samuel Dixon, 1852, DM 24C30(4); Stephen Hempstead, 1863, DM 16C76; Nathan and Olive Boone, DM 6S100.
71 "That's Daddy": Abner Bryan, 1890, DM 4C49; Nathan and Olive Boone, DM 6S99; John P. Hale, *Daniel Boone: Some Facts and Incidents Not Hitherto Published* (Charleston, WV: Lewis Baker, 1889), 10; Isaac Van Bibber, 1854, DM 23C109(1); Pleasant Henderson, n.d., DM 24C36(6); Estill, DM 24C31(2); Dixon, DM 24C30(3); Nathan Reid, DM 24C2(29); Daniel Boone Bryan, 1843, DM 22C5(10); William Phelps, 1868, DM 24C57.
71 Leading up to this moment: Hammon, ed., *John Floyd*, 107–8; Nathan Reid, DM 31C2(26–27); Coshow, DM 21C28; Jones, 1885, DM 21C15(4); John Reid, 1848, DM 10NN104.
72 The search party had journeyed: Phelps, DM 24C57.
72 Boone signaled them: Nathan Reid, DM 31C2(27); Jones, 1889, DM 21C8(4–6); George Bryan, 1844, DM 22C16(14); Hempstead, DM 16C76; Hammon, ed., *John Floyd*, 108.
72 Concealed by the trees: Jones, 1889, DM 21C8(6–7); Lamme, DM 6S305–306; George Bryan, DM 22C16(14); Smith, 420; Nathan Reid, DM 31C2(28); Hammon, ed., *John Floyd*, 108; Morgan and Elizabeth Boone Bryan, 1851, DM 6S301–302.
73 The Shawnee chopping wood: Richard Holder, 1850, DM 24C29(1–2); Lamme, DM 6S305–306; Hammon, ed., *John Floyd*, 108; Hale, *Boone*, 10; L. W. Boggs, 1857, DM 23C27(3).
73 The girls started across the ridge: Daniel Boone Bryan, DM 22C5(10); Phelps, DM 24C57; Nathan and Olive Boone, DM 6S99; Jones, 1889, DM 21C8(7); George Bryan, DM 22C16(14); Elizabeth A. Perkins, *Border Life* (Chapel Hill: University of North Carolina Press, 1998), 89; Dixon, DM 24C30(4).
73 Big Jimmy: Josiah Collins, DM 12CC75; Nathan and Olive Boone, DM 6S99.
74 The rescuers gave the girls blankets: Coshow, DM 21C37(2), 21C43; Richard White, *The Middle Ground: Indians, Empires, and Republics in the Great Lakes Region, 1650–1815* (New York: Cambridge University Press, 2011), 341; Susan Callaway Howell, 1868, DM 23S229–231.

74   The faction of rescuers: Harry G. Enoch and Diane Rogers, *Deposition Book, 1795–1814* (Winchester, KY: 2005), 15; Coshow, DM 21C48(1).
75   As they neared the river: Coshow, DM 21C28, 21C37(2).

Chapter 5: Fallout
79   Word of the kidnapping: Neal O. Hammon, ed., *John Floyd: The Life and Letters of a Frontier Surveyor* (Louisville: Butler Books, 2013), 107; John Filson, *The Discovery, Settlement and Present State of Kentucke* (Wilmington, KY: James Adams, 1784), 39.
79   In Boonesboro and the isolated outposts: Willard Rouse Jillson, *Tales of the Dark and Bloody Ground* (Louisville: C. T. Dearing, 1930), 74, 75; Hammon, ed., *John Floyd*, 109; George W. Ranck, *Boonesborough* (Louisville: John P. Morton, 1901), 189.
81   Cornstalk, the Shawnee chief: Cornstalk's actions on tour drawn in part from William Wilson's report, Sept. 26, 1776, repr. in Peter Force, ed., *American Archives: A Documentary History*, vol. 2 (Washington, DC: M. St. Clair and Peter Force, 1851), 514–18.
82   Cornstalk, as it turned out: Ranck, 238.
82   Now as he heard the news: Force, 514; Charles H. Faulkner, *Massacre at Cavett's Station* (Knoxville: University of Tennessee Press, 2013), 47–48; Spencer Tucker, ed., *The Encyclopedia of the Wars of the Early American Republic, 1783–1812*, vol. 1 (Santa Barbara, CA: ABC-CLIO, 2014), 95–96.
83   Meanwhile, when the three soldiers: Joseph C. Jefferds, *Captain Matthew Arbuckle: A Documentary Biography* (Charleston, WV: Education Foundation, 1981), 80; Colin G. Calloway, *The Shawnees and the War for America* (New York: Viking, 2007), 43; Reuben Gold Thwaites and Louise Phelps Kellogg, *The Revolution on the Upper Ohio, 1775–1777* (Madison: Wisconsin Historical Society, 1908), 41.
83   The three soldiers and the Shawnee chief: Jefferds, 80–81.
84   What Cornstalk actually did: Richard L. Pangburn, *Indian Blood*, vol. 1 (Madison: University of Wisconsin, 1993), 533; Colin G. Calloway, *The Indian World of George Washington* (New York: Oxford University Press, 2018), 196; Force, 514; Edgar W. Hassler, *Old Westmoreland: A History of Western Pennsylvania during the Revolution* (Pittsburgh, PA: J. R. Weldin, 1900), 18–23.
85   "A ducking is very disagreeable": Peter Houston, *A Sketch of the Life and Character of Daniel Boone*, ed. Ted Franklin Belue (Mechanicsburg, PA: Stackpole Books, 1997), 17.
85   With the joyous return: Ranck, 53; Neal O. Hammon and Richard Taylor, *Virginia's Western War, 1775–1786* (Mechanicsburg, PA: Stackpole Books, 2002), 37.
86   With the girls' kidnapping: Anne P. Crabb, *And the Battle Began Like Claps of Thunder* (Richmond, KY: Fort Boonesborough Foundation, 1998), 97; Ranck, 176; Elizabeth A. Perkins, *Border Life* (Chapel Hill: University of North Carolina Press, 1998), 101.
86   Just weeks after the girls' return: Ranck, 53; Lyman C. Draper, *The Life of Daniel Boone*, ed. Ted Franklin Belue (Mechanicsburg, PA: Stackpole Books, 1998), 423; Nathan Reid, n.d., DM 31C2(42); Harry G. Enoch and Anne Crabb, *African Americans at Fort Boonesborough, 1775–1784* (Richmond, KY: Fort Boonesborough Foundation, 2019), 58.
87   Whether Daniel or Squire: Draper, *Life*, 423; Robert Wickliffe, 1859, DM 15CC84.

87   The other girls: S. Paul Jones, 1889, DM 21C8(7); Richard Holder, 1850,
      DM 24C29(4); R. G. Williams, 1861, DM 24C43; Daniel Boone Bryan, 1843,
      DM 22C9(10); Harry G. Enoch, *Colonel John Holder: Boonesborough Defender and
      Kentucky Entrepreneur* (Winchester, KY: Acclaim Press, 2009), 28–36, 38–39, 82–83.
88   Progress was made: Hammon, ed., *John Floyd*, 27, 31–32, 109.
89   As so many fled: Lewis H. Kilpatrick, "The Journal of William Calk,"
      Mississippi Valley Historical Review 7, no. 4 (Mar. 1921): 369; Nathan and Olive
      Boone, 1851, DM 6S85; George W. Stoner, 1868, DM 24C55; John M. Stoner,
      1853, DM 24C53.
89   Another Boonesboro newcomer: Material for Simon Kenton in this section
      drawn from Edna Kenton, *Simon Kenton: His Life and Period* (Garden City, NY:
      Doubleday, Doran, 1930), 22–25, 52, 75–77, 84–85; Sarah McCord, 1851, DM
      5S133–135, 5S142.
90   Boonesboro faced major disappointment: Ranck, 55, 194–198.
91   Henry Hamilton, forty-two, set his sights: Bernard W. Sheehan, "The
      Famous Hair Buyer General," *Indiana Magazine of History* 79, no. 1 (Mar. 1983):
      4–5; H. W. Beckwith, ed., *Collections of the Illinois State Historical Library*, vol. 1
      (Springfield: Illinois State Historical Library, 1903), 173–74.
92   Hamilton was a bureaucrat: Beckwith, ed., 174; John D. Barnhart,
      "Lieutenant Governor Henry Hamilton's Apologia," *Indiana Magazine of History*
      52, no. 4 (1956): 386; Clarence Walworth Alvord, ed., *Collections of the Illinois
      State Historical Library*, vol. 8 (Springfield: Illinois State Historical Library, 1912),
      175.
92   Enlarged repeatedly: Silas Farmer, *History of Detroit and Wayne County*, vol. 1
      (Detroit: S. Farmer & Co., 1889), 222.
92   Later Hamilton would recall: Barnhart, 387; Sheehan, 9–10; Farmer, 244.
93   Cornstalk would be an especially valuable ally: John Sugden, *Blue Jacket:
      Warrior of the Shawnees* (Lincoln: University of Nebraska Press, 2000), 19.
93   During Cornstalk's visit: Force, 516–17.
95   American policy: Southern Campaigns Revolutionary War Pension
      Statements & Rosters, William Alexander pension petition S2344, 1832, http://
      revwarapps.org/s2344.pdf; Keith Krawczynski, *William Henry Drayton: South
      Carolina Revolutionary Patriot* (Baton Rouge: Louisiana State University Press,
      2001), 231.
96   On April 24, 1777, Simon Butler: Nathan and Olive Boone, DM 6S93.
96   Boonesboro's dire circumstances: Draper, *Life*, 435.
96   Boone and as many as a dozen: Filson, 39.
97   "Boys, we are gone": John Gass, 1844, DM 24C73(24); George W. Stoner,
      DM 24C55; George R. Chalfant, *Firearms and Ammunition Used by Fort Defenders
      and Native Americans at Fort Boonesborough 1777 & 1778* (self-published, 2019), 9;
      Bess L. Hawthorne, "The Famous Falls of the Ohio Trip," *Register of the Kentucky
      State Historical Society* 36, no. 117 (Oct. 1938): 371.
97   Now while raising his rifle: Stoner's experiences in this battle drawn from
      Willis A. Bush, 1853, DM 24C59(1–2); George W. Stoner, DM 24C55(5–6);
      Samuel Tribble, c. 1840s, DM 12CC43–44; Nancy O'Malley, *Boonesborough
      Unearthed: Frontier Archaeology at a Revolutionary Fort* (Lexington: University
      Press of Kentucky, 2019), 132.
99   As they tried to reach the fort: Nathan and Olive Boone, DM 6S102; Edna
      Kenton, 88.

Chapter 6: Rise of Blackfish

100 Henry Hamilton finally received the message: John D. Barnhart, "Lieutenant
     Governor Henry Hamilton's Apologia," *Indiana Magazine of History* 52, no. 4
     (1956): 384; Richard C. Adams, "History of the Delaware Indians," Senate
     Document no. 501, 59th Cong., 1st sess. (Washington, DC: Government Printing
     Office, 1906), 23.
101 Hamilton decided to unveil: Hamilton's conference in this section drawn
     from Reuben Gold Thwaites and Louise Phelps Kellogg, eds., *Frontier Defense
     on the Upper Ohio, 1777–1778* (Madison: Wisconsin Historical Society, 1912),
     8–9, 19.
101 When they gathered outside: Silas Farmer, *History of Detroit and Wayne
     County*, vol. 1 (Detroit: S. Farmer & Co., 1889), 246. Governor Cass dates the
     event as 1776, but all circumstances suggest this later meeting.
102 "I constantly addressed the Indians": Barnhart, 384.
102 Hamilton also encouraged the braves: Neal O. Hammon and Richard Taylor,
     Virginia's Western War, 1775–1786 (Mechanicsburg, PA: Stackpole Books, 2002),
     240n28; Bayless Hardin, ed., "Whitley Papers, Volume 9," *Register of the Kentucky
     State Historical Society* 36, no. 116 (July 1938): 192.
102 Captain Matthew Arbuckle, as leader: Joseph C. Jefferds, *Captain Matthew
     Arbuckle: A Documentary Biography* (Charleston, WV: Education Foundation,
     1981), ix, 81–84.
103 Nonhelema's strong build: Jefferds, 70, 74, 83; Thwaites and Kellogg, eds.,
     Documentary History of Dunmore's War, 1774 (Madison, WI: Wisconsin Historical
     Society, 1905), 301.
104 By incorporating Nonhelema's insights: Emilius O. Randall and Daniel J.
     Ryan, *History of Ohio: The Rise and Progress of an American State*, vol. 2 (New
     York: Century History Co., 1912), 183–84; Thwaites and Kellogg, *Frontier
     Defense*, 186.
104 Arbuckle, suspicious by nature: Thwaites and Kellogg, *Frontier Defense*, 126.
105 Rather than looking forward: Thwaites and Kellogg, *Frontier Defense*, 125,
     149, 175.
105 Cornstalk arrived: John Stuart, "Memoir of Indian Wars" in *Collections of the
     Virginia Historical & Philosophical Society*, vol. 1 (Richmond, VA: T. W. White,
     1833), 58.
106 The imprisonment of Cornstalk: Thwaites and Kellogg, *Frontier Defense*, 175.
106 Cornstalk cooperated with demands: Stuart, 62.
106 Having anticipated an Indian siege: Stuart, 59–60.
107 "Let us kill the Indians": Stuart, 60; Thwaites and Kellogg, *Frontier Defense*, 163.
107 The commotion sent a woman inside: Stuart, 61.
108 Daniel Boone continued to recover: Nathan and Olive Boone, 1851, DM
     6S102; George W. Ranck, *Boonesborough* (Louisville: John P. Morton, 1901), 63;
     Nancy O'Malley, *Boonesborough Unearthed: Frontier Archaeology at a Revolutionary
     Fort* (Lexington: University Press of Kentucky, 2019), 102; Samuel Dixon, 1852,
     DM 24C30(6–7).
109 In the wake of Cornstalk's death: Stuart, 62; John Mack Faragher, *Daniel
     Boone: The Life and Legend of an American Pioneer* (New York: Henry Holt, 1993),
     264.
109 Colonel William Preston of Virginia: Stuart, 62; Jefferds, 65, 90; "Fighting
     Chief Cornstalk's Remains Laid to Rest Again," *Charleston Gazette*, Sept. 21,
     1954; Thwaites and Kellogg, *Frontier Defense*, 169, 175, 225, 234.

110 Shawnee war chief Blackfish: Lyman C. Draper, *The Life of Daniel Boone*, ed. Ted Franklin Belue (Mechanicsburg, PA: Stackpole Books, 1998), 460; Thwaites and Kellogg, *Frontier Defense*, 161.

110 Blackfish's warriors: John Filson, *The Discovery, Settlement and Present State of Kentucke* (Wilmington, KY: James Adams, 1784), 39.

110 Only when militias entered the area: Ranck, 60; Ansel Goodman, 1832, DM 11C28–30.

111 Saltmakers would collect sediment-rich water: Draper, *Life*, 459–60.

111 At the encampment: Nathan and Olive Boone, DM 6S282; Faragher, 13.

111 Eeriness continued: Draper, *Life*, 460–61; Nathan and Olive Boone, DM 6S103, 6S125; Joseph Jackson, 1844, DM 11C62(3–4).

112 Boone launched into a run: Draper, *Life*, 461; Nathan and Olive Boone, DM 6S104–105; Filson, 40.

112 The warriors seized Boone's weapons: Draper, *Life*, 461–63; Nathan and Olive Boone, DM 6S105–106; Filson, 40; Daniel Boone Bryan, 1844, DM 22C14(13).

113 This pair had tried to engage the Miami tribe: *Report of the Pioneer and Historical Society of the State of Michigan*, vol. 9 (Lansing, MI: Thorp & Godfrey, 1886), 435.

113 Pompey then escorted Boone: Delinda Boone Craig, 1866, DM 30C57; Elizabeth A. Perkins, *Border Life* (Chapel Hill: University of North Carolina Press, 1998), 89; Nathan and Olive Boone, DM 6S106–107; Draper, *Life*, 463.

Chapter 7: Families

115 Boone had no good choices: Nathan and Olive Boone, 1851, DM 6S107.

115 With his conditions accepted: Nathan and Olive Boone, DM 6S107–108; Lyman C. Draper, *The Life of Daniel Boone*, ed. Ted Franklin Belue (Mechanicsburg, PA: Stackpole Books, 1998), 464; Joseph Jackson, 1884, DM 11C62(4–5); Ansel Goodman, 1832, 11C28–30.

116 The captives were taken: Jackson, DM 11C62(5–7).

117 When a party of travelers trudged: Daniel Boone Bryan, 1843, DM 22C5(11); Patrick Henry, 1778, DM 25S222.

117 A little more than two months: Daniel Trabue, *Westward into Kentucky*, ed. Chester Raymond Young (Lexington: University Press of Kentucky, 2015), 46–47.

118 Trabue and his party: Josiah Collins, 1840s, DM 12CC74; Daniel Boone Bryan, DM 22C5(11–12); Edna Kenton, *Simon Kenton: His Life and Period* (Garden City, NY: Doubleday, Doran, 1930), 83, 89–90, 93–94; Sarah McCord, 1851, DM 5S144; George W. Ranck, *Boonesborough* (Louisville: John P. Morton, 1901), 67; Neal O. Hammon and Richard Taylor, *Virginia's Western War, 1775–1786* (Mechanicsburg, PA: Stackpole Books, 2002), 71; Harry G. Enoch and Anne Crabb, *African Americans at Fort Boonesborough, 1775–1784* (Richmond, KY: Fort Boonesborough Foundation, 2019), 25; John Gass, 1844, DM 24C73(7).

119 The nearby settlement at Harrodsburg: Charles Staples, ed., "History in Circuit Court Records of Fayette County, Ky.," *Register of the Kentucky State Historical Society* 31, no. 95 (Apr. 1933): 113; "Certificate Book of the Virginia Land Commission 1779–80," *Register of the Kentucky State Historical Society* 21, no. 61 (Jan. 1923): 79.

119 In addition to these individuals: Hammon and Taylor, *Virginia's Western War*, 71.

119 Facing the scarcity: Josiah Collins, DM 12CC67.

120 Daniel Boone's absence: Evisa Coshow, 1885, DM 21C45(2–3); Delinda Boone Craig, 1866, DM 30C75; Daniel Boone Bryan, DM 22C5(11); John Filson, *The Discovery, Settlement and Present State of Kentucke* (Wilmington, KY: James Adams, 1784), 44; Josiah Collins, DM 12CC67.

121 A battle of wills: Josiah Collins, DM 12CC67; Draper, *Life*, 481.

121 Jemima's choice to remain: "Colonel Richard Callaway," *Register of the Kentucky State Historical Society* 2, no. 4 (Jan. 1904): 62; Craig, DM 30C78.

122 Reportedly, Callaway was a strict taskmaster: Gass, 1840s, DM 11CC16; John Ferdinand Smyth, *A Tour in the United States*, vol. 1 (London: G. Robinson, 1784), 330.

123 Though she may have felt more secure: Ranck, 163; Reuben Gold Thwaites, *Daniel Boone* (New York: D. Appleton, 1903), 13; Filson, 38, 44.

124 "You have got all the young men": Jackson, DM 11C62(4–5).

124 Deliberations continued: Willis A. Bush, 1853, DM 24C59(6); Jackson, DM 11C62(5–7).

125 They were saved: Filson, 40; Craig, 1866, DM 30C51; Jackson, DM 11C62(8–10).

125 Blackfish appeared: Isaiah Boone, 1846, DM 19C76; Bush, DM 24C59(6).

126 At one point on the march: Bush, DM 24C59.

126 Boone objected: Craig, DM 30C52; Bush, DM 24C59(6).

126 Staring down these parallel columns: Nathan and Olive Boone, DM 6S110, 6S128; Craig, DM 30C52–53; Septimus Schull, 1833, DM 11CC52.

127 The march took almost two weeks: Draper, *Life*, 468–69; Goodman, DM 11C28; Nathan and Olive Boone, DM 6S111; Jerry E. Clark, *The Shawnee* (Lexington: University Press of Kentucky, 2015), 94.

127 They arrived on February 18: Jackson, DM 11C62(8–10).

128 Boone was also in for more tests: Stephen Hempstead, 1868, DM 22S186–187; J. P. Hale, "Daniel Boone, Some Facts and Incidents Not Hitherto Published," *West Virginia School Journal* 2, no. 4 (Feb. 1882): 85–86; David Thompson, c. 1840s, DM 12CC200.

128 Revenge was not the priority: Draper notes, n.d., DM 11C81.

129 Rumors posited: Hempstead, DM 16C76; Stephen Cooper, 1889, DM 11C101.

129 As Boone's notoriety grew: Theodore Roosevelt, *The Winning of the West*, vol. 1 (New York: Putnam, 1889), 52.

130 "What one had": Anne P. Crabb, *And the Battle Began Like Claps of Thunder* (Richmond, KY: Fort Boonesborough Foundation, 1998), 97.

130 Sniping often followed: Harry G. Enoch and Anne Crabb, *Women at Fort Boonesborough, 1775–1784* (Richmond, KY: Fort Boonesborough Foundation, 2014), 5; Nathaniel Hart Jr., c. 1843, DM 17CC195; Deborah Rosen, "Women and Property across Colonial America," *William and Mary Quarterly* 60, no. 2 (Apr. 2003): 355–81.

131 Governor Henry Hamilton was in for a pleasant surprise: *Report of the Pioneer and Historical Society of the State of Michigan*, vol. 9 (Lansing, MI: Thorp & Godfrey, 1886), 431, 435.

132 As winter turned to spring: Nathan and Olive Boone, DM 6S112.

132 As the "principal prisoner": Nathan and Olive Boone, DM 6S112; Ranck, 61; Israel Morrison, 1844, DM 8J145(1); Isaiah Boone, DM 19C72.

133 The governor and the prisoner: *Report of the Pioneer and Historical Society*, 435; Nathan and Olive Boone, DM 6S112–113; Ranck, 62.

133 Hamilton had a choice to make: Sabina Ellis, 1858, DM 7S45–52; Elizabeth Scott, 1863, DM 19S165.

134 Trying his hand at propaganda: Nathan and Olive Boone, DM 6S113.

134 Boone likewise considered propaganda: Robert B. McAfee, "The Life and Times of Robert B. McAfee and His Family Connections," *Register of the Kentucky State Historical Society* 25, no. 75 (Sept. 1927): 228.

134 Hamilton offered the Indians a top price: Filson, 40–41; *Report of the Pioneer and Historical Society*, 435.

135 The conspicuous gap: Nathan and Olive Boone, DM 6S113, 6S117; William Dodd Brown, "The Capture of Daniel Boone's Saltmakers: Fresh Perspectives from Primary Sources," *Register of the Kentucky Historical Society* 83 (1985): 11; James Callaway, 1868, DM 25S258–259; Thomas S. Bouchelle, 1884, DM 9C68(4–5).

136 Boone's secret: Craig, DM 30C53–54; Josiah Collins, DM 12CC76–77.

136 But the Indians still believed: Nathan and Olive Boone, DM 6S114.

137 A war dance was planned: Josiah Collins, DM 12CC76; Craig, DM 30C54.

137 Boone's status: Joseph Scholl, 1868, DM 24S109–111; Moses Boone, 1846, DM 19C9.

138 In contrast with Andrew Johnson's behavior: Abner Bryan, 1890, DM 4C46–47; Susan Callaway Howell, 1868, DM 23S233; Nathan and Olive Boone, DM 6S118.

138 Blackfish addressed Boone as "my son": Nathan and Olive Boone, DM 6S119; Howell, DM 23S224, 23S233; Bettie T. Bryan, 1884, DM 22C28–28(2); Thomas Spotwood Hinde, 1845, DM 20S253–254; John Sugden, *Tecumseh: A Life* (New York: Henry Holt, 2013), 32–33, 416–17n12.

139 Two of Boone's very young sisters: Nathan and Olive Boone, DM 6S118–119; Timothy Flint, *Biographical Memoir of Daniel Boone* (Cincinnati: George Conclin, 1845), 148.

139 Blackfish apparently invited Boone: John Sugden, *Blue Jacket: Warrior of the Shawnees* (Lincoln: University of Nebraska Press, 2000), 15; Clark, 29.

140 Though Boone did not play the fool: Nathan and Olive Boone, DM 6S122; Bettie T. Bryan, DM 22C28–28(2); Filson, 41.

140 In other ways, Boone showed his usefulness: Flint, 148; Nathan and Olive Boone, DM 6S121–122; Harriet Boone Baber, 1861, DM 23C34(1); Filson, 41; Hempstead, 1863, DM 16C76.

140 In May, Blackfish: Josiah Collins, DM 12CC76; Bayless Hardin, ed., "Whitley Papers, Volume 9," *Register of Kentucky State Historical Society* 36, no. 116 (July 1938): 193; Trabue, 54–55.

141 Blackfish now asked Boone: Nathan and Olive Boone, DM 6S116; Josiah Collins, DM 12CC76–77.

142 Johnson's success caused ripples: Nathan and Olive Boone, DM 6S116.

142 Boone had the opposite agenda: Flint, 148; Filson, 41; Nathan and Olive Boone, DM 6S119–120.

143 A story arose about how Boone "proved": Ephraim McLain, 1884, DM 16C7(1–2)–8.

143 Boone also had to find a way to stockpile: Hempstead, DM 16C76.

144 Jemima Boone's long wait: Trabue, 54; Nathan and Olive Boone, DM 6S121; Filson, 41; Daniel Boone Bryan, 1844, DM 22C14(12).

145 Allies who usually would have stood up: Edna Kenton, 96–97.

146 Urgency mounted for Boone to escape: Craig, DM 30C54; Nathan and Olive Boone, DM 6S117.

146 Benjamin Kelly, sixteen, one of the youngest: Hinde, DM 20S253–254; Sugden, *Tecumseh*, 32–33, 416–17n12.

147 As Boone's escape plot came together: Nathan and Olive Boone interview, 1851, DM 6S120–121; Filson, 41; Nathan and Olive Boone, DM 6S121; Bettie T. Bryan, DM 22C28–28(2); Flint, 137.

148 It was announced that Boone would accompany: Thomas Hinde letter, *American Pioneer* 1, no. 11 (Nov. 1842): 374.

148 Half King, or Dowyentet: John Heckewelder, *A Narrative of the Mission of the United Brethren among the Delaware and Mohegan Indians* (Philadelphia: McCarty & Davis, 1820), 236–37; Colin G. Calloway, *The American Revolution in Indian Country* (Cambridge, UK: Cambridge University Press, 1995), 40.

149 Word spread fast about Fort Detroit: Calloway, *American Revolution*, 40; Patrick Griffin, *American Leviathan: Empire, Nation, and Revolutionary Frontier* (New York: Hill & Wang, 2008), 153; James W. McClung, *Historical Significance of Rockbridge County, Virginia* (Staunton, VA: McClure Co., 1939), 24–25; *Virginia Military Records: From the Virginia Magazine of History and Biography* (Baltimore: Genealogical Publishing Co., 1983), 319; Joseph C. Jefferds, *Captain Matthew Arbuckle: A Documentary Biography* (Charleston, WV: Education Foundation, 1981), 65.

149 With the futile court proceedings exhausted: Jefferds, 93; Reuben Gold Thwaites and Louise Phelps Kellogg, eds., *Frontier Defense on the Upper Ohio, 1777–1778* (Madison: Wisconsin Historical Society, 1912), 70, 82.

150 Armed with Nonhelema's intelligence: Jefferds, 93–95; W. Stephen McBride and Kim A. McBride, "Border Warfare in Revolutionary Era West Virginia" in *Partisans, Guerrillas, and Irregulars: Historical Archaeology of Asymmetric Warfare*, eds. Steven D. Smith and Clarence R. Geier (Tuscaloosa: University of Alabama Press, 2019), 26–28; Thwaites and Kellogg, *Frontier Defense*, 72–73.

151 Boone continued to hunt: Hinde, DM 20S253–254.

151 A man named Jimmy Rogers: Elizabeth Musick, 1868, DM 22S168–170; Nathan and Olive Boone, DM 6S122; Stephen Warren, *The Shawnees and Their Neighbors, 1795–1870* (Urbana: University of Illinois Press, 2005), 78; Isaiah Boone, DM 31C2; Clark, 42.

152 Boone was asked to repair: Henry Wilson, n.d., DM 31C2(70); Filson, 41; Nathan and Olive Boone, DM 6S121.

152 Back at the salt springs: Jackson, DM 11C62(11–13); Nathan and Olive Boone, DM 6S123.

153 "Blackfish would be angry": Craig, DM 30C48–49, 30C55; James Galloway, n.d., DM 31C2(65); Isaiah Boone, DM 19C78; Thomas S. Bouchelle, 1884, DM 9C68(4–5); Moses Boone, DM 19C9; Nathan and Olive Boone, DM 6S123; Filson, 41; Coshow, DM 21C24(22); Elijah Bryan, 1885, DM 4C33.

Chapter 8: Risen

157 Daniel Boone was dead: Draper notes, DM 3B18; Nathan and Olive Boone, 1851, DM 6S55–61.

158 The search party held a meeting: Draper notes, n.d., DM 4B203; Nathan and Olive Boone, 1851, DM 6S122; John C. Boone, 1890, DM 16C132 (I follow John Mack Faragher's belief that John C. Boone confuses "Indian Phillips" and Jimmy Rogers); Joseph Scholl, 1868, DM 24S109–111.

158 Upon departing from his "old mamma": Joseph Jackson, 1844, DM
11C62(11–13); Nathan and Olive Boone, DM 6S124–125.

159 Having crossed on his makeshift raft: Stephen Hempstead, 1863, DM
16C76; Jackson, DM 11C62(11–13).

159 That night, exhaustion: Nathan and Olive Boone, DM 6S125; Timothy
Flint, *Biographical Memoir of Daniel Boone* (Cincinnati: George Conclin,
1845), 153; Lyman C. Draper, *The Life of Daniel Boone*, ed. Ted Franklin Belue
(Mechanicsburg, PA: Stackpole Books, 1998), 480.

160 He shot an American buffalo: Nathan and Olive Boone, DM 6S125; John
Filson, *The Discovery, Settlement and Present State of Kentucke* (Wilmington, KY:
James Adams, 1784), 41; Lewis Collins, *History of Kentucky*, vol. 2, ed. Richard H.
Collins (Louisville: John P. Morton, 1924), 555; Draper notes, DM
4B191–92.

160 Since the Shawnee had departed: *Report of the Pioneer and Historical Society of
the State of Michigan*, vol. 9 (Lansing, MI: Thorp & Godfrey, 1886), 435–40.

161 At the same time that Boone was riding: *Report of the Pioneer and Historical
Society*, 442–44.

161 Around the very moment: *Report of the Pioneer and Historical Society*, 446–47.

162 By the time a runner: *Report of the Pioneer and Historical Society*, 452;
Bradley J. Birzer, "French Imperial Remnants on the Middle Ground: The Strange
Case of August de la Balme and Charles Beaubien," *Journal of the Illinois State
Historical Society* 93, no. 2 (Summer 2000): 142.

162 At this latest Fort Detroit gathering: *Report of the Pioneer and Historical
Society*, 454; Nathan and Olive Boone, DM 6S129.

163 Daniel Boone, "emaciated": George W. Ranck, *Boonesborough* (Louisville:
John P. Morton, 1901), 69; "Adventures of Daniel Boone," *Chambers' Edinburgh
Journal* 5, no. 115 (Mar. 14, 1846): 172.

163 Hearing that his family had gone: Nathan and Olive Boone, DM 6S140;
Ranck, 70.

164 Boone came armed: Morton V. Joyes Sr., "Letter by Colonel John Todd, Jr.,
1778," *Filson Club History Quarterly* 2 (1928): 160; Filson, 42.

164 "I found our fortress in a bad state": Delinda Boone Craig, 1866, DM
30C56; Filson, 42; Moses Boone, 1846, DM 19C12; Willis A. Bush, 1853, DM
24C59(7); John Gass, 1844, DM 24C73(2), 24C73(13).

165 As thrilled as Jemima: Daniel Boone Bryan, 1844, DM 22C14(12).

165 William Hancock: Reuben Gold Thwaites and Louise Phelps Kellogg, eds.,
Frontier Defense on the Upper Ohio, 1777–1778 (Madison: Wisconsin Historical
Society, 1912), 114; Robert Hancock, 1853, DM 24C17(1); Josiah Collins, 1840s,
DM 12CC105.

166 Hancock, forty, had lived in Boonesboro: Draper, *Life*, 487n17; Emory G.
Evans, "Byrd, William (1728–1777)" in *Dictionary of Virginia Biography*, vol. 2,
ed. Sara B. Bearss et al. (Richmond: Library of Virginia, 2001), 470–72.

166 In contrast to how Boone ingratiated: Josiah Collins, DM 12CC105.

166 Though Hancock admitted: Thwaites and Kellogg, *Frontier Defense*, 114.

167 After the council: Hancock, DM 24C17(1); Nathan and Olive Boone, DM
6S119–122.

167 To prepare: Hancock, DM 24C17(1–2).

168 He became increasingly disoriented: Hancock, DM 24C17(2); Jackson, DM
11C62(13–14).

168 On July 17, inside the fort: Hancock, DM 24C17(2–3); Nathan and Olive
     Boone, DM 6S129; Filson, 42; Thwaites and Kellogg, *Frontier Defense*, 115.

169 Boone composed his own account: Thwaites and Kellogg, *Frontier Defense*,
     115; Daniel Trabue, *Westward into Kentucky*, ed. Chester Raymond Young
     (Lexington: University Press of Kentucky, 2015), 57; Gass, DM 24C73(2).

169 In addition to gathering intelligence: Hancock, DM 24C22(1).

169 Boone had little patience: Edna Kenton, *Simon Kenton: His Life and Period*
     (Garden City, NY: Doubleday, Doran, 1930), 97; William B. Smith, "Attack
     of Boonsborough [*sic*]," *Ladies' Literary Cabinet* 3, no. 19 (Mar. 17, 1821): 147;
     Harry G. Enoch and Diane Rogers, *Deposition Book, 1795–1814* (Winchester, KY:
     2005), 101; Isaiah Boone, 1846, DM 19C81.

170 Meanwhile, the settlement was being watched: Filson, 42; Trabue, 57.

171 The planners' specific goals: Neal O. Hammon and Richard Taylor, *Virginia's
     Western War, 1775–1786* (Mechanicsburg, PA: Stackpole Books, 2002), 81.

171 Richard Callaway fumed: Trabue, 57.

Chapter 9: Before the Thunder

173 Boone rounded up twenty-nine men: Lyman C. Draper, *The Life of Daniel
     Boone*, ed. Ted Franklin Belue (Mechanicsburg, PA: Stackpole Books, 1998), 498;
     Daniel Trabue, *Westward into Kentucky*, ed. Chester Raymond Young (Lexington:
     University Press of Kentucky, 2015), 55–57; Timothy Flint, *Biographical Memoir
     of Daniel Boone* (Cincinnati: George Conclin, 1845), 156; William B. Smith,
     "Attack of Boonsborough [*sic*]," *Ladies' Literary Cabinet* 3, no. 19 (Mar. 17, 1821):
     147; George W. Ranck, *Boonesborough* (Louisville: John P. Morton, 1901), 63.

174 One big difference: Jesse Hodges, 1817, DM 11C65; Draper, *Life*, 498; Edna Kenton,
     Simon Kenton: His Life and Period (Garden City, NY: Doubleday, Doran, 1930), 98.

174 Butler moved ahead: Draper, *Life*, 499; John Filson, *The Discovery, Settlement
     and Present State of Kentucke* (Wilmington, KY: James Adams, 1784), 42;
     William M. Kenton, 1851, DM 5S104.

175 Just then, Boone: Draper, *Life*, 499, 522n2; Filson, 42.

175 Further evidence: Draper, *Life*, 499, 522n2; Filson, 42; Edna Kenton, 98–99;
     Hodges, 1818, DM 11C66.

176 Blackfish's command: Moses Boone, 1846, DM 19C9; *Report of the Pioneer
     and Historical Society of the State of Michigan*, vol. 9 (Lansing, MI: Thorp &
     Godfrey, 1886), 465.

177 After Boone's escape: *Report of the Pioneer and Historical Society*, 479.

177 Some among the tribes: Joseph Jackson, 1844, DM 11C62(15); Stephen
     Warren, *The Shawnees and Their Neighbors, 1795–1870* (Urbana: University of
     Illinois Press, 2005), 22, 178n10.

178 At Fort Detroit: *Report of the Pioneer and Historical Society*, 465, 479; Daniel
     Boone Bryan, 1843, DM 22C5(13); "American Cities—Detroit," *Appleton's
     Journal* 8, no. 174 (July 27, 1872): 91; Draper, *Life*, 500; Ranck, 73; Bradley J.
     Birzer, "French Imperial Remnants on the Middle Ground: The Strange Case of
     August de la Balme and Charles Beaubien," *Journal of the Illinois State Historical
     Society* 93, no. 2 (Summer 2000): 144.

179 There was irony in the situation: Ranck, 71.

179 Meanwhile, at Boone's position: Daniel Boone Bryan, DM 22C5(13), 1844,
     22C14(12).

179 In a space designated as his "gunsmith shop": Moses Boone, DM 19C18;
     Isaiah Boone, 1846, DM 19C18, 19C57.

180 With Butler, Montgomery: Anne P. Crabb, *And the Battle Began Like Claps of Thunder* (Richmond, KY: Fort Boonesborough Foundation, 1998), 59–62, 65; Trabue, 59; John Gass, 1844, DM 24C73(4).

180 Fanny Holder (née Callaway): Daniel Boone Bryan, DM 22C5(13), 22C14(12); Gass, DM 24C73(1); Hazel Atterbury Spraker, ed., *The Boone Family: A Genealogical History* (Rutland, VT: Tuttle Company, 1922), 116.

180 Boone was standing outside: Draper, *Life*, 500; Moses Boone, DM 19C9, 19C48; Isaiah Boone, DM 19C78.

181 The Indian army marched: Daniel Boone Bryan, DM 22C5(13–14); Moses Boone, DM 19C9; Trabue, 58; Nathan and Olive Boone, 1851, DM 6S130; John C. Boone, 1890, DM 16C132.

181 Boone and Blackfish sat: Willis A. Bush, 1853, DM 24C59(7); Daniel Boone Bryan, DM 22C5(14); Josiah Collins, 1840s, DM 12CC74.

181 Blackfish handed over letters: Nathan and Olive Boone, DM 6S130–131.

182 Blackfish also brought wampum: Daniel Boone Bryan, DM 22C5(14).

182 "If you will surrender": Josiah Collins, DM 12CC74; John Bradford, *The Voice of the Frontier: John Bradford's Notes on Kentucky*, ed. Thomas D. Clark (Lexington: University of Kentucky Press, 1993), 19.

182 Boone used the very real power struggle: Daniel Boone Bryan, DM 22C5(14); Gass, DM 24C73(2); Nathan and Olive Boone, DM 6S131–132; Isaiah Boone, DM 19C80.

183 Moluntha, the chief: Bradford, 19.

183 Like Blackfish, Captain Will: Ephraim McLain, 1884, DM 16C7(9), 16C8(1).

183 Inside the fort: Filson, 42; Gass, DM 24C73(2); Nathaniel Hart Jr., c. 1843, DM 17CC198.

184 They had two more days: Daniel Boone Bryan, DM 22C5(14); Filson, 42; Moses Boone, DM 19C9–11; Gass, DM 24C73(3–4); Isaiah Boone, DM 19C84–85.

184 When the two-day deadline arrived: Gass, 1840s, DM 11CC13; Moses Boone, DM 19C9; Smith, 147; John C. Boone, 1890, DM 16C132.

184 Taken aback: Nathan and Olive Boone, DM 6S132–133; Moses Boone, DM 19C9.

185 Blackfish suggested: Daniel Boone Bryan, DM 22C5(14–15); Nathan and Olive Boone, DM 6S133; Trabue, 58; Filson, 43; Ranck, 251; Gass, DM 24C73(13).

185 Eventually the leaders: Daniel Boone Bryan, DM 22C5(14–15); Harry G. Enoch, *Pioneer Voices* (Winchester, KY: 2012), 76; Gass, DM 24C73(4), 11CC13; Draper, *Life*, 503; Josiah Collins, DM 12CC74; Moses Boone, DM 19C9–11; Isaiah Boone, DM 19C80; Richard French, 1840s, DM 12CC203.

185 Additional clothes were spun: Ranck, 87; Enoch, *Pioneer Voices*, 76.

186 Multiple meetings: Daniel Boone Bryan, DM 22C5(15); Moses Boone, DM 19C25.

186 "Friends and brothers": Daniel Boone Bryan, DM 22C5(15).

186 With this groundwork: Ranck, 88; Moses Boone, DM 19C19, 19C24–25; Gass, DM 24C73(4); Draper, *Life*, 506.

187 An elaborate meal: Gass, DM 24C73(4); Nancy O'Malley, *Boonesborough Unearthed: Frontier Archaeology at a Revolutionary Fort* (Lexington: University Press of Kentucky, 2019), 129; Isaiah Boone, DM 19C80–81.

187 "Brethren," Blackfish said: Daniel Boone Bryan, DM 22C5(16); Moses Boone, DM 19C13–13(1); Nathan and Olive Boone, DM 6S134–135; Gass, DM 24C73(4–5); Trabue, 58.

187 Theodore Roosevelt would later marvel: Theodore Roosevelt, *The Winning of the West*, vol. 1 (New York: Putnam, 1889), 44.

188 According to the accounts of settlers: Daniel Boone Bryan, DM 22C5(15–16); Gass, DM 24C73(5); Isaiah Boone, DM 9C13, 19C82.

188 In hindsight many of these assumptions: Harriet S. Caswell, *Our Life among the Iroquois Indians* (Boston: Congregational Sunday-School and Publishing Society, 1892), 262, shows the handshake format as part of Indian tradition, with another example in Crabb, *And the Battle*, 25; Daniel Boone Bryan, DM 22C5(16); Moses Boone, DM 19C13.

Chapter 10: The Last Siege

190 Marksmen on the high platforms: Daniel Boone Bryan, 1843, DM 22C5(16); Moses Boone, 1846, DM 19C14; Daniel Trabue, *Westward into Kentucky*, ed. Chester Raymond Young (Lexington: University Press of Kentucky, 2015), 58; John Gass, 1840s, DM 11CC13; William B. Smith, "Attack of Boonsborough [*sic*]," *Ladies' Literary Cabinet* 3, no. 19 (Mar. 17, 1821): 148; Josiah Collins, 1840s, DM 12CC74; Isaiah Boone, 1846, DM 19C81.

190 Daniel Boone also struggled free: Nathan and Olive Boone, 1851, DM 6S132, 6S134–135; Moses Boone, DM 19C13–13(1); Hazel Atterbury Spraker, ed., *The Boone Family: A Genealogical History* (Rutland, VT: Tuttle Company, 1922), 119–21; Harry G. Enoch and Anne Crabb, *Women at Fort Boonesborough, 1775–1784* (Richmond, KY: Fort Boonesborough Foundation, 2014), 120–21; Daniel Boone Bryan, DM 22C5(16); Josiah Collins, DM 12CC64.

191 Inside the fort: Isaiah Boone, DM 19C83; Moses Boone, DM 19C14–15; Gass, DM 11CC14.

191 Outside, Boone staggered: Delinda Boone Craig, 1866, DM 30C58; Moses Boone, DM 19C14–15; George Bryan, 1844, DM 22C16(22).

191 Squire was unable: Moses Boone, DM 19C13(1), 15; Gass, 1844, DM 24C73(6), 1840s, 11CC13.

192 Squire fired: Moses Boone, DM 19C15; John Mason Peck, *Makers of American History: Daniel Boone* (New York: University Society, 1904), 56; Ted Igleheart, "Squire Boone, the Forgotten Man," *Filson Club History Quarterly* 44 (Oct. 1970): 357.

192 William Patton, the settler: Trabue, 59.

192 Behind the fort walls: Ephraim McLain, 1884, 16C7(9), 16C8(1); Gass, DM 24C73(6); Moses Boone, DM 19C17.

192 At first, Boone sensed: Craig, 1866, DM 30C59; Gass, DM 24C73(16).

192 Squire continued: Moses Boone, DM 19C15–16; George W. Ranck, *Boonesborough* (Louisville: John P. Morton, 1901), 252; Igleheart, 356, 365.

193 A pattern began: Moses Boone, DM 19C23; Gass, DM 24C73(14); Evisa Coshow, 1885, DM 21C24(5), 21C27; Spraker, 120; Nathan and Olive Boone, DM 6S138.

193 The tribal army: Moses Boone, DM 19C9–11; Abner Bryan, 1890, DM 4C44ff.

194 In the meantime, settlers began to hear: Moses Boone, DM 19C19.

194 With Squire now confined: Moses Boone, DM 19C18, 19C20; Trabue, 58; Enoch and Crabb, *Women at Fort Boonesborough*, 27.

194 The British and Indian forces: Moses Boone, DM 19C20–21; Gass, DM 24C73(10).

194 The settlers had raised an American flag: Moses Boone, DM 19C17–19; Isaiah Boone, DM 19C84; Gass, DM 24C73(7).

195 Pompey reportedly got into a habit: Gass, DM 24C73(9); Joseph Jackson, 1844, DM 11C62(15); Peck, 57–58. Review of different accounts of Pompey included in Ted Franklin Belue, "Did Daniel Boone Kill Pompey, the Black Shawnee, at the 1778 Siege of Boonesborough?," *Filson Club History Quarterly* 67 (1993): 5–22.

195 Provisions in the fort: Draper notes, n.d., DM 4B205; Craig, DM 30C58; Coshow, DM 21C27–33.

195 The settlers caught rainwater: Moses Boone, DM 19C20–22; Gass, DM 24C73(12); Isaiah Boone, DM 19C84; Harry G. Enoch and Diane Rogers, *Deposition Book, 1795–1814* (Winchester, KY: 2005), 101; Nancy O'Malley, *Boonesborough Unearthed: Frontier Archaeology at a Revolutionary Fort* (Lexington: University Press of Kentucky, 2019), 95.

196 The volleys of gunfire: Ranck, 252; Susan Callaway Howell, 1868, DM 23S224; Coshow, DM 21C27–33.

197 From inside: Coshow, DM 21C24(5); Daniel Boone Bryan, DM 22C5(16); Trabue, 59; Moses Boone, DM 19C9, 19C19–20.

197 Indeed, the invading force: Moses Boone, DM 19C20–24; Gass, DM 24C73(9–13); Timothy Flint, *Biographical Memoir of Daniel Boone* (Cincinnati: George Conclin, 1845), 162.

197 To counter the tactic: Coshow, 21C24(5); Moses Boone, DM 19C20; Daniel Boone Bryan, DM 22C5(16); Gass, DM 24C73(9); Trabue, 59.

197 London, the enslaved man: Moses Boone, DM 19C17.

198 Blackfish's troops: Gass, DM 11CC13, 24C73(7), 24C73(10); Lyman C. Draper, *The Life of Daniel Boone*, ed. Ted Franklin Belue (Mechanicsburg, PA: Stackpole Books, 1998), 530, note p.

198 Inside a cabin, Bundrin: Nathan and Olive Boone, DM S6138, 6S142–143; Gass, DM 24C73(7).

198 The settlers scrambled: Draper, *Life*, 515; Moses Boone, DM 19C16–19; Richard French, 1840s, DM 12CC203; Samuel Dixon, 1852, DM 24C30(6); Craig, DM 30C59; George Bryan, DM 22C16(22).

198 William Patton, still confining himself to the woods: Trabue, 59.

199 While on watch at night: Moses Boone, DM 19C17; Draper, *Life*, 512; Gass, DM 24C73(7–8).

199 The campaign to burn: Gass, DM 24C73(11); Daniel Boone Bryan, DM 22C5(16); Spraker, 120.

199 As days passed: Ranck, 96.

199 Flaws in construction: Gass, DM 24C73(11–12); Moses Boone, DM 19C22; Draper, *Life*, 515–16; Ranck, 96.

200 The Indians continued excavating: Gass, DM 24C73(8), 24C73(13); Moses Boone, DM 19C20.

200 Still, casualties mounted: Nathan and Olive Boone, DM 6S142; Gass, DM 24C73(7); Moses Boone, DM 19C16; Howell, DM 23S223.

200 By this time, the young women: W. D. Holder, 1849, DM 24C27(1).

200 At one point as Jemima rushed: Craig, DM 30C58; Nathan and Olive Boone, DM 6S138, 6S142; Anne P. Crabb, *And the Battle Began Like Claps of Thunder* (Richmond, KY: Fort Boonesborough Foundation, 1998), 29; Spraker, 119–21.

201 The night of September 17: Moses Boone, DM 19C21; Gass, DM 24C73(7).

201 At the same time: Trabue, 59.

201 Patton reached Logan's Fort: Trabue, 59.

201 After leaving Paint Creek: Crabb, *And the Battle Began*, 32; Draper, *Life*, 519.
202 Benjamin Logan also absorbed the news: Lowell H. Harrison and James
     C. Klotter, *A New History of Kentucky* (Lexington: University Press of Kentucky,
     1997), 29; Bessie Taul Conkwright, "A Sketch of the Life and Times of General
     Benjamin Logan," *Register of the Kentucky State Historical Society* 14 (Jan. 1916):
     22–24; Lynda Williams Closson, "Battle of Logan's Fort," *Hallowed Ground*
     (Winter 2018), https://www.battlefields.org/learn/articles/battle-logans-fort;
     "Benjamin Logan," in *The Kentucky Encyclopedia*, ed. John E. Kleber (Lexington:
     University of Kentucky Press), 569; Trabue, 47.
203 Hearing that Boonesboro was wiped out: Trabue, 60; *Lincoln County, Kentucky*
     (Paducah, KY: Turner Pub. Co., 2002), 11; Benjamin Briggs, 1844, DM 9J185.
203 An air of martyrdom: Trabue, 60–61, 171n34.
205 After the agonizing wait: Trabue, 61–62.
205 Simon Butler and Alexander Montgomery: Gass, DM 24C73(14); Trabue,
     62; Draper, *Life*, 518.
206 How a couple dozen settlers: Peck, 60; Moses Boone, DM 19C18, 19C21–
     22; Gass, DM 24C73(13); Smith, 148.
206 Indications suggest: Edna Kenton, *Simon Kenton: His Life and Period*
     (Garden City, NY: Doubleday, Doran, 1930), 100–101; Dixon, DM 24C30(6).
207 Settlers almost instantly: Ranck, 258.
207 Though history: Humphrey Marshall, *History of Kentucky*, vol. 1 (Frankfort,
     KY: George S. Robinson, 1824), 62; Ranck, 86, 102; Bradley J. Birzer, "French
     Imperial Remnants on the Middle Ground: The Strange Case of August de la
     Balme and Charles Beaubien," *Journal of the Illinois State Historical Society* 93,
     no. 2 (Summer 2000): 144.
208 Only an hour after the last: Gass, DM 24C73(14); Isaiah Boone, DM
     19C85; Craig, DM 30C58; Nathan and Olive Boone, DM 6S138, 6S142; Draper,
     Life, 515.
208 Jemima would always remember: Coshow, DM 21C27; Conkwright, 29.

Chapter 11: Aftershocks

210 The Boones were in the fight of their lives: Edna Kenton, *Simon Kenton: His
     Life and Period* (Garden City, NY: Doubleday, Doran, 1930), 101; William B.
     Smith, "Adventure with the Indians" in *The Museum of Perilous Adventures and
     Daring Exploits* (New York: G. & F. Bill, 1859), 417–18.
210 The injured Benjamin Logan: Bessie Taul Conkwright, "A Sketch of the Life
     and Times of General Benjamin Logan," *Register of the Kentucky State Historical
     Society* 14 (Jan. 1916): 29; *Proceedings of the Twenty-Second Annual Meeting of the
     Kentucky State Bar Association* (Covington, KY: Press of Westerfield-Bonte, 1923),
     249.
212 "If any commander": "Articles of War; September 20, 1776," Section 13,
     Articles 22 and 19, *Journals of the Continental Congress*, ed. Worthington Chauncey
     Ford, Avalon Project, https://avalon.law.yale.edu/18th_century/contcong
     _09-20-76.asp.
212 Logan had to preside: Conkwright, 29; Daniel Trabue, *Westward into
     Kentucky*, ed. Chester Raymond Young (Lexington: University Press of Kentucky,
     2015), 63; Joseph Martin, 1844, DM 24C41(2–3).
213 With all the dangers: Martin S. Lederman, "Of Spies, Saboteurs, and Enemy
     Accomplices: History's Lessons for the Constitutionality of Wartime Military
     Tribunals," *Georgetown Law Journal* 105 (2017): 1529–1680, at 1624.

214 As his first charge: Trabue, 63.

214 Depicting Boone's captivity: Trabue, 57, 63; John Mack Faragher, *Daniel Boone: The Life and Legend of an American Pioneer* (New York: Henry Holt, 1993), 200; Ala Alryyes, "War at a Distance: Court-Martial Narratives in the Eighteenth Century," *Eighteenth Century Studies* 41, no. 4 (Summer 2008): 526.

215 Callaway also introduced: Trabue, 63; Willis A. Bush, 1853, DM 24C59(7); Richard French, 1840s, DM 12CC203.

216 As for the events at the Lower Blue Licks: Trabue, 63; *Report of the Pioneer and Historical Society of the State of Michigan*, vol. 9 (Lansing, MI: Thorp & Godfrey, 1886), 435; Willard R. Jillson, "Squire Boone, 1744–1815," *Filson Club History Quarterly* 16, no. 3 (July 1942): 154.

217 The divergent experiences: Noble Callaway, 1868, DM 25S125; Ted Franklin Belue, "Terror in the Canelands: The Fate of Daniel Boone's Salt Boilers," *Filson Club History Quarterly* 68, no. 1 (Jan. 1994): 14.

217 In contrast, the Shawnee: Belue, "Terror in the Canelands," 13; James Callaway, 1832, DM 21C75.

217 While Hamilton was away: Edna Kenton, 101, 106–8, 113–18; Rockne Ehle, "The Captivity of Simon Kenton," *Upper Ohio Valley Historical Review* 10, no. 12 (Spring/Summer 1981): 12; Sarah McCord, 1851, DM 5S148.

218 After a failed escape attempt: Edna Kenton, 121–26, 132–33; Ehle, 13, 20n57.

219 Mingo chief Logan: Edna Kenton, 130–36.

219 Rather than being placed in the prison cell: Edna Kenton, 135, 137; William Dodd Brown, "The Capture of Daniel Boone's Saltmakers: Fresh Perspectives from Primary Sources," *Register of the Kentucky Historical Society* 83 (1985): 13; Ehle, 13.

219 While Butler was in Fort Detroit: John D. Barnhart, ed., *Henry Hamilton and George Rogers Clark in the American Revolution* (Crawfordsville, IN: R. E. Banta, 1951), 60, 74–78, 83.

220 Seven months removed: Barnhart, ed., *Henry Hamilton*, 197.

220 That June, Hamilton: Edna Kenton, 140–43; William Kenton, 1851, DM 5S112.

220 But Butler's true liberation: McCord, DM 5S135, 5S159; Edna Kenton, 142; William Kenton, DM 5S117.

221 Henry Hamilton found himself: Barnhart, ed., *Henry Hamilton*, 36; John D. Barnhart, "Lieutenant Governor Henry Hamilton's Apologia," *Indiana Magazine of History* 52, no. 4 (1956): 393; Reasons for not accepting parole in answer to Governor Jefferson's demands by Henry Hamilton, Sept. 27, 1780, MS Eng 508.1 (10a), Henry Hamilton Papers, Houghton Library, Harvard University, Cambridge, MA.

221 After spending part of 1779: Charles W. Bryan Jr., "Richard Callaway, Kentucky Pioneer," *Filson Club History Quarterly* 9 (Jan. 1935): 47–48; Anne P. Crabb, *And the Battle Began Like Claps of Thunder* (Richmond, KY: Fort Boonesborough Foundation, 1998), 97; Eudocia Estill, 1852, DM 24C32; John Gass, 1840s, DM 11CC16.

222 In a chilling moment: Joseph Jackson, 1844, DM 11C62(28); Anne Crabb, "'What Shall I Do Now?, The Story of the Indian Captivities of Margaret Paulee, Jones Hoy, and Jack Callaway," *Filson Club History Quarterly* 70 (Oct. 1996): 399; George W. Ranck, *Boonesborough* (Louisville: John P. Morton, 1901), 67.

222 After the siege: "Bowman's Expedition Against Chillicothe" in *Ohio Archaeological and Historical Publications*, vol. 19 (Columbus, OH: Fred J. Herr,

1910), 446–55; John Sugden, *Tecumseh: A Life* (New York: Henry Holt, 2013), 33; Colin G. Calloway, "'We Have Always Been the Frontier': The American Revolution in Shawnee Country," *American Indian Quarterly* 16, no. 1 (Winter 1992), 43.

223 Even tribal leaders: Joan R. Gunderson, "Nonhelema" in *Women and War: A Historical Encyclopedia from Antiquity to Present*, vol. 1, ed. Bernard A. Cook (Santa Barbara, CA: ABC-CLIO, 2006), 434; Robert Morgan, *Boone: A Biography* (Chapel Hill, NC: Algonquin Books, 2008), 363–64; C. A. Weslager, *Delaware Indians: A History* (New Brunswick, NJ: Rutgers University Press, 1972), 306; Joseph C. Jefferds, *Captain Matthew Arbuckle: A Documentary Biography* (Charleston, WV: Education Foundation, 1981), 28.

224 Hanging Maw, who carried out the kidnapping: Robert Conley, *A Cherokee Encyclopedia* (Albuquerque: University of New Mexico Press, 2007), 113.

224 Theodore Roosevelt later posited: Theodore Roosevelt, *The Winning of the West*, vol. 1 (New York: Putnam, 1889), 46.

225 The 1778 siege: Ranck, 109, 115; Draper notes, n.d., DM 5B56–68.

226 The Boones continued to move around: Delinda Boone Craig, 1866, DM 30C78; Kenneth Williams, "Life on the Kentucky Frontier: A Roundtable Discussion," *Register of the Kentucky Historical Society* 102, no. 4 (Autumn 2004): 483n23.

227 Saving Boonesboro: Neal O. Hammon and Richard Taylor, *Virginia's Western War, 1775–1786* (Mechanicsburg, PA: Stackpole Books, 2002), 204; Craig, DM 30C78.

227 Boone indeed treasured: "Daniel Boone and His Sons in Missouri," *Lawrence Chieftain*, Sept. 2, 1880; Craig, DM 30C50–51.

228 Nineteen years after: Harry G. Enoch and Diane Rogers, *Deposition Book, 1795–1814* (Winchester, KY: 2005), 15–17; Nathan and Olive Boone, 1851, DM 6S221; Ted Igleheart, "Squire Boone, the Forgotten Man," *Filson Club History Quarterly* 44 (Oct. 1970): 365.

228 Familiar faces: Hazel Atterbury Spraker, ed., *The Boone Family: A Genealogical History* (Rutland, VT: Tuttle Company, 1922), 552; George W. Stoner, 1868, DM 24C55(10–11).

229 Kenton smiled: McCord, DM 5S171–172; Edna Kenton, 251–55, 262; Nathan and Olive Boone, DM 6S93; John James, 1851, DM 5S172.

229 Boone came across as a stoic man: David Meriwether, *My Life in the Mountains and on the Plains* (Norman: University of Oklahoma Press, 1965), 29–30; Susan Callaway Howell, 1868, DM 23S248.

229 Rebecca Boone passed: Nathan and Olive Boone, DM 6S279–280; Craig, DM 30C81–83.

230 When James Fenimore Cooper's: John Alexander McClung, *Sketches of Western Adventure* (Cincinnati: U. P. James, 1839), 40.

230 When her life was memorialized: George Bryan, 1844, DM 22C16(21); Martha Levy Luft, "Charles Wimar's *The Abduction of Daniel Boone's Daughter by the Indians*, 1853 and 1855: Evolving Myths," *Prospects* 7 (1982): 300–314; June Namias, *White Captives: Gender and Ethnicity on the American Frontier* (Chapel Hill: University of North Carolina Press, 1993), 106–107; Nancy O'Malley, *Boonesborough Unearthed: Frontier Archaeology at a Revolutionary Fort* (Lexington: University Press of Kentucky, 2019), 137; C. C. Ousley, *Kentucky at the Jamestown Tercentennial Exposition* (Louisville: circa 1907), 47.

231 Jemima did dictate her stories: Craig, DM 30C48–49, 30C68–69; Faragher, 132; Isaac Van Bibber, 1854, DM 23C109(1).

INDEX

ABOUT THE AUTHOR

MATTHEW PEARL's novels have been international and *New York Times* bestsellers and have been translated into more than thirty languages. He edits *Truly*Adventurous* magazine, and his nonfiction writing has appeared in the *New York Times*, the *Boston Globe*, and *Slate*. He has been chosen as Best Author in *Boston* magazine's "Best of Boston" issue and received the Massachusetts Book Award for Fiction. *The Taking of Jemima Boone* is his nonfiction debut.